Social System and Social Structure

SOCIAL SYSTEM AND SOCIAL STRUCTURE

Dr. Suman Ghosal

CENTRUM PRESS
NEW DELHI-110002 (INDIA)

CENTRUM PRESS
H.O.: 4360/4, Ansari Road, Daryaganj,
New Delhi-110002 (India)
Tel: 23278000, 23261597, 23255577, 23286875

B.O.: No. 1015, Ist Main Road, BSK IIIrd Stage,
IIIrd Phase, IIIrd Block, Bengaluru-560085 (INDIA)
Tel: 080-41723429

Email: centrumpress@gmail.com
Visit us at: www.centrumpress.com

Social System and Social Structure

First Edition, 2012

ISBN 978-93-81293-68-3

PRINTED IN INDIA

Printed at Tarun Offset, Delhi

Contents

Preface

Social system is a concept used relatively early in sociology by functionalists. And from the very beginning a social system was considered as complex. The concept of a system indicates the society is an entity. It also points out the intrinsic social forces that rule the system and prevent it form collapsing. At the same time the systemic approach to society has been strongly criticized in sociology mainly because of organic analogies and psychological terms used to describe specific social phenomena. To understand what it is the complexity of a social system different aspects and different levels of social phenomena must be considered. Explanation of the system might point out the dynamic or static aspect of a system. The dynamic approach to social system explores such phenomena as equilibrium, relations of the elements, conflict, development etc., while the static approach deals with such notions as structure, normative system, social control, individuals, groups, institutions, culture, and collective actions, however many of these can be analyse in both perspective.

Social structure can also be divided into microstructure and macrostructure. Microstructure is the pattern of relations between most basic elements of social life, that cannot be further divided and have no social structure of their own. Macrostructure is thus a kind of 'second level' structure, a pattern of relations between objects that have their own structure. Some types of social structures that modern sociologist differentiate are *relation structures, communication structures* and sociometric structures.

India is justly famous for its complex social systems. Indian society is multifaceted to an extent perhaps unknown in any other of the world's great civilizations. Virtually no generalization made about Indian society is valid for all of the nation's multifarious groups. Comprehending the complexities of Indian social structure has challenged scholars and others observers over many decades. The book is meant for detailing and analysing the fundamentals of our social system since ancient period to till date in a very lucid way. Keeping in view the expected consequences of socio-economic development as an instrument of change in the structure and culture, the present work mainly deals with agrarian social structure, caste structure, power structure, culture and changing conditions of women. Social Structure and Change has given me maximum satisfaction. It has reached out to students of various disciplines and pursuits, and has not remained confined to senior school students only. College and university students and those preparing for competitive examinations have equally found it useful.

Indian society is traditionally male-dominated. However, females are given due respect. Since they form an essential part of society, their rights to liberty, education, employment, etc. have been safeguarded by the constitution of India. This book is a comprehensive and exhaustive study, dealing with various aspects of Indian social system, at micro level.

—Editor

1

Social System

Social system is a central term in sociological systems theory. The term draws a line to ecosystem, biological organisms, psychical systems and technical systems. They all form the environment of social systems. Minimum requirements for a social system is interaction of at least two personal systems or two persons acting in their roles.

Characteristics of Social Systems

Jay Wright Forrester describes three counterintuitive behaviours as important: causes from symptoms are often far removed in time and space, identifying leverage points, conflicting short + long-term consequences.

Approaches of Parsons and Luhmann

In sociological systems theory there is a controversy what kind of structural elements a social system consists of. For Talcott Parsons it is actions, while Niklas Luhmann considers communication processes which constitute a social system. Though communication is also an action (e.g. speech acts) and on the surface this seems to be a discussion about terms only, the selection of basic terms has theoretical and empirical consequences.

Social Systems and Digital/Online Worlds

Social systems sciences is a loose term for engineered environments which, if successful, attract users to participate. The advent of computers and the internet has enabled new types of social systems to take form. There are multiple methods of measuring participation within a social system. Reach, engagement, frequency of participation – all tell something about the success of a social system.

All social systems have commonalities. One is that they become more fun and interesting as more people play and participate. Another is that with each iteration, or version, very quickly the population or interest reaches a plateau.

Indeed, the world is one large social system, split into many smaller social systems.

- Digital social systems
- Virtual worlds
- Role-playing games as social systems.

When the Internet first reached the hands of the populace, people took the existing model of dungeons and dragons and created their own digital versions of the worlds once played by people in their living rooms and basements. These first text-based online role-playing games attracted people who enjoyed the social aspect of battling for gold and riches. Hundreds of new worlds sprouted up. Some of these worlds were designed more successfully than others. In terms of reach, some of these worlds supported thousands of users, while some only tens to hundreds.

DragonRealms

DragonRealms was a highly regulated, highly immersive experience. Through a system where progression was based not only on fighting and questing within the world, it also depended on contribution to the world itself. To advance, an adventurer was required to role-play, or act their character at all times. *DragonRealms* had a particularly high administrator to player ratio, approximately one administrator for every player. This made it possible for the admins to silently watch the players. Players would be awarded by admins with 'favor points' for creative advancement. Every five levels, a player would need 1 favor point to progress. In *DragonRealms*, there were five main guilds (Inquisitor, Red gauntlelt,...). Each of these guilds had a role in the world. Alliances were formed, betrayed. Favor points could also be used by guilds to build in the world. Special weapons, abilities, and castles, unique to the favor point wielder, were granted by the admins. At the height of this world, an average of 1300 players were interacting with this world.

This system was highly engaging; most players spent multiple hours per day in this world. Eventually though, the costs associated with moderating such a game were too much for the creators and the game was taken offline.

Virtual World Evolution

These role-playing games took popular aspects from thousands of MUDs, and built a graphic interface around them. With each successive iteration and advance in graphics, these games became more interesting, and addictive.

Ultima Online (UO)

By 1996 Ultima Online's simple, 2-D graphic interface served some 50,000 daily users.

EverQuest

By 2000 EverQuest became the first virtual world to reach 500,000. By 2000 this number ballooned to almost over two million users. Because of the addictive nature of the game, and the amount of time needed to be a Hero in this world, the game was coined EverCrack.

World of Warcraft (WoW)

World of Warcraft was launched in November 2004. Within two months, WoW had surpassed *EverQuest* for largest virtual world. Within a year, over 10 million people were paying a monthly subscription fee to take part in this environment. WoW took many ideas from *EverQuest*, while fixing many of the aspects that frustrated users.

Second Life

Second Life was different from the role-playing virtual worlds. The progression system was not on fighting monsters and battling opponents. Instead, *Second Life* aimed to represent the real world. Players could build homes, islands, open businesses, casinos. Players could design clothing, actions, dance moves by using an open source design. By selling or renting their creations, users could get 'rich' and be successful in this virtual worlds. While some expected *Second Life* to be wildly popular, as of 2008, *Second Life* homes some three million players, only 200,000 of which are online at a given time. This is less than 1/5 the number of players as *World of Warcraft*.

Social Classes:

- Upper class contained nobles, priests, government officials and warriors.
- Merchants, traders and artisans made up a Middle or "Freeman" Class.
- Slavery existed.

Early in Sumerian civilization, eighty to ninety percent of those who farmed did so on land they considered theirs rather than communal property. Here, too, the Sumerians were expressing a trend that was common among others. Another individual effort was commerce, and with a growth in commerce the Sumerians had begun using money, which made individual wealth more easily measured and stored. Commerce required initiative, imagination, an ability to get along with people and luck, and, of course, some merchants were more successful than were others. Farming took stamina, strength, good health, good luck and organization. And some farmers were more successful than were other farmers.

Those farmers who failed to harvest enough to keep themselves in food and seed borrowed from those who had wealth in surplus. Those who borrowed hoped that their next harvest would give them the surplus they needed to repay their loan. But if the next harvest were also inadequate, to meet their obligations they might be forced to surrender their lands to the lender or to work for him. When Sumerians lost their land, they or their descendants might become sharecroppers: working the lands of successful landowners in exchange for giving the landowners a good portion of the crops they grew.

Accompanying divisions in wealth was a division in power, and power among the Sumerians passed to an elite. Sumerian priests who had once worked the fields alongside others, soon were separated from commoners. A corporation run by priests became the greatest landowners among the Sumerians. The priests hired the poor to work their land and claimed that land was really owned by the gods. Priests had become skilled as scribes, and in some cities they sat with the city's council of elders. These councils wielded great influence, sometimes in conflict with a city's king.

Common Sumerians remained illiterate and without power, while kings, once elected by common people, became monarchs. The monarchs were viewed as agents of and responsible to the gods. It was the religious duty of his subjects to accept his rule as a part of the plan of the gods. Governments drafted common people to work on community projects, and common people were obliged to pay taxes to the government in the form of a percentage of their crops, which the city could either sell or use to feed its soldiers and others it supported. And priests told commoners that their drudgery was necessary to allow the gods their just leisure.

Clinging to their belief in the goodness and power of their gods and wondering about their sin and the toil and strife with which they lived, the Sumerians imagined a past in which people lived in a god-created paradise. This was expressed in the same poetic tale that described the conflict between the king of Uruk and the distant town of Arrata the earliest known description in writing of a paradise and the fall of humankind. The poem describes a period when there were no creatures that threatened people - no snakes, scorpions, hyenas, or lions a period in which humans knew no terror. There was no confusion among various peoples speaking different languages, with everyone praising the god Enlil in one language. Then, according to the poem, something happened that enraged the god Enki (the god of wisdom and water who had organized the earth in accordance with a general plan lay down by Enlil). The clay tablet on which the poem was written is damaged at this point, but the tablet indicates that Enki found some sort of inappropriate behavior among humans. Enki decided to put an end to the Golden Age, and in the place of the golden age came conflict, wars and a confusion of languages.

On another clay tablet, surviving fragments of a poem describe the gods as having decided that humans were evil and the gods as having created a flood "to destroy the seed of humanity," a flood that raged for seven days and seven nights. The tablet describes a huge boat commanded by a king named Ziusudra, who was preserving vegetation and the seed of humankind. His boat was "tossed about by the windstorms on the great waters." When the storm subsided, the god Utu — the sun — came forward and shed light on heaven and earth. The good king Ziusudra opened a window on the boat and let in light from Utu. Then Ziusudra prostrated himself before Utu and sacrificed an ox and a sheep for the god.

Women

Woman were not free. Men dominate women as they were physically stronger. They often ruled women by brute force always making the decisions. The Sumerians put the domination of men over women into law. If a husband died, the widow came under the control of her former husband's father or brother, or if she had a grown son under his control. A woman in Sumer had no recourse or protection under the law. A woman's only power, if she had any, was the influence of her personality within her family.

If the wife of a man followed after another man and he slept with her, they shall slay that woman, but that male shall be set free. If a man proceeded by force, and deflowered the virgin slavewoman of another man, that man must pay five shekels of silver.

Education

Early in Sumerian civilization, schooling was associated with the priesthood and took place in temples. But this changed, and an education apart from the temples arose for the children of affluent families, who paid for this education — and with men dominating women, most if not all students were males. The students were obliged to work hard at their studies, from sun up to sun down. Not believing in change, there was no probing into the potentials of humankind or study of the humanities. Their study was "practical" — rote learning of complex grammar and practice at writing. Students were encouraged with praise while their inadequacies and failures were punished with lashes from a stick or cane.

War and Slavery

Serfs and slaves made up majority of population and were responsible for all manual labour. As Sumerian cities grew in population and expanded, the virgin swamps that had insulated city from city disappeared. And, like other peoples, the Sumerians were inclined to empathize more with those closer to themselves and inclined to see their own interests more clearly than those distant from them. Sumerians from different cities were unable or unwilling to resolve their conflicts over land and the availability of water, and wars between Sumerian cities erupted — wars they saw as between their gods.

Eventually, the Sumerians made slaves of other Sumerians they had captured in their wars with each other, but originally they acquired their slaves from peoples beyond Sumer. The Sumerian name for a female slave was mountain girl, and a male slave was called mountain man. The Sumerians used their slaves mainly as domestics and concubines. And they justified their slavery as would others: that their gods had given them victory over an inferior people. Wars with distant people were fuelled by the greed and ambitions of kings. The Sumerians described this in a poetic tale of conflict between the king of Uruk and the distant town of Arrata, a tale written by a Sumerian some five hundred years after the event, a tale of which only fragments remain. Here was reporting as it would be for more than three thousand years, as it would be with Homer and his Iliad, the sacred writings of Hindus and with the Old Testament, with gods in command and not disapproving of war.

Among the Sumerian cities was an impulse to be supreme, and, around 2800 BCE, Kish had become the first of the cities to dominate the whole of Sumer. Then Kish's supremacy was challenged by the city of Lagash, which launched a bloody conquest against its Sumerian neighbors and extended its power beyond Sumerian lands. A bas-relief sculpture uncovered by archaeologists depicts a king of Lagash celebrating his victory over the city of Umma, the king's soldiers, with helmets, shields and pikes, standing shoulder to shoulder and line behind line over the corpses of their defeated enemy.

Dissents

The variety of populous, civilized life produced differing opinions, and dissent - something authoritarians would never be able to extinguish. Sumerians complained. One wrote that he was a "thoroughbred steed" but drawing a cart carrying "reeds and stubble." Another complained in writing of the stupidity in one city taking enemy lands and then the enemy coming and taking its lands. Rather than docility, people in the city of Lagash instigated history's first recorded revolt. This came after Lagash's rulers had increased local taxes and restricted personal freedoms. Lagash's bureaucrats had grown in wealth. And the people of Lagash resented this enough that they overthrew their king and brought to power a god-fearing ruler named Urukagina, who eliminated excessive taxation and rid the city of usurers, thieves and murderers - the first known reforms.

WHAT IS SOCIAL SYSTEM

Social system is a concept used relatively early in sociology by functionalists. And from the very beginning a social system was considered as complex ('the father' of sociology, August Comte regarded society as the most complex level of reality). The concept of a system indicates the society is an entity. It also points out the intrinsic social forces that rule the system and prevent it form collapsing. At the same time the systemic approach to society has been strongly criticized in sociology mainly because of organic analogies and psychological terms used to describe specific social phenomena.

To understand what it is the complexity of a social system different aspects and different levels of social phenomena must be considered. Explanation of the system might point out the dynamic or static aspect of a system. The dynamic approach to social system explores such phenomena as equilibrium, relations of the elements, conflict, development etc., while the static approach deals with such notions as structure, normative system, social control, individuals, groups, institutions, culture, and collective actions, however many of these can be analyse in both perspective.

Let us assume that society is a system. What does it mean? And what is a complex system?

At least few features are important in the definition of a social system:

- System is the entity consisting of elements which are bounded which means that components constitutes a system. The relations among the elements are themselves important parts of the system. Elements of the system might be quite heterogeneous and yet they are interrelated. The relations also may alter. Interdependence of the elements in the system is one of most important assumption for systemic approach in sociology.

- Social system is an emergent structure, a new type of social order appears on particular level of structure (individual, group, institution). System-level properties are of new quality: "system-level exists solely as emergent properties characterizing the system action as a whole". Macro-level outcomes is often the result of interdependence of social actors. The interdependence of social actors (microlevel) means that the systemic level is not merely the outcome of aggregated individuals.
- There are many sub-systems on different levels (e.g. micro and macrolevel) or areas (e.g. economic, political, religious institutions of a society). The relation between individual (micro) and systemic level (macro) is on of the crucial in sociology. The question is whether each subsystem has its own specificity and to what extent it must be taken into consideration in explanation.

Complexity of Social System

Complexity of social system represents different types of social phenomena and at the same time emphasises multidimensional nature of social world. Social system is formed by the characteristic of it components. One of the typical definition of complex system is as follows: complex systems are systems with multiple interacting components whose behaviour cannot be simply inferred from the behaviour of the components. This definition precisely points out the constitutive features of complex system. James Coleman proposes to explain "the behaviour of social systems by means of three components: the effects of properties of the system on the constraints or orientations of actors; the actions of actors who are within the system; and the combination or interaction of those actions, bringing bout the systemic behaviour".

In order to show how complex is the social system I would like to analyse few aspects of complexity. There are many forms and types of social relations and they can generate different social forms: one can distinguish so called weak and incidental interactions, more petrified relations, up to social ties and social structure. If the system is complex then its elements are numerous and they are in mutual relations. One can see it analysing the relations of the system. Let's examine 'few' important features of social relation itself:

- the size of the group,
- the type of relation (mutual and no mutual relations, unilateral, bilateral, multilateral relations),
- recurrence, durability and stability of relations,
- the formal and informal aspect of relations,
- the communicational aspect o relations,
- the power, dependence, and control as the dimension of relations,
- the aspect of emotional ties, interest ties etc. of social relations and much more.

This particular example shows how complicated may be analysing the social relations. Other elements of social reality may take also diverse forms. Each subsystem consists of various levels of social organisation: from simple through more complicated: individuals, social entities, groups, communities, institutions. One of the most typical examples showing how parts of a system give rise to the collective behaviours of the system is to compare the individual actions and collective actions.

The interrelations of collective actions are usually more complex and the effects of such activity are different. It must be emphasized that most sociologists would agree that action takes place at the level of individual actors and the more complex level exist as emergent properties characterizing the system of action as a whole. "It is only in this sense that there is behavior of the system". If one considers the institutional aspect of social system then, again, one has to deal with patterns of behaviour, system of norms and social rules. At this point culture as a object of analysis appears. Culture is always an important part of each social system and sometimes is treated as a separate system by sociologists (it is a complex entity consisting of subsystems of values, norms, patterns of behaviour etc.). Thus, complexity of a social system represents a multidimensional social reality. Researching social system is to answer the question which elements of that complex entity play the main role in explanation of some aspects of social reality.

A Prison as a Social System

A prison as a social system is a special subject of research for several reasons. First, a prison is a relatively isolated social system and may be analysed much easier in terms of social system than other cases, especially a society as a whole is too complex system to research it directly. Second, the correctional institution is an example of total institution which consists of two communities or subsystems: the inmates and the staff. Third, this kind of institution is relatively separated and differs from other organizations in degree of control mechanisms, but it has also connections with outside environment. A macro scale perspective shows the connection between the mega system and subsystems and its consequences. Two levels of analysis are proposed here: medium scale social system, specific social relations in prison community, and the relations between super-system (macrosystem) and sub-system (prison). The nature of the relations themselves is a separate issue. The aim of the article is to present several examples and brief analysis on social system and discuss the issue of system complexity. I believe such an investigation allows to understand the specificity of social reality and enables better research.

Researching the complexity of prison as a social system demands to explore the organisational aspect of system first. At least three aspects are important:

- type of prison,
- size of prison and prison community,
- spatial distribution and arrangements of space.

Depending on conditions of imprisonment and type of sentence there are different kinds of prisons: closed and open (in fact there are two types of open prisons: semi-open and open, but for this analysis I will ignore the difference).

The grade of confinement is crucial because it supports various type of structure, group relations and communication system. Thus one can see how one single feature (open/closed organisation) influences the system. There is diversity in connectivity among the individuals. The open system makes it easier, while the closed one does not. Consequently, the communication channels in open system are numerous and in the closed system are limited. The other issue is the role of communication in forming collectivity, for instance community. It must be emphasised that the conditions of communication have further consequences. The quality of space distribution and social interaction generate different type of social relations and groups. In result, in closed system there are stronger social ties in cell-groups, weak ties in prison community and little mobility whereas in open system there are less integrated community, weak ties, lack of trust. Moreover, these set of conditions are conducive to specific style of behaviours of the system, for instance the probability of conflicts, the strength and resolution of the conflicts would diverge. All these features are the consequence of communications system.

Relation between an individual and group is of great importance. The action of the individual in group are under the influence of more complex level, that is group level. Individuals actions are determined (to some extent) by the groups. It means that "the members of solidary groups act in ways that are consistent with collective standards of conduct, norms, because they are obliged to do so".

All these following features are bounded to each other and this is one of the important criterion of system. The structure of prison community is another interesting aspect of complexity of the system. The structure is one of the most important element of the system because it has the capacity for structuring other aspect of the social reality. The structure gives the interdependence to the individuals' actions and it is not only the feedback processes. Actions of social actor have systemic character thanks to the interdependence. The societal organization of prison consists of two groups: the inmates and the staff. What is more, the inmates are not homogenous collectivity, several groups may constitute it. This is in fact some simplification, but let us assume that there are two groups of inmates: the members of subculture group and the 'ordinary' prisoners who do not belong to subculture groups.

It is often underlined that social world being a complex system is multidimensional. It can be observed inside the prison community where the mutual relations and the structure develop several elements of the system. The social interactions among members of the subculture groups are different than the interactions between non-subculture members and the staff. There are numerous norms that rules their relations and communication. How complex is the communication subsystem? Prison communication system contains informal and formal subsystem. Moreover, the system of communication consists of – at least – several elements such as tattoos, set of symbols and signs, the social norms that control contacts. The norms inform how to communicate? In what way? To whom? And all those elements may vary depending on type of prison system (closed or open). The list of elements is not complete, I do not intend however at this point to analyse the whole system, thoroughly. This limited presentation is to emphasise merely the complexity of societal system.

Concluding, if complexity is a research problem it is necessary to consider several variables that determine the human behaviour and the significance of these elements for the system.

Dynamics of Complex System

Social change is an example of complexity of societal system. First of all, the dynamic approach to the system reveal the connections among the elements and the results of their interplay – interdependence. Second, it enables to follow the change of the system which probably is visible only if one treats the social entity as a system. A single element may react to other element of a system starting the chain reaction in a social process. "Actions of each actor are somehow connected to those of others at an earlier point in time. This sequence of effects can continue into the future".

An example that illustrates how system may change is the process of adaptation to the environment. Let's consider the relations between communication system and other elements. Communication system creates several elements of social system such as the social structure, the group identity and group solidarity. An interesting phenomenon is 'prison life within the language'. Language must be consider here in boarder sense as an area where verbal acting replaces 'real' behaviours. It is of course the result of adaptation of the system to the given conditions i.e. numerous constraints. It is obvious that free acting is restricted. In such conditions inmates use verbal act as real behaviours, e.g. stigmatisation in closed small community or group is much stronger and more effective than in open society where individual mobility is high. The secret language (or precisely: vocabulary) of prisoners is another example of adaptation to environment. The reason to create such a language is the inmates' need to communicate without control of personnel in prison.

An interesting issues is how does spatial distribution affect the communication channels and change the social system in the end. Communication and language as a main area of social life become more influential as a part of the whole system. For instance the rumours, the stigmatisation, the ascribed social role or opinions would create the social structure and impose the execution of social norms. Generally, communication especially verbal contacts are the area of social action much more developed because they take over the functions of social actions.

The case proves that social relations, especially communication have an effect on different forms of social life and processes. Communication practices and language uses play an important role for they construct social reality within the language and beyond the language reality. The tattoos have the same role as the signs, they denote the social roles and social identities of prisoners. The subculture norms also can be treated as the effect of adaptation, most of the norms are suited to specific living conditions in the prison. Concluding, in general the prison subculture is the result of adaptation of the system. Let us analyse closer another example: the process of the influence of the relations within social structure. Social relations form the social structure in prison. The type of the structure depends on:

- type of communications links,
- the formal structure and organisation of prison, and
- spatial distribution.

The communication competence of individuals is also important factor. For instance if an individual who has a high communication competence exchange different kind of goods (cigarettes, coffee, or even very rare goods as narcotics) such an exchange starts the process of building social position of an individual. Successful exchange and good relations generate the high position and prestige. All these variables interact in forming specific type of social structure. These factors construct the system of distribution of interest and the structure of power. Thus, social interactions form the social system. The frequency of contacts determine the quality of social relation. Frequent interactions may turns into social ties, and consequently, if there is unequal distribution of power and control, into social structure.

Interdependence of Micro System and Macro System

One of the crucial problem for sociological theory is to explain the relation between the micro and macro level. This kind of relation is understood as the connection between (macro) system and subsystem.

Let us assume that the outside social environment is the macro system and the prison is subsystem (the sub-system of prison) and that there is dependence of microsystem from macrosystem. One of the primary assumption is that the sub-system reflects the mechanisms of macrosystem, as it is its part. The dominant factors of the macrosystem become dominant in subsystem, too. And this is the case of the correctional system in Poland.

The influence of the macro-system on the prison as social system is complicated itself because the macro system consists of several subsystems: society, economic and political institutions, culture, law etc. Which sub-system might be important for prison sub-system? Among many features the free market economy and political change would be the main factors that changed the macro system and consequently changed the subsystem of prison. The market economy altered the circumstances that govern the structure, which means that money is the main resources that redistributes the power, and influences the social relationships. As to political change, the democratisation of the system is also the feature of subsystem. The attitude towards the criminals, the politics of punishment and the law are the subject of political decisions. All these changes of the outside environment determine the conditions of imprisonment.

Political change was performed on the macrolevel by administrative decisions. The conditions of living and the rights of the inmates improved significantly after 1990 as a consequence of new regulations implemented as the macro-to–micro transition. Whereas the market economy was much more the area of micro-to-macro transformation of the prison subsystem. Gradually, new resources (money) started to shape the social reality and formed the social structure, changed the social ties, and above all introduced conflicts that destroyed group solidarity. One of the significant and widely recognised result of free market is the change of social solidarity. Free market promotes erosion of social solidarity because it causes very often the conflicts of interests. This sometimes is perceived as the threat to social order, which is wrong. Free market supports rather new kind of social ties, and it is responsible for social change. It stimulate the new social order that implies more conflicts and less collective actions but still it is some social order.

The relation between the prison and the environment is at first glance simple: the sub-system take over the features of the mega system. But if one follows further consequences it appears that new elements may appear as the result of the specificity of the subsystem. Why is that? The particular set of features inside the prison interact with each other and can generate the specific feature of subsystem that can not be predictable merely from the features of environment. Therefore one can distinguish the two types of system that are formed by different outside environment (mega system): totalitarian prison vs free-market prison. This clear distinction illustrates the great social change of macro system. Here are the characteristics of totalitarian and democratic prison subsystem that reflects the conditions of the outside environment:

Totalitarian Prison

- the restricted system of institutional control,

- the limited access to the material goods,
- the social status depend less on one's economic status and more on social identity,
- the high level of deprivation of economic, social and psychical needs,
- the group interests and individual interest converge,
- the mobility in population of criminals is little.

'Democratic' Prison

- less restricted system of institutional control,
- wider access to goods,
- the social status of individual depends on one's socio-economic relation with other member of community,
- the social distance increases that divides community in much distinct way: the poor – the rich,
- the individuals' interest and group interests are in contradictions,
- the social mobility population of criminals increases (new kinds of crime).

This brief presentation specifies the main differences of subsystem that are the consequences of the macrosystem. In democratic prison subculture gradually disappears because it is hostile environment that support the appearance and development of subculture strong community. The main function of that community was to survive. In comparison with totalitarian prison democratic prison takes over the function (or rather takes much more care) of supplying goods for the inmates. The interdependence of microsystem to macrosystem causes the change in subsystem.

SOCIAL SYSTEM OF ISLAM

Equality of Mankind

Allah created a human couple to herald the beginning of the life of mankind on earth, and everybody living in the world today originates from this couple. The progeny of this couple were initially a single group with one religion and the same language. But as their numbers gradually increased, they spread all over the earth and, as a natural result of their diversification and growth, were divided into various tribes and nationalities. They came to speak different languages; their models of dress varied; and their ways of living also differed widely climates and environments affected their colour and physical features. All these differences exist in the world of reality and Islam does not seek to ignore them. But it disapproves of the prejudices which have arisen among mankind because of these differences in race, colour, language and nationality. Islam makes clear to all men that they have come from the same parents and are therefore brothers and equal as human beings. Allah created a human couple to herald the beginning of the life of mankind on earth, and everybody living in the world today originates from this couple.

The progeny of this couple were initially a single group with one religion and the same language. But as their numbers gradually increased, they spread all over the earth and, as a natural result of their diversification and growth, were divided into various tribes and nationalities. They came to speak different languages; their models of dress varied; and their ways of living also differed widely climates and environments affected their colour and physical features. All these differences exist in the world of reality and Islam does not seek to ignore them. But it disapproves of the prejudices which have arisen among mankind because of these differences in race, colour, language and nationality. Islam makes clear to all men that they have come from the same parents and are therefore brothers and equal as human beings. Allah created a human couple to herald the beginning of the life of mankind on earth, and everybody living in the world today originates from this couple. The progeny of this couple were initially a single group with one religion and the same language. But as their numbers gradually increased, they spread all over the earth and, as a natural result of their diversification and growth, were divided into various tribes and nationalities. They came to speak different languages; their models of dress varied; and their ways of living also differed widely climates and environments affected their colour and physical features. All these differences exist in the world of reality and Islam does not seek to ignore them. But it disapproves of the prejudices which have arisen among mankind because of these differences in race, colour, language and nationality. Islam makes clear to all men that they have come from the same parents and are therefore brothers and equal as human beings.

Islam says that if there is any real difference between man and man it cannot be one of race, colour, country or language, but of ideas, beliefs and principles. Two children of the same mother, though they may be equal from the point of view of a common ancestry, will have to go their different ways in life if their beliefs and moral conduct differ. On the contrary, two people, one in the East and the other in the West, even though geographically and outwardly separated by vast distances, will tread the same path in life if they share the same code of moral behavior. On the basis of this fundamental tenet, Islam seeks to build a principled and ideological society very different from the racial, nationalistic and parochial societies existing in the world today.

The basis of co-operative effort among men in such a society is not the place of one's birth but a creed and a moral principle. Anyone, if he believes in *Allah* as his Master and Lord and accepts the guidance of the Prophets as the law of his life, can join this community, whether he is a resident of America or Africa, whether he belongs to the Semitic race or the Aryan, whether he is black or fair-skinned, whether he speaks a European language or Arabic. All those who join this community will have the same rights and social status. They will not be subjected to any racial, national or class distinctions. No one will be regarded as high or low. There will be no untouchability. There will be no special restrictions upon them in making marriages, eating and drinking and social contracts. No one will be looked down upon because of his birth or work. No one will claim any distinctive rights by virtue of his caste, community or ancestry. Man's merit will not depend on his family connections or riches, but only on whether he is better than others in moral conduct or excels others in piety and righteousness.

Such social order, transcending as it does geographical boundaries and the barriers of race, colour and language, is appropriate for all parts of the world; on its foundations can be raised the universal brotherhood of man. In societies based on race or nationality only those people can join who belong to a particular race or nation, but in Islam anyone who accepts its creed and moral standards can become a member, possessing equal rights with everyone else. Those who do not accept this creed, while obviously not being received into the community, are treated with tolerance and humanity and guaranteed all the basic human rights.

It is clear that if two children of the same mother differ in their ideas, their ways of life will be different; but this does not mean that they cease to be brothers. In the same way, if two nations or two groups of people living in the same country differ in their fundamental beliefs, principles and ideology, their societies will also certainly differ; yet they will continue to share the common ties of humanity. Hence, the Islamic society offers to non-Muslims societies and groups the maximum social and cultural rights that can possibly be accorded.

Institution of the Family

The foremost and fundamental institution of human society is the family unit. A family is established by the coming together of a man and a woman, and their contact brings into existence a new generation. This then produces ties of kinship and community, which, in turn, gradually develop further ties. The family is an instrument of continuity which prepares the succeeding generation to serve human civilization and to discharge its social obligations with devotion, sincerity and enthusiasm. This institution does not merely recruit cadets for the maintenance of human culture, but positively desires that those who are to come will be better members of society. In this respect the family can be truly called the source of the progress, development, prosperity and strength of human civilization. Islam therefore devotes much attention to the issues relating to the family and strives to establish it on the healthiest and strongest possible foundations.

According to Islam the correct relationship between man and woman is marriage, a relationship in which social responsibilities are fully accepted and which results in the emergence of a family. Sexual permissiveness and other similar types of irresponsible behavior are not dismissed by Islam as mere innocent pastimes or ordinary transgressions. Rather, they are acts which strike at the very roots of society. Hence,

Islam holds all extra-marital sex as sinful and forbidden (*haram*) and makes it a criminal offence. Severe punishments are prescribed to deter would-be offenders.

Veil, which regulates the free association of men and women, restriction on erotic music and obscene pictures and the discouragement of the spread of all forms of pornography, are other weapons used in the fight to protect and strengthen the institution of the family.

Islam does not look on adult celibacy simply with disfavor, it calls on every young man to take upon himself the social responsibilities of married life just as his parents did in their time. Nor does Islam regard asceticism and lifelong celibacy merely as being of no benefit; it sees them as departures from the nature of man and as acts of revolt against the Divine scheme of things.

It also strongly disapproves of those rites, ceremonies or restrictions which tend to make marriage a difficult affair. Islam tries to make marriage the easiest and fornication the most difficult thing in society, and not vice versa as it is in most societies today. Hence, after debarring certain blood relatives from entering into matrimony with one another, it has legalized marriage with all other near and distant kith and kin. It has removed all distinctions of caste and community, and permitted matrimony of any Muslim with any other Muslim. It has urged that the *mehr* (dower) should be fixed at a figure which can be easily borne by both sides. It has dispensed with the necessity of priests and register offices. In an Islamic society marriage is a plain and simple ceremony which can be performed anywhere before two witnesses, though it is essential that the proceedings should not be kept secret. Society must know that the couple are now going to live as husband and wife.

Within the family itself Islam has assigned to the man a position of authority so that he can maintain order and discipline as the head of the household. Islam expects the wife to obey her husband and look after his well-being; and it expects the children to behave accordingly to their parents. Islam does not favor a loose and disjointed family system devoid of proper authority, control and discipline. Discipline can only be maintained through a central authority and, in the view of Islam, the position of father in the family is such that it makes him the fittest person to have this responsibility. But this does not mean that man has been made a house-hold tyrant and woman has been handed over to him as a helpless chattel. According to Islam the real spirit of material life is love, understanding and mutual respect. If woman has been asked to obey her husband, the latter has been called on make the welfare of his family his top priority.

Although Islam places great emphasis on the marital bond, it only wants it to remain intact as long as it is founded on the sweetness of love or there exists at least the possibility of lasting companionship. If neither of these two conditions obtain, it gives man the right of divorce and woman the right of separation; and under certain conditions, where married life has become a source of misery, the Islamic courts of justice have the authority to annul the marriage.

Relatives and Neighbours

After the limited circle of the family, the next social sphere is that of kinship and blood relationship. Islam wants all those who are related through common parents, common brothers and sisters or marriage to be affectionate, cooperative and helpful to each other. In many places in the Qur'an good treatment of the near relations (*Dhawi-al-qurba*) is enjoined. In the Hadith of the Prophet, blessings and peace be on him, proper treatment of one's blood relations has been strongly emphasized and counted among the highest virtues. A person who cold-shoulders his relations or treats them indifferently is looked on by Islam with great disfavor.

But this does not mean that it is an Islamic virtue to favor one's relations. If such support or bias towards one's relations results in injustice, it is repugnant to Islam, and is condemned as an act of *Jahiliyyah* (ignorance). Similarly, it is utterly against the principles of Islam for a government official or public servant to support his relations at public expense or to favor his kith and kin in his official decisions: this would actually be a sinful act. Fair treatment of one's relations, as enjoined by Islam, should be at one's own expense and within the limits of justice and fair-play.

After relations come one's neighbours. The Qur'an has divided them into three categories: a neighbor who is also a relation; a neighbor who is a stranger; and a casual or temporary neighbor with whom one happens to live or travel for a certain time. All of them are deserving of sympathy, affection, kindness and fair treatment. The Prophet, blessings and peace be on him, once said that the right of the neighbor were so strongly emphasized by the angel Gabriel that he thought neighbours might even share one's inheritance. (*Bukhari* and *Muslim*)

In one Hadith the Prophet, blessings and peace be on him, said: Anyone whose neighbor is not safe from his misdeeds is not a true Believer. (*Bukhari* and *Muslim*) Again, he said: A person who enjoys a meal while his neighbor is starving is not a true Believer. (*Ahmad, Baihaqi*). The Prophet, blessings and peace be on him, was once asked about the fate of a woman who performed many Prayers and fasted extensively and who was a frequent almsgiver, but whose neighbours complained of her abusive tongue. He said: Such a woman shall be in the Hell-fire. He was, then, asked about another woman who did not possess these virtues but did not trouble her neighbours either, and he said: She would be in Paradise. (*Ahmad, Baihaqi*) The Prophet, blessings and peace be on him, has laid so much emphasis on being considerate to neighbours that he has advised that whenever a Muslim brings home fruit for his children he should either send some to his neighbours as a gift, or at least take care not to offend them by throwing the peelings away outside their door. On another occasion he said: A man is really good if his neighbours regard him as such, and bad if they consider him so. (*Ibn Majah*)

Islam, therefore, requires all neighbours to be loving and helpful and to share each other's sorrows and happiness. It enjoins them to establish social relations in which one can depend upon the other and regard his life, honour and property safe among his neighbours. A society in which two people, separated only by a wall, remain unacquainted with one another for years, and in which those living in the same area of a town have no interest or trust in one another, can never be called Islamic.

Next to these come the wider relationships covering the whole of society. The broad principles on which Islam wants people to structure their social lives are:

To co-operate in acts of goodness and righteousness and not to co-operate in acts of sin and injustice. (al-Maidah 5: 2)

One's friendship should be only for seeking the pleasure of *Allah*: whatever you give should be given because *Allah* likes it to be given, and whatever you withhold should be withheld because *Allah* wishes to. (*Trimidhi*)

You are the best community ever raised among mankind; your duty is to command people to do good and prevent them from committing evil. (Al- 'Imran 3: 110)

Do not think evil of each other, nor probe into each other's affairs, nor incite one against the other. Avoid hatred and jealousy. Do not unnecessarily oppose each other. Always remain the slaves of Allah, and live as brothers to each other. (*Muslim*)

Do not help a tyrant, knowing him to be such. (*Abu Daud*)

To support the community when it is in the wrong is like falling into a well while catching the tail of your camel which was about to fall into it. (*Abu Daud; Mishkawt*)

No one among you shall be a true believer unless he likes for others what he likes for himself. (*Bukhari* and *Muslim*)

ENTERPRISE SOCIAL NETWORKING

Enterprise social networking focuses on the use of online social networks or social relations among people who share business interests and/or activities. Enterprise social networking utilizes enterprise social software (regarded as a primary component of Enterprise 2.0), which is essentially social software used in "enterprise" (business/commercial) contexts. It encompasses modifications to corporate intranets and other classic software platforms used by large companies to organize their communication, collaboration and other aspects of their intranets. Enterprise social networking is also generally thought to include the use of a standard external social networking service to generate visibility for an enterprise.

Emerging trends in Enterprise Social Networking

Many companies are starting to implement social networks to promote collaboration amongst their employees. Vendors are now starting to use this as a way to help out the different companies. Some companies are starting to teach their employees about cloud computing and SaaS. These new technologies are being added to the enterprise social networks. These networks are being implemented to get employees collaborating and sharing tips and ideas about how to improve the workplace. Some social networks are homegrown systems that are built internally. Companies are using social networks to trade information amongst team members or other people who are part of the company. Sometimes this might also mean trading documents in real time. Based on research that Gartner has completed, 50% of enterprises will be using some sort of social network within the next two years.

BUSINESS IMPACTS

Companies such as IBM have recently been doing research to see how social networking can impact enterprise networks. Different companies have embraced social networking and they are creating their own internal social networking sites. IBM is one example and they have created Beehive. Many companies are encouraging the employees to use their social networks so they can connect with other employees, help people socialize when they take a break, or even help contribute to other work related issues. Some companies are even joining the typical social networking sites like Facebook or MySpace to gain more clients, communicate with their clients, or target certain individuals based on their likes. These companies want to gain the trust of their clients.

Applications

The year 2009 saw 92% of Inc. 500 companies using at least one social media channel, a dramatic increase over the 77% reported in 2008.

Medpedia is one of about 70 medical wikis that allows physicians and researchers to share information. While the information is free and publicly available, contributions are limited to those provided by medical professionals.

Deloitte has been a pioneer in its use of the corporate social networking applications for consulting. The adoption of social networking in sales organizations has recently been given a new name, S2.0 or Sales 2.0. Implementing a private sales social network provides a means to quickly disburse company sales knowledge. Smart companies are using social media tools to outsource their work to their customers. In addition to using social networking to market the enterprise, companies are involving customers in the design process. Chicago company Threadless invites their customers to submit their T-shirt designs to the Threadless web site for review by other customers. Smart companies are also involving their customers in technical support using enterprise social networking. eBay was an early adopter of the practice of allowing users to assist each other online.

To build brand loyalty through support of charitable giving, Pepsi decided to forego Super Bowl ads in favor of launching the Pepsi Refresh Project that helps people improve their communities through a variety of projects submitted and chosen through web voting by the general public funded by the Pepsi.

Issues: Lack of Familiarity with Social Networking

Employees may have had little or no experience using social networking tools and conventions, such as working with wikis or blogs. In addition, they may have never been exposed to networking conventions such as tagging information or including links in data. This is especially true of employees in nontechnical businesses.

Lack of Adoption

If training in the use of enterprise social networking tools is not provided to employees who do not have experience using them, they are unlikely to be widely adopted. The use of enterprise social networking must be championed at the highest levels of the enterprise to provide the resources needed and promote adoption throughout the organization.

Transparency

The sharing of information across the enterprise through via social networking creates a transparency that may or may not necessarily be welcomed by all sectors of the organization.

Perception

There is often an assumption that social networking will not work well in a particular industry or that its use may be perceived as unprofessional. In addition the ability to justify use of enterprise social networking, based on return on investment is not always readily apparent.

Privacy and Security

Privacy issues associated with social networking sites can be seen from many perspectives. Some people will argue that this is just a part of globalization and the growth of technology, while others will still believe that it is a right for any citizen, and will never change their views and perspectives about their privacy. With the increase in popularity of social networking, many users have given up their personal privacy in order to join these networks. Social media privacy issues didn't begin with social networking sites; they have historically been persistent issues with many other types of social media such as text messaging, instant messaging and computer-supported collaboration work.

According to Oscar Gandy, in the age of digital media we probably do not have privacy. He states: "the panoptic sort is an antidemocratic system of control that cannot be transformed because it can serve no purpose other than that for which it was designed — the rationalization and control of human existence." Gandy demanded creation of an agency that would ensure the survival of privacy.

From a policy perspective, according to Schement and Curtis, privacy is seen "as security against intrusion by government". According to Garfinkel (2000) "Privacy isn't just about hiding things. It's about self–possession, autonomy, and integrity."

Because social tools make many things that were normally private much more public, including all types of corporate data, many organizations would rather wait for best practices or to see what their peers are doing before delving very far into social networking. Privacy can become a huge issue at the enterprise level, when customer and employee data are at stake. Security concerns must be addressed prior to embarking upon creation of an enterprise social network.

SOCIAL CONSTRUCTIONISM

Social constructionism and social constructivism are sociological theories of knowledge that consider how social phenomena or objects of consciousness develop in social contexts.

Within constructionist thought, a social construction (social construct) is a concept or practice that is the construct (or artifact) of a particular group. When we say that something is socially constructed, we are focusing on its dependence on contingent variables of our social selves rather than any inherent quality that it possesses in itself. Take, for example, the concept of marriage: what this term includes and doesn't include and what it means to society does not exist "out there" in the world, but only in and through the social institutions that give it meaning within a culture. The underlying assumptions on which social constructivism is typically seen to be based are reality, knowledge, and learning.

Social constructs are generally understood to be the by-products of countless human choices rather than laws resulting from divine will or nature. This is not usually taken to imply a radical anti-determinism, however. Social constructionism is usually opposed to essentialism, which instead defines specific phenomena in terms of inherent and transhistorical essences independent of conscious beings that determine the categorical structure of reality. A major focus of social constructionism is to uncover the ways in which individuals and groups participate in the construction of their perceived social reality. It involves looking at the ways social phenomena are created, institutionalized, known, and made into tradition by humans. The social construction of reality is an ongoing, dynamic process that is (and must be) reproduced by people acting on their interpretations and their knowledge of it. Because social constructs as facets of reality and objects of knowledge are not "given" by nature, they must be constantly maintained and re-affirmed in order to persist. This process also introduces the possibility of change: what "justice" is and what it means shifts from one generation to the next. Ian Hacking noted in "The Social Construction of What?" that social construction talk is often in reference not only to worldly items, like things and facts – but also to beliefs about them. It is relevant to note that this perspective is often correctly closely connected with many contemporary theories, perhaps most notably the developmental theories of Vygotsky and Bruner.

Although both social constructionism and social constructivism deal with ways in which social phenomena develop, they are distinct. Social constructionism refers to the development of phenomena relative to social contexts while social constructivism refers to an individual's making meaning of knowledge within a social context (Vygotsky 1978). For this reason, social constructionism is typically described as a sociological concept whereas social constructivism is typically described as a psychological concept. However, while distinct, they are also complementary aspects of a single process through which humans in society create their worlds and, thereby, themselves.

Social constructivism has been studied by many educational psychologists, who are concerned with its implications for teaching and learning. For more on the psychological dimensions of social constructivism, see the work of Ernst von Glasersfeld and A. Sullivan Palincsar.

Constructionism became prominent in the U.S. with Peter L. Berger and Thomas Luckmann's 1966 book, The Social Construction of Reality. Berger and Luckmann argue that all knowledge, including the most basic, taken-for-granted common sense knowledge of everyday reality, is derived from and maintained by social interactions. When people interact, they do so with the understanding that their respective perceptions of reality are related, and as they act upon this understanding their common knowledge of reality becomes reinforced. Since this common sense knowledge is negotiated by people, human typifications, significations and institutions come to be presented as part of an objective reality, particularly for future generations who were not involved in the original process of negotiation. For example, as parents negotiate rules for their children to follow, those rules confront the children as externally produced "givens" that they cannot change. It is in this sense that it can be said that reality is socially constructed. The specific mechanisms underlying Berger and Luckmann's notion of social construction are discussed further in social construction. Berger and Luckmann's social constructionism has its roots in phenomenology. It links to Heidegger and Edmund Husserl through the teaching of Alfred Schutz. Schutz was Berger's PhD adviser.

During the 1970s and 1980s, social constructionist theory underwent a transformation as constructionist sociologists engaged with the work of Michel Foucault and others as a narrative turn in the social sciences was worked out in practice. This had a particular impact on the emergent sociology of science and the growing field of science and technology studies. In particular, Karin Knorr-Cetina, Bruno Latour, Barry Barnes, Steve Woolgar, and others used social constructionism to relate what science has typically characterized as objective facts to the processes of social construction, with the goal of showing that human subjectivity imposes itself on those facts we take to be objective, not solely the other way around. A particularly provocative title in this line of thought is Andrew Pickering's *Constructing Quarks: A Sociological History of Particle Physics*. At the same time, Social Constructionism shaped studies of technology - the Sofield, especially on the Social construction of technology, or SCOT, and authors as Wiebe Bijker, Trevor Pinch, Maarten van Wesel etc. Despite its common perception as objective, mathematics is not immune to social constructionist accounts. Sociologists such as Sal Restivo and Randall Collins, mathematicians including Reuben Hersh and Philip J. Davis, and philosophers including Paul Ernest have published social constructionist treatments of mathematics.

Social Constructionism and Postmodernism

Social constructionism can be seen as a source of the postmodern movement, and has been influential in the field of cultural studies. Some have gone so far as to attribute the rise of cultural studies (the cultural turn) to social constructionism. Within the social constructionist strand of postmodernism, the concept of socially constructed reality stresses the on-going mass-building of worldviews by individuals in dialectical interaction with society at a time. The numerous realities so formed comprise, according to this view, the imagined worlds of human social existence and activity, gradually crystallised by habit into institutions propped up by language conventions, given ongoing legitimacy by mythology, religion and philosophy, maintained by therapies and socialization, and subjectively internalised by upbringing and education to become part of the identity of social citizens.

Degrees of Social Construction

Though social constructionism contains a diverse array of

theories and beliefs, it can generally be divided into two camps: Weak social constructionism and strong social constructionism. The two differ mainly in degree, where weak social constructionists tend to see some underlying objective factual elements to reality, and strong social constructionists see everything as, in some way, a social construction. This is not to say that strong social constructionists see the world as ontologically unreal. Rather, they propose that the notions of "real" and "unreal" are themselves social constructs, so that the question of whether anything is "real" is just a matter of social convention.

Weak Social Constructionism

Harvard psychologist Steven Pinker writes that "some categories really are social constructions: they exist only because people tacitly agree to act as if they exist. Examples include money, tenure, citizenship, decorations for bravery, and the presidency of the United States."

In a similar vein, Stanley Fish has suggested that baseball's "balls and strikes" are social constructions. Both Fish and Pinker agree that the sorts of objects indicated here can be described as part of what John Searle calls "social reality". In particular, they are, in Searle's terms, ontologically subjective but epistemologically objective. "Social facts" are temporally, ontologically, and logically dependent on "brute facts." For example, "money" in the form of its raw materials (rag, pulp, ink) as constituted socially for barter (for example by a banking system) is a social fact of "money" by virtue of (i) collectively willing and intending (ii) to impose some particular function (purpose for which), (iii) by constitutive rules atop the "brute facts." "Social facts have the remarkable feature of having no analogue among physical [brute] facts". The existence of language is itself constitutive of the social fact, which natural or brute facts do not require. Natural or "brute" facts exist independently of language; thus a "mountain" is a mountain in every language and in no language; it simply is what it is.

Searle illustrates the evolution of social facts from brute facts by the constitutive rule: X counts as Y in C. "The Y terms has to assign a new *status* that the object does not already have just in virtue of satisfying the Y term; and there has to be collective agreement, or at least acceptance, both in the imposition of that status on the stuff referred to by the X term and about the function that goes with that status. Furthermore, because the physical features [brute facts] specified by the X term are insufficient by themselves to guarantee the fulfilment of the assigned function specified by the Y term, the new status and its attendant functions have to be the sort of things that can be constituted by collective agreement or acceptance."

Finally, against the strong theory and for the weak theory, Searle insists, "it could not be the case, as some have maintained, that all facts are institutional [i.e., social] facts, that there are no brute facts, because the structure of institutional facts reveals that they are logically dependent on brute facts. To suppose that all facts are institutional [i.e., social] would produce an infinite regress or circularity in the account of institutional facts. In order that some facts be institutional, there must be other facts that are brute [i.e., physical, biological, natural]. This is the consequence of the logical structure of institutional facts." Ian Hacking, Canadian philosopher of science, insists, "the notion that everything is socially constructed has been going the rounds. John Searle [1995] argues vehemently (and in my opinion cogently) against universal constructionism". "Universal social constructionism is descended from the doctrine that I once named linguistic idealism and attributed, only half in jest, to Richard Nixon. Linguistic idealism is the doctrine that only what is talked about exists, nothing has reality until it is spoken of, or written about. This extravagant notion is descended from Berkeley's idea-ism, which we call idealism: the doctrine that all that exists is mental" "They are a part of what John Searle [1995] calls social reality. His book is titled the *Construction of Social Reality,* and as I explained elsewhere [Hacking, 1996], that is not a *social* construction book at all"

Hacking observes, "the label 'social constructionism' is more code than description" of every Leftist, Marxist, Freudian, and Feminist PostModernist to call into question every moral, sex, gender, power, and deviant claim as just another essentialist claim—including the claim that members of the male and female sex are inherently different, rather than historically and socially constructed. Hacking observes that his 1995 simplistic dismissal of the concept actually revealed to many readers the outrageous implications of the theorists: Is child abuse a real evil, or a social construct, asked Hacking? His dismissive attitude, "gave some readers a way to see that there need be no clash between construction and reality", inasmuch as "the metaphor of social construction once had excellent shock value, but now it has become tired". Informally, they require human practices to sustain their existence, but they have an effect that is (basically) universally agreed upon. The disagreement lies in whether this category should be called "socially constructed". Ian Hacking argues that it should not. Furthermore, it is not clear that authors who write "social construction" analyses ever mean "social construction" in Pinker's sense. If they never do, then Pinker (probably among others) has misunderstood the point of a social constructionist argument.

Strong Social Constructionism

Strong social constructionists oppose the existence of "brute" facts. That a mountain is a *mountain* (as opposed to just another undifferentiated clump of earth) is socially engendered, and not a *brute* fact. That the concept of mountain is universally admitted in all human languages reflects near-universal human consensus, but does not make it an objective reality. Similarly for all apparently real objects and events: trees, cars, snow, collisions.

SOCIAL CONSTRUCTIONIST ANALYSIS

"Social construction" may mean many things to many people. Ian Hacking, having examined a wide range of books and articles with titles of the form "The social construction of X" or "Constructing X", argues that when something is said to be "socially constructed", this is shorthand for at least the following two claims:

- In the present state of affairs, X is taken for granted; X appears to be inevitable.
- X need *not* have existed, or need *not* be at all as it is. X, or X as it is at present, is *not* determined by the nature of things; it is *not* inevitable.

Hacking adds that the following claims are also often, though not always, implied by the use of the phrase "social construction":

- X is quite bad as it is.
- We would be much better off if X were done away with, or at least radically transformed.

Thus a claim that gender is socially constructed probably means that gender, as currently understood, is not an inevitable result of biology, but highly contingent on social and historical processes. In addition, depending on who is making the claim, it may mean that our current understanding of gender is harmful, and should be modified or eliminated, to the extent possible.

According to Hacking, "social construction" claims are not always clear about exactly what isn't "inevitable", or exactly what "should be done away with." Consider a hypothetical claim that quarks are "socially constructed". On one reading, this means that quarks themselves are not "inevitable" or "determined by the nature of things." On another reading, this means that our *idea* (or conceptualization, or understanding) of quarks is not "inevitable" or "determined by the nature of things".

Hacking is much more sympathetic to the second reading than the first. Furthermore, he argues that, if the second reading is taken, there need not always be a conflict between saying that quarks are "socially constructed" and saying that they are "real". In our gender example, this means that while a legitimate biological basis for gender may exist, *some* of society's perceptions of gender may be socially constructed.

The stronger first position, however, is more-or-less an inevitable corollary of Willard Van Orman Quine's concept of ontological relativity, and particularly of the Duhem-Quine thesis. That is, according to Quine and like-minded thinkers (who are not usually characterized as social constructionists) there is no single privileged explanatory framework that is closest to "the things themselves"—every theory has merit only in proportion to its explanatory power.

As we step from the phrase to the world of human beings, "social construction" analyses can become more complex. Hacking briefly examines Helène Moussa's analysis of the social construction of "women refugees". According to him, Moussa's argument has several pieces, some of which may be implicit:

1. Canadian citizens' idea of "the woman refugee" is not inevitable, but historically contingent. (Thus the idea or category "the woman refugee" can be said to be "socially constructed".)
2. Women coming to Canada to seek asylum are profoundly affected by the category of "the woman refugee". Among other things, if a woman does not "count" as a "woman refugee" according to the law, she may be deported, and forced to return to very difficult conditions in her homeland.
3. Such women may modify their behavior, and perhaps even their attitudes towards themselves, in order to gain the benefits of being classified as a "woman refugee".
4. If such a woman does not modify her behavior, she should be considered un-Canadian and as such should not be admitted to citizenship.

Hacking suggests that this third part of the analysis, the "interaction" between a socially constructed category and the individuals that are actually or potentially included in that category, is present in many "social construction" analyses involving types of human beings.

Environmental Leftist Social Constructionism

The Postmodern social construction of nature is a theory of postmodernist continental philosophy that poses an alternative critique of previous mainstream, promethean dialogue about environmental sustainability and ecopolitics. Whereas traditional criticisms of environmentalism come from the more conservative "right" of politics, leftist critiques of nature pioneered by postmodernist constructionism highlight the need to recognise "the other".

The implicit assumption made by theorists like Wapner is that a new "response to eco-criticism would require critics to acknowledge the ways in which they themselves silence nature and then to respect the sheer otherness of the nonhuman world."

This is because postmodernism prides itself on criticizing the urge toward mastery that characterizes modernity. But mastery is exactly what postmodernism is exerting as it captures the nonhuman world within its own conceptual domain. That in turn implies postmodern cultural criticism can deepen the modernist urge toward mastery by eliminating the ontological weight of the nonhuman world. "What else could it mean to assert that there is no such thing as nature?". Thus, the issue becomes an existentialist query about whether nature can exist in a humanist critique, and whether we can discern the "other's" views in relation to our actions on their behalf. This theorem has come to be known as "The Wapner Paradigm."

SOCIAL DYNAMICS

Social dynamics is the study of the ability of a society to react to inner and outer changes and deal with its regulation mechanisms. Social dynamics is a mathematically inspired approach to analyse societies, building upon systems theory and sociology. Sociologists, ethnologists, economists, social psychologists, criminologists, anthropologists and biologists are utilizing it in their studies of systems and behavior.

Society and culture are things to which we are emotionally bound and for which we have no immediate alternative.

Sociology and psychology deal with ratings, with subjectivity, they are supposed to provide objective findings to serve subjective needs. (Of course different people have more or less different feelings, goals and opinions, this must be discussed, as cultures found upon least common denominators.) Cut short, sociology sits on the fence, it is a mix of human and nature sciences, philosophy and politics. As this has stalled the progress of sociology, some people meant to bring new life into it by applying mathematics and systemics to sociology: On a certain level, life and societies are nothing more than systems dealing respectively with genes and culture (for life-like behavior in the latter, see meme). Therefore we can try to describe social systems by signals which become modified by transmission functions.

The analogy with biological and social systems can be taken too far and systems and approaches that work in natural sciences often do not account for the complexity in the social world. Edward O. Wilson has referred to the social sciences as 'hypercomplex'. While memetics is one of a history of approaches in Darwinising culture, there is a fundamental issues, and some would argue crudity in the way that social phenomena are ill-fitted into this view of heredity and transmission. On any measure this approach can only lead to a drifting from Darwinism and a more neo-Lamarckian framing of culture. As to what that might mean for memetics and culture as a neo-Darwinian understanding, the jury is clearly still out.

So while there are connections with the natural sciences and important areas of collaboration there has to be a respect for the social sciences as a range of epistemology on its/her own. If physics is used we can see approaches like mathematical sociology, socio-cybernetics and sociophysics emerging in recent years and again these offer further insights into the workings of culture.

These approaches offer something far more dynamic and quite different from the potentially sluggish terms of heredity and transmission. In 'actor network theory' social science already has an understanding that is quite conducive to physics' ideas of fields and potentially quantum theory.

So whether it is referred to as social dynamics, or culture dynamics any approach has to unify all these positions without losing task of the most important goal of all, and that is to illuminate the complex layers underpinning the human social and cultural experience, locally and globally, individually and collectively.

SOCIAL FLOOR

A social floor, also called a social minimum, is the concept that there is baseline level of social services and human rights to which every human being should have access. A social floor encompasses a system of Social protection, or a Social safety net, that would create a minimum "bundle of resources that a person needs in order to lead a minimally decent life in their society." The purpose of a social floor is to "prevent people from falling into destitution."

Components of a Social Floor

A social floor is the resources and services that every member of a society should have access to. Varying points of view exist on which services and resources should be included in the social minimum. The widely-accepted definition of a Social Protection Floor, as defined by the International Labour Organization (ILO) and the United Nations (UN), includes the following 4 guarantees: 1. Universal access to basic healthcare 2. Child/family benefits: guaranteed income security for children 3. Social assistance for the poor and unemployed 4. Guaranteed income security for the elderly and disabled

Some organizations believe that a social floor should also include additional services. For example, some scholars argue that a social floor should include public works, access to education, housing, land, and credit. Although there may not be agreement on the exact definition of a social floor, there is consensus that those who cannot provide for themselves, including children, unemployed, elderly, and disabled, should still have access to a minimum amount of services and resources.

Arguments for a Social Floor

The argument in favor of a social floor is based in the concept of morality and Social justice. The idea is that human beings should have the opportunity to lead a decent life in their society. This requires a minimum level of resources. The social floor would exist to provide these resources or the ability to attain these resources for those that cannot acquire them on their own. The principle of Social justice is equality and social unity. By necessity, this "demands prioritizing the worst off." According to proponents of a social floor, universal Social protection would help decrease poverty and inequality, and would benefit everyone by improving society overall. The social floor could also potentially have an economic benefit. Economies require a productive workforce in order to function. The view in favor of a social floor argues that increased Social protection and universal access to healthcare have been shown to increase productivity and decrease poverty, which leads to overall political stability and economic growth. According to the proponents implementing a social minimum would increase capabilities which ultimately would increase income. A central argument of those in favor of a social floor is that providing a universal social minimum can also provide a myriad of other benefits such as improving the economy by allowing people to have more purchasing power and be more self- sufficient.

Arguments against a Social Floor

One of the key argument against Social protection is affordability. Doubt exists as to if it is possible to fund a social minimum, especially in underdeveloped countries. Critics argue that a social floor is impossible, impractical, or unfair to fund. The idea that a social floor is impossible or impractical to fund is fairly straightforward. Providing the level of social services required to meet a social minimum would be a significant portion of the GDP of any given country. Some critics of the social floor concept argue that it is unrealistic to implement a social floor, simply because there is not enough money to fund it, especially in developing countries. Another argument, that funding a social minimum is unfair, is similar to the classic argument against Welfare: it takes away money from people that have earned it and rewards people who have not worked for it. Proponents of the social floor deny that the social floor is unfair with an appeal to social justice and morality. The International Labour Organization addresses the problem of affordability, claiming that a social floor is not only affordable, but economically beneficial. The idea is that, over time, Social protection will pay for itself through increased economic productivity. According to the International Labour Organization, a Cost-benefit analysis shows that the benefits of universal Social protection far outweigh the costs. The United Nations agrees, stating that "social protection systems are an economic investment" that can provide stability during times of economic downturn.

Besides the affordability argument against Social Protection there is a moral argument against seizing unearned property. Critics also contend that paying individuals not to work leads to further systemic poverty.

Proposed Policy for a Social Floor

Assuming that the social floor is a practical and realistic goal, the next step in implementing this universal social minimum would be reaching a consensus on what is included in a social floor. The social floor would be different for every country depending on what is the minimum level of income and capabilities required to live a decent life, a life of dignity, in that society. The International Labour Organization and the

United Nations have already developed a definition of the social floor that could be universally applied: universal access to basic healthcare, child/family benefits, social assistance for the poor and unemployed, and guaranteed income security for the elderly and disabled.

But for this concept of a social floor to be practically implemented, "governments must commit themselves to a political programme for a universal social minimum." Although potentially some aspects of Social protection could be funded through International aid, undoubtedly much of the funding would need to come from the government of the individual country. Universal social protection would require a significant percentage of the output of the host country.

2

Social Structure

Social structure is a term used in the social sciences to refer to patterned social arrangements which form the society as a whole, and which determine, to some varying degree, the actions of the individuals socialized into that structure. The meaning of "social structure" differs between various fields of sociology. On the macro scale, it can refer to the system of socioeconomic stratification (e.g., the class structure), social institutions, or, other patterned relations between large social groups. On the meso scale, it can refer to the structure of social network ties between individuals or organizations. On the micro scale, it can refer to the way norms shape the behavior of actors within the social system.

These meanings are not always kept separate. For example, recent scholarship by John Levi Martin has theorized that certain macro-scale structures are the emergent properties of micro-scale cultural institutions (this meaning of "structure" resembles that used by anthropologist Claude Lévi-Strauss). Marxist sociology also has a history of mixing different meanings of social structure, though it has done so by simply treating the cultural aspects of social structure as epiphenomena of its economic ones. Since the 1930s, the term has been in general use in social science, especially as a variable whose sub-components needed to be distinguished in relationship to other sociological variables.

Overview

The notion of social structure *as relationships between different entities or groups* or as *enduring and relatively stable patterns of relationship* emphasises the idea that society is grouped into structurally related groups or sets of roles, with different functions, meanings or purposes. One example of social structure is the idea of "social stratification", which refers to the idea that society is separated into different strata (levels), guided (if only partially) by the underlying structures in the social system. This approach has been important in the academic literature with the rise of various forms of structuralism. It is important in the modern study of organizations, because an organization's structure may determine its flexibility, capacity to change, and many other factors. Therefore, structure is an important issue for management.

Social structure may be seen to influence important social systems including the economic system, legal system, political system, cultural system, and others. Family, religion, law, economy and class are all social structures. The "social system" is the parent system of those various systems that are embedded in it.

Society: self contained, self sufficient population united by social relationships, bounded from other populations by geographic locations

Stratification: unequal distribution of valued goods or holdings in a population (i.e. class, status, resources, grades, wealth, positional goods, etc.)

Network - pattern of relationships in a population of actors

Social Structure Variables: Pattern of relationships, size of institution, income distribution, and concurrency of social relationships

History

The early study of social structures has informed the study of institutions, culture and agency, social interaction, and history. Alexis de Tocqueville was apparently the first to use the term social structure; later, Karl Marx, Herbert Spencer, Max Weber, Ferdinand Tönnies, and Émile Durkheim all contributed to structural concepts in sociology. Weber investigated and analyzed the institutions of modern society: market, bureaucracy (private enterprise and public administration), and politics (e.g. democracy).

One of the earliest and most comprehensive accounts of social structure was provided by Karl Marx, who related political, cultural, and religious life to the mode of production (an underlying economic structure). Marx argued that the economic base substantially determined the cultural and political superstructure of a society. Subsequent Marxist accounts, such as that by Louis Althusser, proposed a more complex relationship that asserted the relative autonomy of cultural and political institutions, and a general determination by economic factors only "in the last instance".

In 1905, the German sociologist Ferdinand Tönnies first published his study *The Present Problems of Social Structure* in the U.S.A, in: arguing that only the *constitution* of a multitude into a unity creates a "social structure" (basing this approach on his concept of social will).

Émile Durkheim (drawing on the analogies between biological and social systems popularized by Herbert Spencer and others) introduced the idea that diverse social institutions and practices played a role in assuring the functional integration of society — the assimilation of diverse parts into a unified and self-reproducing whole. In this context, Durkheim distinguished two forms of structural relationship: mechanical solidarity and organic solidarity. The former describes structures that unite similar parts through a shared culture; the latter describes differentiated parts united through exchange and material interdependence.

Georg Simmel develop Weber did but more generally), competition, division of labour, formation of parties, representation, inner solidarity coupled with exclusiveness toward the outside, and many similar features in the state, in a religious community, in an economic association, in an art school, and in family and kinship networks (however diverse the interests that give rise to these associations, the forms in which interests are realized may yet be identical (Crothers, 1996)).

The notion of social structure was extensively developed in the 20th century, with key contributions from structuralist perspectives drawing on the theories of Claude Lévi-Strauss, Feminist or Marxist perspectives, from functionalist perspectives such as those developed by Talcott Parsons and his followers, or from a variety of analytic perspectives. Some follow Marx in trying to identify the basic dimensions of society that explain the other dimensions, most emphasizing either economic production or political power. Others follow Lévi-Strauss in seeking logical order in cultural structures. Still others, notably Peter Blau, follow Simmel in attempting to base a formal theory of social structure on numerical patterns in relationships—analysing, for example, the ways in which factors like group size shape intergroup relations.

The notion of social structure is intimately related to a variety of central topics in social science, including the relation of structure and agency. The most influential attempts to combine the concept of social structure with agency are Anthony Giddens' theory of structuration and Pierre Bourdieu's practice theory. Giddens emphasizes the duality of structure and agency, in the sense that structures and agency cannot be conceived apart from one another. This permits him to argue that structures are neither independent of actors nor determining of their behavior, but rather sets of rules and competencies on which actors draw, and which, in the aggregate, they reproduce. Giddens's analysis, in this respect, closely parallels Jacques Derrida's deconstruction of the binaries that underlie classic sociological and anthropological reasoning (notably the universalizing tendencies of Lévi-Strauss's structuralism). Bourdieu's practice theory also seeks a more supple account of social structure as embedded in, rather than determinative of, individual behavior.

Other recent work by Margaret Archer (morphogenesis theory), Tom R. Burns and collaborators (actor-system dynamics theory and social rule system theory), and Immanuel Wallerstein (World Systems Theory) provided elaborations and applications of the sociological classics in structural sociology.

Definitions and Concepts

As noted above, social structure has been identified as

(i) the relationship of definite entities or groups to each other,

(ii) enduring patterns of behaviour by participants in a social system in relation to each other, and

(iii) institutionalised norms or cognitive frameworks that structure the actions of actors in the social system.

Lopez and Scott (2000) distinguish between *institutional structure* and *relational structure*, where in the former:

"*...social structure is seen as comprising those cultural or normative patterns that define the expectations of agents hold about each other's behaviour and that organize their enduring relations with each other.* "

whereas in the latter:

"*...social structure is seen as comprising the relationships themselves, understood as patterns of causal interconnection and interdependence among agents and their actions, as well as the positions that they occupy.* "

Social structure can also be divided into microstructure and macrostructure. Microstructure is the pattern of relations between most basic elements of social life, that cannot be further divided and have no social structure of their own (for example, pattern of relations between individuals in a group composed of individuals - where individuals have no social structure, or a structure of organizations as a pattern of relations between social positions or social roles, where those positions and roles have no structure by themselves). Macrostructure is thus a kind of 'second level' structure, a pattern of relations between objects that have their own structure (for example, a political social structure between political parties, as political parties have their own social structure). Some types of social structures that modern sociologist differentiate are *relation structures* (in family or larger family-like clan structures), *communication structures* (how information is passed in organizations) and sociometric structures (structures of sympathy, antipathy and indifference in organisations - this was studied by Jacob L. Moreno).

Social rule system theory reduces the structures of (3) to particular rule system arrangements, that is, the types of basic structures of (1 and 2). It shares with role theory, organizational and institutional sociology, and network analysis the concern with structural properties and developments and at the same time provides detailed conceptual tools needed to generate interesting, fruitful propositions and models and analyses.

Sociologists also distinguish between:

- normative structure — pattern of relations in given structure (organisation) between norms and modes of operations of people of varying social positions
- ideal structure — pattern of relations between beliefs and views of people of varying social positions
- interest structure — pattern of relations between goals and desires of people of varying social positions
- interaction structure — forms of communications of people of varying social positions

Origins and Evolution

Some believe that social structure is naturally developed. It may be caused by larger system needs, such as the need for labour, management, professional and military classes, or by conflicts between groups, such as competition among political parties or among elites and masses. Others believe that this structuring is not a result of natural processes, but is socially constructed.

It may be created by the power of elites who seek to retain their power, or by economic systems that place emphasis upon competition or cooperation. The most thorough account of the evolution of social structure is perhaps provided by structure and agency accounts that allow for a sophisticated analysis of the co-evolution of social structure and human agency, where socialised agents with a degree of autonomy take action in social systems where their action is on the one hand mediated by existing institutional structure and expectations but may, on the other hand, influence or transform that institutional structure.

Critical Implications

The notion of social structure may mask systematic biases, as it involves many identifiable subvariables, for example, gender. Some argue that men and women who have otherwise equal qualifications receive different treatment in the workplace because of their gender, which would be term a "social structural" bias, but other variables (such as time on the job or hours worked) might be masked. Modern social structural analysis takes this into account through multivariate analysis and other techniques, but the analytic problem of how to combine various aspects of social life into a whole remains.

WHAT IS A SOCIAL STRUCTURE?

Are there such things as "social structures"? In what do they consist? What sorts of social powers do they exercise? Consider a few candidates: the global trading system, the Federal government, the Chinese peasantry of the 1930s, the English class system, the Indian marriage system, race in the United States, the city of Chicago. Are these items examples of "social structures"?

Several ideas appear to be core features in our ordinary understanding of this concept. A social structure consists of rules, institutions, and practices. A social structure is socially embodied in the actions, thoughts, beliefs, and durable dispositions of individual human beings. A social structure is effective in organizing behavior of large numbers of actors. A structure is coercive of individual and group behavior. A social structure assigns roles and powers to individual actors. A social structure often has distributive consequences for individuals and groups. A social structure is geographically dispersed. Social structures can cause social outcomes involving both persistence and change.

We might try to reduce these intuitions to a definition: a social structure is a system of geographically dispersed rules and practices that influence the actions and outcomes of large numbers of social actors.

Now back to our original question: do such things exist? Before proceeding to a answer, a few points are evident. Any social entity must possess microfoundations in human mentalities and actions. There is no such thing as a social entity that lacks human embodiment—any more than there are works of art that lacks material embodiment. Social entities "supervene" upon human individuals.

This point also applies to any statements we might make about the putative causal powers of a social entity. So claims about the causal properties of social structures must be supplemented by a theory of the microfoundations of those powers. How does an extended social structure exert influence over the actions of located individuals?

And there is a final parallel point about claims about the geographical scope and coherence of a social entity. If we want to maintain that an entity exercises influence as a coherent and extended entity, we need to be able to specify the mechanisms through which this takes place. How does the Federal state exert its control and influence over the vast scope of the United States and its population?

So, with these qualifications about the unavoidable need for providing microfoundations—are there social structures?

Several of the instances offered above fit the terms of our provisional definition. They are large complexes of rules and practices that influence behavior and outcomes. And it is straightforward to begin to provide a description of the microfoundations upon which they exist: the social components through which these structures are embodied and through which they exercise influence on individuals and groups. The US Federal Government functions as a system of branches of government, each with its own departments governed by formal and informal rules. And the "reach" of the state down to the local and individual level is secured by the socially implemented forms of power that are locally expressed (bank inspectors, law enforcement agencies, tax auditors,...).

This is an example of a large social structure that operates through a high degree of formal institutionalization. But some of the examples mentioned above depend primarily on informal mechanisms — the workings of widespread beliefs and attitudes, along with a diffused willingness of individuals to "enforce" the requirements of the structure. Structures relying primarily on informal mechanisms include the Indian marriage system or the English class system.

Is "race" a structure in American society? Plainly it possesses some of the key elements identified above. The reality of race leads to an uneven distribution of opportunities and outcomes, so "race" is a social fact with distributive consequences. It has the element of coercion: racial prejudice and patterns of discrimination are imposed on individuals without an "opt-out" possibility. And we can identify many of the social mechanisms through which race and racial discrimination work; so the category possesses microfoundations. Today many of those mechanisms are "informal" rather than "formal"; but of course the legal institutionalization of racial discrimination is a recent fact in American history. So "race" is a structural feature of American society.

Several of the examples mentioned above appear to fall outside the category of social structure, however; for example, "Chinese peasantry". These examples appear to be large factors that play a role in large social structures, but are more akin to elements than systems. So the structure that defines "Chinese peasantry" is the system of property, agriculture, and kinship that defines the peasant's role and opportunities in society; the category of "peasant" identifies one node within that system or structure.

What about "the city of Chicago"? Is this a structure or some other category of social entity? I am inclined to say that the city of Chicago is a complex social entity, not a structure. It falls *within* a variety of structures in America and the world—the global trading system, the electoral process, and the politics of national funding for large cities; and it embodies within it a variety of smaller structures—the public school system, lending practices, nepotism. But the city itself does not function as a regulative system coordinating the activities of large numbers of individuals. Rather, it is a complex social entity composed of a mix of social practices, behaviours, systems, and relationships.

THE STRUCTURE OF SOCIAL ACTION

"Who now reads Spencer? It is difficult for us to realise how great a stir he made in the world.... He was the intimate confidant of a strange and rather unsatisfactory God, whom he called the principle of Evolution. His God has betrayed him. We have evolved beyond Spencer." Professor Brinton's verdict may be paraphrased as that of the coroner, "Dead by suicide or at the hands of person or persons unknown." We must agree with the verdict. Spencer is dead. But who killed him and how? This is the problem.

Of course there may well be particular reasons why Spencer rather than others is dead, as there were also particular reasons why he rather than others made such a stir. With these this study is not concerned. But in the " crime," the solution of which is here sought, much more than the reputation of, or interest in, a single writer has been done to death. Spencer was, in the general outline of his views, a typical representative of the later stages of development of a system of thought about man and society which has played a very great part in the intellectual history of the English-speaking peoples, the positivistic-utilitarian tradition. What has happened to it? Why has it died?

The thesis of this study will be that it is the victim of the vengeance of the jealous god, Evolution, in this case the evolution of scientific theory. In the present chapter it is not proposed to present an account either of what has evolved or of what it has evolved into; all that will come later. It is necessary to preface this with a tentative statement of the problem, and an outline of some general considerations relevant to the way the present task is to be undertaken, and how the present study should be judged.

Spencer's god was Evolution, sometimes also called Progress. Spencer was one of the most vociferous in his devotions to this god, but by no means alone among the faithful. With many other social thinkers he believed that man stood near the culminating point of a long linear process extending back unbroken, without essential changes of direction, to the dawn of primitive man. Spencer, moreover, believed that this culminating point was being approached in the industrial society of modern Western Europe. He and those who thought like him were confident that evolution would carry this process on almost indefinitely in the same direction cumulatively.

A good many students have lately become dubious of these propositions. Is it not possible that the future holds in store something other than "bigger and better" industrialism? The conception that, instead of this, contemporary society is at or near a turning point is very prominent in the views of a school of social scientists who, though they are still comparatively few, are getting more and more of a hearing.

Spencer was an extreme individualist. But his extremism was only the exaggeration of a deep-rooted belief that, stated roughly, at least in the prominent economic phase of social life, we have been blest with an automatic, self-regulating mechanism which operated so that the pursuit by each individual of his own self-interest and private ends would result in the greatest possible satisfaction of the wants of all. All that was necessary was to remove obstacles to the operation of this mechanism, the success of which rested on no conditions other than those included in the conception of rational pursuit of self-interest. This doctrine, too, has been subjected to increasingly severe criticism from many quarters, by no means all relevant to the purposes of this study. But another article of faith about the workings of the social world has been breaking down.

Finally, Spencer believed that religion arose from the prescientific conceptions of men about the empirical facts of their own nature and their environment. It was, in fact, the product of ignorance and error. Religious ideas would, with the progress of knowledge, be replaced by science. This was only a phase of a much wider deification of science. Indeed the interest of the Spencerian type of social scientist in religion has thus been virtually confined to primitive man - the question was, how has science developed out of primitive religion? In this field, too, there is increasing scepticism of the Spencerian view. It has been possible above to cite views on only a few questions. It is, however, enough to indicate that a basic revolution in empirical interpretations of some of the most important social problems has been going on. Linear evolutionism has been slipping and cyclical theories have been appearing on the horizon. Various kinds of individualism have been under increasingly heavy fire. In their place have been appearing socialistic, collectivistic organic theories of all sorts. The role of reason and the status of scientific knowledge as an element of action have been attacked again and again. We have been overwhelmed by a flood of anti-intellectualistic theories of human nature and behaviour, again of many different varieties. A revolution of such magnitude in the prevailing empirical interpretations of human society is hardly to be found occurring within the short space of a generation, unless one goes back to about the sixteenth century. What is to account for it?

It is, of course, very probable that this change is in considerable part simply an ideological reflection of certain basic social changes. This thesis would raise a problem, the answer to which would be difficult to find in terms of Spencerian thought. But to deal adequately with this problem would far transcend the limits of this study.

It is no less probable that a considerable part has been played by an "immanent" development within the body of social theory and knowledge of empirical fact itself. This is the working hypothesis on which the present study has been made. The attempt will be made to trace and evaluate the significance of one particular phase of this process of development which can be discerned and analysed in detail in the work of a limited group of writers in the social field, mostly known as sociologists. But before entering upon this enterprise it is necessary to make a few preliminary methodological remarks about the nature of a "body of social theory and knowledge of empirical fact." What are the main relations of the principal elements in it to each other, and in what sense and by what kind of process may such a "body" be thought to be undergoing a process of development? Only then can it be stated explicitly what kind of study is here proposed and what order of results may reasonably be expected from it.

Theory and Empirical Fact

In the following discussion some fundamental methodological propositions will be laid down without any attempt to give them a critical foundation. It will, however, turn out that the question of the status of these views will form one main element of the subject matter of the whole study. Their soundness is to be judged not in terms of the arguments brought forward in their defence in the present introductory discussion but in terms of the way they fit into the structure of the study as a whole and its outcome.

There is, more often implicit than explicit, a deep-rooted view that the progress of scientific knowledge consists essentially in the cumulative piling up of "discoveries" of "fact." Knowledge is held to be an entirely quantitative affair. The one important thing is to have observed what had not been observed before. Theory, according to this view, would consist only in generalisation from known facts, in she sense of what general statements the known body of fact would justify. Development of theory would consist entirely in the process of modification of these general statements to take account of new discoveries of fact. Above all, the process of discovery of fact is held to be essentially independent of the existing body of "theory," to be the result of some such impulse as "idle curiosity."

It is evident that such terms as "fact" are much in need of definition This will come later. At the present juncture against the view just roughly sketched may be set another, namely, that scientific " theory " - most generally defined as a body of logically interrelated "general concepts" of empirical reference - is not only a dependent but an independent variable in the development of science. It goes without saying that a theory to be sound must fit the facts but it does not follow that the facts alone, discovered independently of theory, determine what the theory is to be, nor that theory is not a factor in determining what facts will be discovered, what is to be the direction of interest of scientific investigation.

Not only is theory an independent variable in the development of science, but the body of theory in a given field at a given time constitutes to a greater or less degree an integrated "system." ' That is, the general propositions (which may be, as will be seen later, of different kinds) which constitute a body of theory have mutual logical relations to each other. Not, of course, that all the rest are deducible from any one - that would confine theory to the one proposition - but in the sense that any substantive change in the statement of one important proposition of the system has logical consequences for the statement of the others. Another way ff of putting this is to say that any system of theory has a determinate logical structure.

Now obviously the propositions of the system have reference to matters of empirical fact; if they did not, they could have no claim to be called scientific. Indeed, if the term fact is properly interpreted it may be said that a theoretical proposition, if it has a place in science at all, is either itself a statement of fact or a statement of a mode of relations between facts. It follows that any *important* change in our knowledge of fact in the field in question must of itself change the statement of at least one of the propositions of the theoretical system and, through the logical consequences of this change, that of other propositions to a greater or lesser degree. This is to say, the structure of the theoretical system is changed. All this seems to be in accord with the empiricist methodology sketched above.

But, in the first place, it will be noted that the word "important" used above was italicised. What does an important change in our knowledge of fact mean in this context? Not that the new facts are vaguely "interesting," that they satisfy "idle curiosity, " or that they demonstrate the goodness of God. But the *scientific* importance of a change in knowledge of fact consists precisely in j its having consequences for a system of theory. A scientifically unimportant discovery is one which, however true and however interesting for other reasons, has no consequences for a system of theory with which scientists in that field are concerned. Conversely, even the most trivial observation from any other point of new - a very small deviation of the observed from the calculated position of a star, for instance - may be not only important but of revolutionary importance, if its logical consequences for the structure of theory are far-reaching. It is probably safe to say that all the changes of factual knowledge which have led to the relativity theory, resulting in a very great theoretical development, are completely trivial from any point of view except their relevance to the structure of a theoretical system. They have not, for instance, affected in any way the practice of engineering or navigation.

This matter of the importance of facts is, however, only one part of the picture. A theoretical system does not merely state facts which have been observed and that logically deducible relations to other facts which have also been observed. In so far as such a theory is empirically correct it will also tell us what empirical facts it should be possible to observe in a given set of circumstances. It is the most elementary rule of scientific integrity that the formulator of a theoretical proposition must take into account all the relevant known facts accessible to him. This process of verification, fundamental to science, does not consist merely in reconsideration of this applicability to known facts by others than the original formulator of the theory, and then simply waiting for new facts to turn up. It consists in deliberately investigating phenomena with the expectations derived from the theory in mind and seeing whether or not the facts actually found agree with these expectations.

This investigation is one of situations which have been studied either never at all before or not with these particular theoretical problems in mind. Where possible the situations to be investigated are experimentally produced and controlled. But this is a matter of practical technique, not of logic.

In so far as the expectations from the theory agree with the facts found, making allowance for "errors of observation," etc., the theory is "verified." But the significance of the process of verification is by no means confined to this. If this does not happen, as is often so, either the facts may be found to disagree with the theoretical expectations, or other facts may be found which have no place in the theoretical system. Either result necessitates critical reconsideration of the system itself. There is, then, a reciprocal process: direction, by the expectations derived from a system of theory, toward fields of factual investigation, then reaction of the results of this investigation on the theory.

Finally, verification in this sense is not the only important relation of a theoretical system to the direction of empirical investigation. Not only are specific theoretical propositions which have been directly formulated with definite matters of fact in view subject to verification. But further, a theoretical system built up upon observations of fact will be found, as its implications are progressively worked out, to have logical consequences for fields of fact with which its original formulators were not directly concerned. If certain things in one field are true, then other things in another, related field must also be true. These implications also are subject to verification, which in this case takes the form of finding out what are the facts in this field. The results of this investigation may have the same kind of reaction on the theoretical system itself.

Thus, in general, in the first instance, the direction of interest in empirical fact will be canalised by the logical structure of the theoretical system. The importance of certain problems concerning the facts will be inherent in the structure of the system. Empirical interest will be in the facts so far as they are relevant to the solution of these problems. Theory not only formulates what we know but also tells us what we want to know, that is, the questions to which an answer is needed. Moreover, the structure of a theoretical system tells us what alternatives are open in the possible answers to a given question. If observed facts of undoubted accuracy will not fit any of the alternatives it leaves open, the system itself is in need of reconstruction.

A further point is of importance in the present connection. Not only do theoretical propositions stand in logical interrelations to each other so that they may be said to constitute "system but it is in the nature of the case that theoretical systems should attempt to become "logically closed." That is, a system starts with a group of interrelated propositions which involve reference to empirical observations within the logical framework of the propositions in question. Each of these propositions has logical implications. The system becomes logically closed when each of the logical implications which can be derived from any one proposition within the system finds its statement in another proposition in the same system. It may be repeated that this does not mean that all the other propositions must be logically derivable from any one - on the contrary, if this were true scientific theory would be sheer tautology.

The simplest way to see the meaning of the concept of a closed, system in this sense is to consider the example of a system of simultaneous equations. Such a system is determinate, i.e., closed, when there are as many independent equations as there are independent variables. If there are four equations and only three variables, and no one of the equations is derivable from the others by algebraic manipulation then there is another variable missing. Put in general logical terms: the propositions stated in the four equations logically involve an assumption which is not stated in the definitions of the three variables.

The importance of this is clear. If the explicit propositions of a system do not constitute a logically closed system in this sense it may be inferred that the arguments invoked rest for their logical cogency on one or more unstated assumptions. It is one of the prime functions of logical criticism of theoretical systems to apply this criterion and, if gaps are found, to uncover the implicit assumptions. But though all theory tends to develop logically closed systems in this sense it is dangerous to confuse this with the " empirical " closure of a system. To this issue, that of "empiricism," it will be necessary often to return.

The implications of these considerations justify the statement that all empirically verifiable knowledge even the commonsense knowledge of everyday life - involves implicitly, if not explicitly, systematic theory in this sense. The importance of this statement lies in the fact that certain persons who write on social subjects vehemently deny it. They say they state merely facts and let them "speak for themselves." But the fact a person denies that he is theorising is no reason for taking him at his word and failing to investigate what implicit theory is involved in his statements. This is important since " empiricism " in this sense has been a very common methodological position in the social sciences.

From all this it follows what the general character of the problem of the development of a body of scientific knowledge is, in so far as it depends on elements internal to science itself. It is that of increasing knowledge of empirical fact, intimately combined with changing interpretations of this body of fact - hence changing general statements about it - and, not least, a changing a structure of the theoretical system. Special emphasis should be laid on this intimate interrelation of general statements about empirical fact with the logical elements and structure of theoretical systems.

In one of its main aspects the present study may be regarded as an attempt to verify empirically this view of the nature of science and its development in the social field. It takes the form of the thesis that intimately associated with the revolution in empirical interpretations of society sketched above there has in fact occurred an equally radical change in the structure of theoretical systems. The hypothesis may be put forward, to be tested by the s subsequent investigation, that this development has been in large part a matter of the reciprocal interaction of new factual insights and knowledge on the one hand with changes in the theoretical system on the other. Neither is the "cause" of the other. Both are in a state of close mutual interdependence.

This verification is here attempted in monographic form. The central focus of attention is in the process of development of one coherent theoretical system, that to be denoted as the *voluntaristic theory of action*, and the definition of the general concepts of which this theory is composed. In the historical aspect the primary interest is in the process of transition from one phase of its development to another, distinctly different, one. Of the first phase Spencer may be regarded as a late, and in some points extreme, but nevertheless a typical representative. For convenience of reference and for no other purpose this has been designated as the "positivistic" system of the theory of action, and its variant, - which is most important to the present study, the "utilitarian." Both these terms are used in technical senses in this work and they will be defined, where the main logical structure of the positivistic system is outlined.

It is, however, a striking fact that what is in all essential respects the same system may be found emerging by a similar process of transition from the background of a radically different theoretical tradition which may be designated as the "idealistic." One dominant case of this latter transition, the work of Max Weber, will be dealt with at length. It goes without saying that this convergence, if it can be demonstrated, is a very strong argument for the view that correct observation and interpretation of the facts constitute at least one major element in the explanation of why this particular theoretical system has developed at all.

As has been said, interest will be focused in the process of emergence of a particular theoretical system, that of the "voluntaristic theory of action".' But the above considerations indicate the great importance of dealing with this in the closest connection with the empirical aspects of the work of the men whose theories are to be treated. So for each major thinker at least a fair sample of the major empirical views he held will be presented, and the attempt made to show in detail the relations of these to the theoretical system in question. In each case the thesis will be maintained that an adequate understanding of how these empirical views were arrived at is impossible without reference to the logical structure and relations of the theoretical concepts employed by the writer in question. And in every case except that of Marshall the attempt will be made to demonstrate that the conspicuous change in his empirical views from those current in the tradition with which the writer in question was most closely associated cannot be understood without reference to the corresponding change in the structure of his theoretical system from that dominant in the tradition in question. If this can be demonstrated it will have important general implications. It will be strong evidence that he who would arrive at important empirical conclusions transcending common sense cannot afford to neglect considerations of systematic theory.

The choice of writers to be treated here has been dictated by a variety of considerations. The central interest of the study is in the development of a particular coherent theoretical system, as an example of the general process of "immanent" development of science itself. This process has been defined as a matter of the logical exigencies of theoretical systems in close mutual interrelation with observations of empirical fact and general statements embodying these facts. Hence a choice of authors is indicated which will serve to isolate these elements as far as possible from Others, such as influence of the general "climate of opinion," irrelevant to the purposes of this study.

The first criterion is actual concern with the theory of action Among those who are satisfactory in this respect it is desirable to have represented as great a diversity of intellectual tradition, social milieu and personal character as possible. The inclusion of Marshall is justified by the fact that economic theory and the question of its status involve a crucial set of problems in relation to the theory of action in general and to the positivistic system, especially its utilitarian variant.

This question is as will be seen, the most important single link between utilitarian positivism and the later phase of the theory of action. Pareto also was deeply concerned with the same set of problems, but in relation to distinctly different aspects of the positivistic tradition, and in the midst of a strikingly different climate of opinion. The comparison of the two is most instructive.

Durkheim's starting point was also positivistic, indeed by far the most explicitly so of the three. But it was the variant of the positivistic system most radically foreign to that of utilitarian individualism in which Marshall was primarily immersed, and Pareto also, though to a less extent. In personal character and background more violent contrasts are scarcely imaginable than between Marshall, the strongly moralistic middle-class Englishman; Durkheim, the Alsatian Jewish, radical, anticlerical, French professor; Pareto, the aloof, sophisticated Italian nobleman; and, finally, Weber, a son of the most highly cultured German upper middle class, who grew up on the background of German idealism and was trained in the historical schools of jurisprudence and economics. These intellectual influences were of no real importance in the formation of the thought of any of the other three. Moreover, Weber's personal character was radically different from any of the other three.

Another point strongly in favour of this choice is that although all four of these men were approximately contemporary, there is with one exception not a trace of direct influence of any one on any other. Pareto was certainly influenced by Marshall in the formulation of his technical economic theory, but with equal certainty not in any respect relevant to this discussion. And this is the only possibility of any direct mutual influence. In fact, within the broad cultural unit, Western and Central Europe at the end of the nineteenth and beginning of the twentieth century, it would scarcely be possible to choose four men who had important ideas in common who were less likely to have been influenced in developing this common body of ideas by factors other than the immanent development of the logic of theoretical systems in relation to empirical fact.

Certain other considerations are relevant. The main concern of the study is with the outline of a theoretical system. Its minor variations from writer to writer are not a matter of concern to this analysis. It is, however, necessary to work out its logical structure and ramifications in the clearest form attainable. Hence the choice has been made of intensive analysis from the relevant point of view of the work of a small number of the most eminent men. Marshall was, by many in his field, thought to be the most eminent economist of his generation. But the interest of the present study in him is more limited than in the others. The other three are all generally known as sociologists. There can be little question of their eminence in their generation in their field. A list of the first six sociologists of the last generation which failed to include all three names could hardly be taken seriously. This is not to say they are the only equally eminent ones, but for the purposes of this study they are distinctly the most suitable. In order to avoid all possibility of misunderstanding, it should be reiterated: This study is meant to be a monographic study of one particular problem in the history of recent social thought, that of the emergence of the theoretical system which has been called the "voluntaristic theory of action." It follows that there are a number of related things which this study is not and is not meant to be. In the first place it is not a history of sociological theory in Europe in, roughly, the last generation. It deliberately avoids the inclusiveness with regard both to problems and to men which such a task would require. If there is anything at all in its results, it follows that the process under investigation is one element of the history of European sociological theory in that period. Then this study will constitute a monographic contribution to this history, but that is all.

In the second place, it is not a general secondary interpretation of the work of any or all of the men dealt with. Its aim is neither secondary exposition as such nor critical evaluation of them. With respect to each of the theorists the aspects which this study rests are of great, sometimes of central, importance to their work " a whole. But in the treatment of none will the attempt be made to evaluate this importance relatively to that of other aspects. That must be left to other studies. Finally, in harmony with all this, there has been no attempt to discuss all aspects of the work of these men or all the secondary literature about them. Practically all the existing secondary literature about them has been read, but has been cited only where it seemed particularly relevant to the immediate context. Failure to cite is not to be interpreted as implied criticism, only lack of important bearing. Also, with the texts themselves, encyclopedic completeness has not been aspired to. Nor has every passage that could be construed as relevant to the purpose in hand been cited but only enough, taken in terms of the structure of the writers' theories as a whole, to establish the points at issue.

Perhaps one more word with reference to interpretation may be permitted. This study is conceived to be an organic whole, concerned with ideas which are logically interrelated and permeate the whole study. The reader should keep this in mind in weighing whatever critical remarks he may be inclined to make. Particularly in a study of this character, it is legitimate to ask that a fact cited or a statement made be taken not only in its immediate intrinsic character and meaning but also in relation to the total structure of which it forms a part.

Residual Categories

Two or three further preliminary questions should be taken up so as not to leave the reader in doubt on some matters that are bound to arise in his mind. In the first place, one further conclusion about the character of scientific development follows from the position already taken. It is possible to have scattered and unintegrated bits of knowledge', and to assent to the "truth" of further scattered bits as they are called to one's attention. This type of knowledge does not, however, constitute "science " in the sense in which this study is interested in it.

The latter is present only in so far as these bits of knowledge have become integrated with reference to fairly clear-cut theoretical systems. In so far as this has happened, two things can be said. It is at least unlikely that such a system should play an important part in canalising the thought of a considerable number of highly intelligent men over a period of time, if it were not that the propositions of the system involved empirical references to phenomena which were real and, within the framework of the conceptual scheme, on the whole correctly observed.

At the same time the structure of the conceptual scheme itself inevitably focuses interest on a limited range of such empirical facts. These may be thought of as a " spot" in the vast encircling darkness, brightly illuminated as by a searchlight. The point is, what lies outside the spot is not really "seen" until the searchlight moves, and then only what lies within the area into which its beam is newly cast. Even though any number of facts may be "known" outside this center, they are not scientifically important until they can be brought into relation with a theoretical system.

This fact is of the greatest importance as a canon of interpretation. In studying a man's empirical work the questions asked will not merely be, what opinions did he hold about certain concrete phenomena. nor even. what has he in general contributed to our knowledge of these phenomena? The primary questions will, rather, be, what theoretical reasons did he have for being interested in these particular problems rather than others, and what did the results of his investigation contribute to the solution of his theoretical problems? Then, in turn, what did the insights gained from these investigations contribute to the restatement of his theoretical problems and through this to the revision of his theoretical system? Thus, in connection with Durkheim the real point of interest is not in his having established the fact that the suicide rate in the French army was, during a certain period, considerably higher than in the civil population. Those interested in this fact for its own sake can consult his study. The present interest is, rather, why did Durkheim study suicide anyway, and what is the significance for his general theory of this and the other facts he established in the course of his investigation of it?

Something should also be said about the general character of the process by which this awakening of new scientific interest in fields of fact proceeds, and theoretical problems shift. Every system, including both its theoretical propositions and its main relevant empirical insights, may be visualised as an illuminated spot enveloped by darkness. The logical name for the darkness is, in general, "residual categories." Their role may be deduced from the inherent necessity of a system to become logically closed. On whatever level it operates, a theoretical system must involve the positive definition of certain empirically identifiable variables or other general categories. The very fact that they are defined at all implies that they are distinguished from others and that the facts which constitute their empirical reference are thereby, in certain aspects at least, specifically differentiated from others.

If, as is almost always the case, not all the actually observable facts of the field, or those which have been observed, fit into the sharply, positively defined categories, they tend to be given one or more blanket names which refer to categories negatively defined, that is, of facts known to exist, which are even more or less adequately described, but are defined theoretically by their failure to fit into the positively defined categories of the system. The only theoretically significant statements that can be made about these facts are negative statements - they are not so and so. But it is not to be inferred that because these statements are negative they are therefore unimportant.

It is true that in the work of the mediocre proponents of a theoretical system the qualifications of their empirical deductions from theory which are necessitated by the existence of these residual categories are often ignored, or so vaguely stated as to be virtually meaningless. In the case of the dogmatists of the system their existence, or at least their importance for the system, may even be vehemently denied. Both procedures are vastly encouraged by an empiricist methodology. But in the work of the ablest and most clear-headed proponents of a system these residual categories will often be not merely implicit but explicit, and will be quite clearly stated. In this sense, the best place to go to find the starting points of the breakdown of a system is to the work of the ablest proponents of the system itself. This more than any other reason is the explanation of why the work of so many of the greatest scientific theorists is "difficult." Only the lesser lights can bring themselves to dogmatise about the exclusive importance and adequacy of their own positively defined categories.

It follows from this that the surest symptom of impending change in a theoretical system is increasingly general interest in such residual categories. Indeed, one kind of progress of theoretical work consists precisely in the carving out from residual categories of definite positively defined concepts and their verification in empirical investigation. The obviously unattainable, but asymptotically approached goal of the development of scientific theory is, then, the elimination of all residual categories from science in favour of positively defined, empirically verifiable concepts- For any one system there will, to be sure, always be residual categories of fact, but they will be translatable into positive categories of one or more other systems. For the empirical application of any one system these residual elements will be found to be involved in the necessary data.

The process of the carving out of positive concepts from residual categories is also a process by which the reconstruction of theoretical systems is accomplished as a result of which they may eventually be altered beyond all recognition. But this should be said: The original empirical insights associated with the positive categories of the original system will be restated in different form, but unless they entirely fail to stand up to the combined criticism of theory and renewed empirical verification, they will not be eliminated. Indeed, as has been noted above, this is unlikely to happen. This fact is the essential basis for the justification of talk of the "progress" of science. Theoretical systems change. There is not merely a quantitative accumulation of "knowledge of fact" but a qualitative change in the structure of theoretical systems. But in so far as verification has been valid and sound, this change leaves behind it a permanent precipitate of valid empirical knowledge. The form of statement may well change, but the substance will remain. The older statement will generally take the form of a "special case" of the new. The utilitarian branch of positivistic thought has, by virtue of the structure of its theoretical system, been focused upon a given range of definite empirical insights and related theoretical problems. The central fact. - a fact beyond all question. - is that in certain aspects and to certain degrees, under certain conditions, human action is rational. That is, men adapt themselves to the conditions which they are placed and adapt means to their ends in such a way as to approach the most efficient manner of achieving these ends. And the relations of these means and conditions to the achievement of their ends are "known" to be intrinsically verifiable by the methods of empirical science.

Of course this statement contains a considerable number of terms which have been, and still are, ambiguous in general usage. Their definition is one of the prime tasks of the study as a whole. This range of factual insight and the theoretical problems involved in it, and this alone, is the theme of the first analysis. The task of the first two parts of the study is to trace its development from one well-defined theoretical system to another. The process has been essentially that just sketched, a process of focusing attention on, and carving positive theoretical concepts out of, the residual categories to be found in the various versions of the initial system.

Perhaps it is permissible to state here, or to repeat in a somewhat different form, a vital canon of interpretation for a study of this kind. It is in the nature of the enterprise that many facts and theoretical considerations that are important from any one of a large number of different possible points of view will have been neglected. A specific criterion has just been laid down of what scientific "importance" is considered to mean, and the remarks just made serve further to elucidate the meaning of this criterion. If a critic is to charge neglect of the importance of such things, he should be able to show either (a) that the neglected consideration bears specifically on the limited range of theoretical problems to which this study has been deliberately limited and that its correct consideration would significantly alter the conclusions about them or (b) that the whole conception of the nature of science and its development here advanced is so fundamentally wrong that these criteria of importance are inapplicable.

Theory, Methodology and Philosophy

Out of these considerations grows directly another range of problems which must be commented upon briefly. It will be asked whether a study of this character will find it possible to confine itself to "science" or will not find it necessary to embark upon the perilous waters of philosophy. Such a venture will, indeed, prove necessary at certain points and it is hence advisable to make a general statement of the relevant relations of these two kinds of discipline to each other and to the kind of study here attempted. Like the other statements in this chapter it will be brief and without critical foundation.

The main outline of a view of the general character of empirical science has already been presented. The distinction of science from all the philosophical disciplines is vital. It will turn out to be so at every stage of the ensuing study. But this is not to be taken to mean that the two kinds of discipline are without significant mutual interrelations and that each can afford to ignore the other. For the purposes of this study. - not necessarily for others. - it is legitimate to define philosophy as a residual category. It is the attempt to achieve a rational cognitive understanding of human experience by methods other than those of empirical science.

That there are important mutual relations of philosophy and science, once the distinction between them is established, is a simple deduction from the most general nature of reason itself. The tendency of theoretical systems in science to become logically closed is a special case. The general principle is that it is in the nature of reason to strive for a rationally consistent account of all experience which comes within its range at all. In so far as both philosophical and scientific propositions are brought to the attention of the same mind, there is in the nature of the case, a tendency to bring them into relations of logical consistency with one another. It likewise follows that there are no logically watertight compartments in human experience. Rational knowledge is a single organic whole.

The methodological principles already laid down yield a canon for use in this context as well as others. Since the present concern is with the character and development of certain specific theoretical systems in science, and the interest in these systems is scientific, philosophical questions will be treated only when they become important to these systems in the sense strictly defined. Discussion will be deliberately limited to important philosophical questions in this specific sense. But equally there will be no attempt to avoid them on the plea that they are philosophical or "metaphysical" and hence have no place in a scientific study. This is often a facile way of evading the clear decision of vital but embarrassing issues.

It is important briefly to indicate a few of the main ways in which philosophical questions will be found to impinge upon the problems of this study. In the first place, while scientific knowledge is not the only significant cognitive relation of man to his experience, it is a genuine and valid one. This means that the two sets of disciplines stand in a relation of mutually corrective criticism. In particular, the evidence gained from scientific sources, observation of fact and the theoretical consequences of these facts constitutes, in so far as it is sound, valid ground for criticism of philosophical views.

If, then, scientific evidence which there is reason to believe is correct and has a bearing on important problems, is in conflict with philosophical views explicitly or implicitly involved in the works studied, this will be taken as an indication of the necessity to inquire into the basis of these views on a philosophical level. The object will be to discover whether the philosophical grounds for them are so cogent as to leave no alternative but to revise the earlier impression of the validity of what purported to be scientific evidence. A number of instances of such conflicts will be encountered where philosophical ideas do conflict with crucially important and relevant empirical evidence. However, in none of these has it been possible to discover sufficiently cogent philosophical grounds for discarding this evidence.

But this necessity of criticising philosophical positions from a scientific point of view is not the only important relation of the two sets of disciplines. Every system of scientific theory involves by implication philosophical consequences, both positive and negative. This is nothing more than a corollary of the rational unity of cognitive experience. Then it is also true that every system of scientific theory involves philosophical assumptions.

These may lie in a number of different directions. But the ones to which special attention should be called now are the "methodological." That is, the questions of the grounds of empirical validity of scientific propositions, the kinds of procedures which may on general grounds be expected to yield valid knowledge, etc., impinge directly on the philosophical fields of logic and epistemology.

Indeed it is scarcely too much to say that the main preoccupation of modern epistemology from, approximately, Locke on has been with precisely this question of the philosophical grounds for the validity of the propositions of empirical science. Since all through the study questions of validity will be of pressing importance, discussions of their philosophical aspects cannot safely be neglected. This is important especially in one context. A group of methodological views will be encountered which, again for convenience of reference and that purpose alone, have been brought together under the term "empiricism." The common characteristic of them is the *identification* of the meanings of the concrete specific propositions of a given science, theoretical or empirical, with the scientifically knowable totality of the external reality to which they refer. They maintain, that is, that there is an immediate correspondence between *concrete* experienceable reality and scientific propositions, and only in so far as this exists can there be valid knowledge. In other words, they deny the legitimacy of theoretical abstraction. It should already be evident that any such view is fundamentally incompatible with the view of the nature and status of theoretical systems which is a main foundation of this whole study. Hence discussion of the philosophical grounds advanced to support it cannot be avoided.

It is in this sense of the borderline field between science on the one hand, logic and epistemology on the other, that the term "methodology" as used in this work should be understood Its reference is thus not primarily to "methods" of empirical research such as statistics, case study, interview and the like. These latter it is preferable to call research techniques.

SOCIAL STRUCTURE AND SOCIAL ORGANIZATION

The terms 'social structure' and 'social organization' have long had slightly different implications, although the distinction between them has not always been as clear-cut as some commentators would have preferred. 'Social organization' has tended to be used loosely to refer to the sum total of activities performed in a given social context. 'Social structure' has usually been employed for the social context itself, or more precisely for the set of social relations which link individuals in a society. Yet the definition of 'social structure' varies according to the theoretical perspective of the writer and the degree of precision required by his or her perspective.

Writers who are mainly concerned with social action tend to concentrate on *social organization,* which defines the †roles individuals play in relation to one another. Those who are concerned more with the formal relations between people tend to concentrate on *social structure,* which defines the †statuses of actors performing such roles. Thus, social organization is of greater interest to Malinowskian functionalists, and to some extent processualists, notably †Raymond Firth (1951). Social structure is of greater interest to those whose approaches are descended from classic †structural-functionalist and *structuralist traditions.

For Radcliffe-Brown, 'social structure' includes the relations between individual people—he uses the example of a hypothetical Tom, Dick and Harry. Structural form, in contrast, is at a higher level of abstraction—the positions Tom, Dick or Harry occupy in relation to one another. Tom may be Dick's father-in-law, and thus the structural form defines relations between father-in-law and sons-in-law in general, for a particular society. Essentially, Radcliffe-Brown saw social structure as a network of real people in a real society. Structural form entailed the cultural constants which enabled one to say that the grandchildren of these people would live in a society with a *similar* social structure, albeit one in which social processes had left changes to be understood and analysed in terms of an evolving structural form. In his 1953 letter to Lévi-Strauss, illustrating the difference between social structure and structural form, he used the analogy of sea shells: each individual shell has its own structure, but shells of the same species will share a structural form. Radcliffe-Brown was consciously constructing an anthropology analogous to biology, with its like concerns of structure and function. Functional (as opposed to structural) relations were more part of the social organization through which social structure was played out.

Lévi-Strauss, and many other anthropologists, have consistently employed the term 'social structure' for what Radcliffe-Brown called 'structural form'. Lévi-Strauss even uses 'social structure' to refer to a still higher degree of abstraction—the structure of social relations in all societies, as well as that within a particular society (RadcliffeBrown's 'structural form'). In fact, Lévi-Strauss was simply doing the kind of universal crosscultural comparison Radcliffe-Brown had long advocated but never practised, and indeed Radcliffe-Brown himself frequently slipped and used the term 'social structure' to refer to what he said *should* be called 'structural form'. Where they truly differed was in their respective understandings of the locus of structure (or structural form). Lévi-Strauss's conception of it is at the level of the mind, even the human mind in general. His concern is often with the structure of all possible structures, e.g. in the study of *kinship. RadcliffeBrown, on the other hand, always regarded structures and forms as accessible only empirically, from Tom, Dick and Harry upwards to generalizations based on the comparison of their statuses to those of other individuals, in the same society, or ultimately in diverse societies.

3

Indian Society

THE SOCIAL STRUCTURE OF SOCIETY

Social structure - is a stable relationship of elements in the socialsystem. The main elements of the social structure of society areindividuals holding certain positions (status) and carryingcertain social functions (roles), the union of these individuals tobasis of their status in the group attributes, socio-territorial,ethnic and other community and etc. Social structure is an objectivedivision of society into the community, roles, layers, groups, etc., pointing topeople's different positions relative to each other on numerouscriteria. Each of the elements of social structure, in turn,is a complex social system with its subsystems and connections.

The concept of social structure. The Marxist theory of classes as a basic element of social structure notion of social structure in society generally used in the following basic meaning. In a broad sense, the social structure - a structure of society as a whole system of connections between all its key elements. This approach social structure of the characterizes all of the many types of social commonalities and relationships between them. In the narrow sense of the term "social structure" often applies to social class and social-group communities. The social structure in this sense - is a set of interrelated and interacting with other classes, social strata and groups.

In sociology, there are a lot of concepts of social structure of society, historically one of the first is a Marxist teaching. In Marxist sociology played a leading role of socio -class structure of society. Social-class structure of society, according to this direction is the interaction of three major elements: classes, social strata and social groups. Core social structures are classes. Availability of classes in society noted in science and to Marx in the early XIX century. This concept is widely used French historians Francois Guizot, Thierry O. and English and Frenchpolitical economists Adam Smith and David Ricardo. But the greatest development of the doctrine of grades received in Marxism. Marx and Engels founded the economic causes of classes. They argued that the division of society into classes is the result of the social division of labour and the formation of proprietary relations. The process of class formation occurred in two ways: through the allocation of the clan exploitative elite, originally consisted of hereditary aristocracy, and by contacting slavery of prisoners of war, as well as impoverished tribesmen who fell into debt bondage.

This economic approach to the classes recorded in the famous defining classes, which formulated by Lenin in his work "The Great initiative "and that became a textbook in Marxism, for 70 years.

Classes are large groups of people differing in their place in historically determined system of social production, by their relation (in most cases fixed and formulated in law) to means of production, for their role in the social organization of labour, and therefore, on how to obtain and size of the share of public wealth they possess. Classes - are groups of people, from which one can appropriate the labour of another owing to the different places they occupy indefinite system of social economy. " Thus, according to Lenin, main feature of the class - relationship to the means of production (ownership or not ownership) determine the role of classes in the social organization of labour (managers and managed), the system of government (ruling and controlled), their wealth (rich and poor). The class struggle is driving force of social development.

Marxism divides classes on basic and non-core. Basic classes are those whose existence directly stems from the ruling in the socio-economic structure economic relations, especially relations of property: slaves and slave-owners, peasants and lords, proletariat and bourgeoisie.

Non-core - are the remnants of the old classes in the new socio -economic structure or the emerging classes, which will replace the core and form the basis of class division in the new formation. Apart essential and non-structural element of the classes of society are social strata (or layers).

Social strata - are intermediate or transitional group, without pronounced specific relationship to the means of production and, therefore, do not possess all the attributes of the class. Social strata are be vnutriklassovymi (part of the class) between classes. The former can be attributed large, medium,. Small, urban and rural monopolistic and non-monopolistic bourgeoisie, industrial and rural proletariat, working aristocracy etc. A historical example of interclass layers is "Third Estate", the ripening of the first bourgeois revolution in Egypt - Burgesses, handicrafts. In modern society — intelligentsia. In turn, the interclass elements of a modern structure may have its internal division. Thus, the intelligentsia is divided into proletarian and petty-bourgeois. Thus, the socio -layered structure is not completely coincide with the class. Using the concept social system of ideas of Marxist sociology, allows concretize the social structure of society, to point out its manifold and dynamism.

Despite the fact that in terms of ideological dictates and prosperity dogmatism in Marxist sociology was the absolute domination of Lenin definition of classes, based not purely economic approach, part Marxist sociologists realize that the classes - it is more widely education. Consequently, the concept of social-class structure society should include the political, spiritual and other links relations. In a broader approach to the interpretation of social structure society a significant place is given the concept of "social interests?.

Interests - this is real-life aspirations of individuals, groups, and other communities in which they consciously or unconsciously, guided in their actions and which condition their objective position in the social system. In social interests are the most generalized expression actual needs of representatives of various social communities.

Awareness of interests is carried out continuously during what is happening in social process of social comparison, i.e comparing the life comparing the situation of other social groups. To understand the classes is essential to the term "fundamental social interests, which reflects the presence of a major social interests, which determine its existence and social position. On the basis of the foregoing can offer a definition of classes: classes - a great social groups differing in their role in all spheres of society, which are formed on the basis of fundamental social interests. Classes have general socio-psychological characteristics, values.

"Code" of conduct. Every social community is the subject of work and relationships. Classes as a socio-political community are common to all its Members of the program activities. This program is consistent with the fundamental interests of this or that class, working out of his ideology.

Social strata in this approach are social community, uniting people on the basis of some private interests.

The Theory of Social Stratification and Social Mobility

Marxist Theory of classes as the basis of social structure in non-Marxist sociology is opposed to the Western theory of social stratification. The representatives of this theory argue that the notion of class, probably suitable for analysing the social structure of past societies, including industrial and capitalist society, but in today post industrial society, it does not work, because in this society in broad-based shareholding, as well as off the main holders shares from the scope of production management and replacing them with salaried managers property relations have been eroded, lost its certainty.

Therefore the notion of "class" should be replaced with the term "stratum" (from Latin stratum - the layer) or the notion of a social group, and replaced theory of social and class structure of society must come to the theory social stratification.

Theories of social stratification based on the idea that stratum, the social group, is a real, empirically indurated community that connects people to some common positions ora common cause, which leads to the design of the community in social structure of society and the opposition of other social communities. The theory of stratification are bringing people together in groups and contrasted with other groups on the grounds of a status: imperious property, professional, educational, etc. This offered various criteria of stratification.

The West sociologist R. Dahrendorf suggested that the basis of social stratification put political notion of "authority", which, in his opinion, the most accurate characterizes the relations of power and struggle between social groups for power. Based on this notion R. Dahrendorf divides modern society of rulers and the ruled. In turn, managers divides into two subgroups: control of owners and managers nesobstvennikov —bureaucratic managers. Controlled Group also heterogeneous. It can allocate at least two subgroups: the highest - "labour aristocracy" and lower, low-skilled workers. Between these two social groups is an interim "new middle class" - a product assimilation of the labour aristocracy and the servants of the ruling class — managers.

The term "social mobility" was introduced in sociology in 1927 PA Sorokin, who considered the social mobility as any change social status, and not just individuals and families transition from one social group to another. According to the views of PA Sorokin, social mobility means the movement of the social ladder in two ways: 1) vertically - moving up and down, 2) horizontal - the movement to one tomzhe and social level.

A discussion of the theory of social mobility is the question of whether the social mobility shift of one individual from this social group to another group or social movement in the true sense occurs only when the new status is assigned to the family this individual, and hence social mobility occurs when social status varies among different generations. French sociologists P. Berta, and R. Bourdon argued that social mobility means the transition of individuals from one social category to another to Throughout his biographical or professional life, on the basis comparing its position with the social status of his parents. Thus, here for the postulate social origin. The weakness of this position is that it would imply a steady-state condition society, but society is changing rapidly, and therefore social statuses different generations may not be comparable. Looking for such criteria which would allow to take into account changing social structure of society.

Devoted to problems of social mobility, many concrete sociological studies in various countries. Data on social mobility to some extent give an indication of the degree of openness of society, its democracy. People are important to know how a particular society provides an opportunity to advance individuals and generations of lower categories in the highest, which is formed by the ruling elite of society, whether penetration of the ruling elite from other social groups.

Social Mobility in Modern Society

Modern Western society is justified and for the USSR and today. To what extent we can say that there are classes in the era of so-called "socialism" and Now, what classes exist or exist in our country? If Lenin's use of classes, then we can not fix either way called the working class or peasantry. Under nationwide ownership of the land and the basic means of production it forms a class attribute. You can only talk about various aspects of employment of people: industry worker, employee agricultural sector, the employee culture, education, etc. At the same time, impossible to deny the existence of common interests, the difference in social situation in various segments of the population. We can therefore agree with those domestic social scientists who believe that the notion of class analysis of our society is not applicable. In this society it is impossible to isolate a large element of social structure. There are more working concept proposed by proponents of the theory of social stratification - a stratum (layer) or social group. These groups can be inferred from various criterion: the level of income, place in the power system, based on occupation and etc., it is also possible the allocation of certain social groups for some Integral criteria.

Attempt such a synthetic approach taken in the 1987 - 1989 gg. academics TI Zaslavskaya and Professor RV Ryvkina. Based on Lenin definition of classes, they identified the following key social groups Soviet society of the period: 1) vertical groups of power differing nature of its (party, government and economic power), as well as the volume of this power (of the upper, middle and lower level in the management hierarchy), 2) groups associated with spheres and sectors of the economy, as well as departments differing power, prestige and material base (e.g, military Office and scope of the domestic economy), 3) group of farmsennyh managers differ rank authorities (heads of associations, enterprises and units) 4) the group of intellectuals, which differ profile of employment (for example, engineers and creative professionals, and others), 5) group employed in the field of home economics and self-employment activities; 6) declassed elements.

Thus, on the basis of concrete case studies and statistics revealed that the Soviet society on the integrated criteria, consisting of 5 indicators (income, power, education, etc.), is structured into 6 groups. However, even in the 80-ies differences between income groups were insignificant character. The difference between rich and poor had 5 - 7-fold expression. In recent years there has been more profound differentiation society. Now the difference in income between the poorest and most wealthy groups up to 20 times or more. And this, according sociologists, is critical for determining the level of social tension. Attempt to analyse the trend of development of social structure modern society has made AV Dmitriev (Sociological Study 1993. Number 9). In his opinion, in general, there is originality

"Decomposition" of social structure, which is inherent in growing gap nature of work, income, education level and prestige. Previously sway contradiction between workers and nomenclature, which controlled unchallenged power and property, then now possible to allocate 5 large social groups: 1) administrative elite (the ruling elite), consisting of old parthoznomenklatury first and second levels, fused with the new political elite, and 2) the working class, which breaks up into groups industry, qualifying, demographic and other characteristics, 3) intellectuals, is also subdivided into a number of social groups on various parameters, 4) "new bourgeoisie" - entrepreneurs, bankers, etc., 5) peasantry.

Proposed AV Dmitricv social stratification of modern's society relies on the old Marxist notion of classes, does not reveal more specific social groups within those or other classes. For example, now hardly possible to speak about the class of peasants, because in rural areas can be clearly divided into at least two social groups of the peasantry: socialized (co-operatives) peasantry, and the private (farmer). It should be noted that research on the social stratification of society in currently very difficult due to the high dynamics of social processes.

INDIA SOCIETY : SOCIAL SYSTEMS IN INDIA

Indian society is multifaceted to an extent perhaps unknown in any other of the world's great civilizations. Virtually no generalization made about Indian society is valid for all of the nation's multifarious groups. Comprehending the complexities of Indian social structure has challenged scholars and other observers over many decades.

The ethnic and linguistic diversity of Indian civilization is more like the diversity of an area as variable as Europe than like that of any other single nation-state. Living within the embrace of the Indian nation are vast numbers of different regional, social, and economic groups, each with different cultural practices. Particularly noteworthy are differences between social structures in the north and the south, especially in the realm of kinship systems. Throughout the country, religious differences can be significant, especially between the Hindu majority and the large Muslim minority; and other Indian groups—Buddhists, Christians, Jains, Jews, Parsis, Sikhs, and practitioners of tribal religions—all pride themselves on being unlike members of other faiths.

Access to wealth and power varies considerably, and vast differences in socioeconomic status are evident everywhere. The poor and the wealthy live side by side in urban and rural areas. It is common in city life to see a prosperous, well-fed man or woman chauffeured in a fine car pass gaunt street dwellers huddled beneath burlap shelters along the roadway. In many villages, solid cement houses of landowners rise not far from the flimsy thatched shacks of landless laborers. Even when not so obvious, distinctions of class are found in almost every settlement in India.

Urban-rural differences can be immense in the Indian Society. Nearly 74 percent of India's population dwells in villages, with agriculture providing support for most of these rural residents. In villages, mud-plastered walls ornamented with traditional designs, dusty lanes, herds of grazing cattle, and the songs of birds at sunset provide typical settings for the social lives of most Indians. In India's great cities, however, millions of people live amidst cacophony—roaring vehicles, surging crowds, jammed apartment buildings, busy commercial establishments, loudspeakers blaring movie tunes—while breathing the poisons of industrial and automotive pollution.

Gender distinctions are pronounced. The behavior expected of men and women can be quite different, especially in villages, but also in urban centres. Prescribed ideal gender roles help shape the actions of both sexes as they move between family and the world outside the home.

Crosscutting and pervading all of these differences of region, language, wealth, status, religion, urbanity, and gender is the special feature of Indian society that has received most attention from observers: caste. The people of India belong to thousands of castes and castelike groups—hierarchically ordered, named groups into which members are born. Caste members are expected to marry within the group and follow caste rules pertaining to diet, avoidance of ritual pollution, and many other aspects of life.

CULTURAL HERITAGE OF INDIA-UNITY IN DIVERSITY

Our Indian history is very ancient, it begins with the Indus valley civilization 3250 - 2759 B.C. The people of India are largely the product of successive invasions from immemorial times who had swept into the country. The existence of various types of people in our country created a spirit of tolerance among the people. We have developed a secular outlook from the ancient period.

The term culture is expressed through language, literature, art, religion, architecture, philosophy, social customs and tradition. Indian culture co-existed for centuries under all our invaders from the 'Harappan civilization' to the modern days. Due to the foreign contacts and intermingling with the pre-existing cultures, our Indian culture instead of loosing its identity has only benefited. By absorbing the good features of other cultures we have indeed enriched our Indian culture.

Evolution of Indian Society

India is a huge country with people belonging to different cultural background making the people distinct from one another. The early Indian society was governed by 'Dharmasastra', the works of great sages helped to lead a harmonious life. According to 'Manu Smriti', early Indian society was divided into Aryans and Non-Aryans. The Aryans were further divided into four groups, the Brahmanas, Kshatriyas, Vaishayas, and Sudras. The brahmins occupied highest place in the society. Their duty was to teach vedic literature and to perform various sacrifices. They should maintain a high standard of morality and should lead a very simple life. The Kshatriya's main duty was to defend the country. The Vaishyas were required to attend to agriculture, trade, and commerce. The Sudras formed the majority of the society their duty was to serve the other communities. As time passed each one of these subdivisions became a 'caste' itself and became very rigid. The early society gave much importance to 'Varnasrama Dharma'. The life of an individual was divided into four stages known as 'Asramas'. They are Bramacharia or a student, Grihasta or a married house holder, Vanaprastha a forest hermit and Sanyasin an ascetic who renounced the world. Women were not given a place of honour, they were not allowed to study vedas.

The early Indian society gradually lost its glory due to many kinds of abuses and superstitious beliefs in it. The Brahmins for their own benefit encouraged the superstitions. It was at this juncture, Buddhism and Jainism appeared in India. Buddha and Mahavira preached in the language of common people. They opposed castesim, animal sacrifice and other superstitious rituals. They raised their voices against the evils and showed a new path to the people. They taught equality, universal peace, non-violence and kindness to all living things. They greatly reformed the society through their moral rules and new order of life.

Influence of Islam on Indian society

During the early medieval period the conquests of 'Arabs' and' Turks' resulted in the introduction of a new religion called 'Islam' in India. The society was divided into two communities namely the 'Hindus' and the 'Muslims'. Many Hindus converted themselves into Islam. The impact of Islam on Indian society led to the 'Bkakthi Movement'. The saints who preached 'Bhakthi' taught 'tolerance' and 'devotion' to God. They proclaimed that there is only supreme God and absolute devotion to God is a means of 'Salvation'. They stressed the equality of all human beings and declared that it was only through 'Bhakthi' that man could experience God. They emphasized friendly relations between the two communities. Indian art, architecture and music also received new dimensions due to Islamic contacts. Hindi and urdhu literature flourished.

The pioneers of Bhakthi cult were Ramanandha, Kabir, Guru nanak, Chaitanya, Tulasidas and Surdas. They tried to harmonize Islam and Hinduism. The Bhakthi movement started in south India during 7th and 8th centuries by' Alwars' and 'Nayanmars'. They sang devotional songs. The great saints like' Aathi Sangarar', 'Ramanujam' and 'Madhwa' tried to bring about a revival of the old Hindu beliefs. Bhakthi cult was a movement of social integration. It united the Hindu and Muslim sentiments. People followed the preaching of their saints and abandoned superstitious beliefs and followed oneness of god.

Impact of British Rule on Indian Society

The most important impact of the British rule in India was the Westernization of the Indian society the western education awakened a spirit of reform among the various classes of Indian society. It modifies the ideas and customs of the educated Indians. It created a feeling of brotherhood among the Indians and enabled the people to think India as their motherland and united them. Knowledge of English helped to bring about development in every field from our government, industry, technology, education, arts, sciences etc.

English education helped Indians learn nationalism and liberalism from the west. This period saw the birth of modern Indians who became more self-reliant and self-confident. Critical outlooks of past and new aspirations for the future developed. This new spirit made Indians to question the authority, reason and judgment over the blind faith and superstitious beliefs. Thus there was growth and development in our culture. our Indian society is a grand synthesis (combination) of cultures. This synthesis has made India a unique Mosaic of Cultures as described by our late prime minister Jawaharlal Nehru.

Unity in Diversity

Diversity in Geographical features: The physical features of a country influence to a great extent the life and history of its people. India has diverse geographical features. India is separated from rest of Asia by the Himalayas, with its western and eastern ranges. Mountains of the north, the northern fertile plain, the Thar desert, the Deccan plateau, western and eastern Ghats from part of its physical features: The vast dimensions of India, the varied climatic conditions across the various regions of India resulted in racial and linguistic differences. Yet there is a common bond among the people.

Geographical conditions play an important part in responding to human activities. Cherrapunji in Meghalaya receives highest rain fall and the dry Thar desert in Rajasthan receives only scanty rainfall. The Himalayan mountain ranges are snow clad peaks while the southern parts of India records highest average temperature. Animal and plant life also varies according to the climatic conditions. The soil is too variable, it is fertile at the northern plains and saline dry soil is found at Rajasthan. This also brought about diversity in the life of the people.

Population

Indian population is 16% of the world's population. The huge population is made up of different ethnic groups, following different religions, speaking different languages, observing different customs and traditions. It is this marvellous diversity of people in India, which has made it both museum and a laboratory for the study of man. Hence India is called as 'ethnological Museum'.

Diversity in Language, Customs and Traditions

In India people speak about 845 languages and has 545 dialects. At present 22 official languages are recognized by the Indian government. The people of north India speak the Indo-Aryan group of languages and the Dravidian languages are spoken primarily in southern India. Hindi is the national language and English the concurrent language. People differ in race, figure, and mode of dress, food, customs, and habits from region to region.

Diversity in Religion

India is the birth place of many religions. Hinduism, Buddhism, Jainism, and Sikhism have their origin in India.

Vedic religion is an ancient religion of our country. In the first century B.C St. Thomas an Apostle of christ first brought Christianity to India. The persians brought 'Zoroastrianism'. Muslim conquest of India brought Islam into India. Religious tolerance is found in our country from the past till today. People are free to profess, practice, and propagate any religion of their choice. Different Festivals are celebrated in India. Diwali, Muharram, Bakrid, Mahaveer jayanthi, Guru naanak jayanthi, Christmas, Onam, pongal, Dassara etc. are celebrated with religious fervor and gaiety in India.

Diversity in Literature

The Vedas are the earliest literary works of our country. The Vedic hymns were composed in Sanskrit. Prakrit and Sanskrit were spoken throughout our country. The vedic literature are the Brahmanas, Aranyakas and upanishads. The Ramayana and Mahabharatha are the two epics of India.' Thirukural' by Thiruvalluvar is the greatest literary work in Tamil. The Bagavath geetha is the holy book of Hinduism. The hymns of Alwars and Nayanmars are compiled under the name of Naalayira Thivya Prabandham and Devaram.

Art and Architecture

Different styles of art and architecture are found in India. The north Indian temples have towers like structure over the shrines and the Sikara bulges in the middle and ends almost in a point.The south Indian Sikara looks like a pyramid made up of successive storeys, each smaller than the one beneath it. Hindustani and carnatic music are the classical music of north India and South India respectively. Famous dance forms of North India are Manipuri, Kathak and Bhangra whereas in the south Bharathanatiyam, Kathakali and Kuchipudi are the famous dances. The pilgrim centres are found all over India. Amarnath, Badrinath, Kedarnath, Kasi, Rameshwaram, Nagappatinam, Nagoor, Velankanni etc. are the religious centres visited by people all over India. The universities of Naalantha, Taxila, Kanchi and Vickramashila were the ancient centres of learning.

Magnificient palaces, Chaityas, Viharas and Stupas were built by the kings like Ashoka and Chandra Gupta Maurya. The inscriptions on the Rumindi pillar remain perfect even today. The Ghandhara and Madhura art flourished during the Kushan period. The paintings at Ajantha and Ellora caves are examples of Gupta's art. Rajput built large marble temples, forts, palaces in Rajasthan. The Chalukyas, Rastrakudas, Hoysalas, Pallavas, Cholas, Cheras, and Pandyas were also patrons of architecture.

The Pallavas of Kanchipuram laid the foundation of the Dravidiyan art. The Temples and sculptures of Pallavas at Mahabalipuram, the Pragatheeswarar temple at Tanjore, Godess sri Meenakshi Amman Temple at Madurai, Sri Ramanatha swamy temple at Rameshwaram and the Thirumalai nayak palace at Maduraiare the best examples of south Indian or Dravidian Art.

The medieval art of Sultanates and Moguls were Qutub Minar,the jamma Masjid, the Gol Gumbaz, Fatepur Sikri, the tombs of imperial Mughals, the Taj mahaletc. are fine examples of the Indo-Islamic architecture. It developed due to the fusion of Hindu and Islamic cultures. During the British rule many buildings were built in western styles in big cities.

During the British rule the whole country was brought under one rule. Sardar Vallabhai Patel integrated all the princely states into one political unit soon after independence.

INDIA -UNITY IN DIVERSITY

The culture of India has been shaped by the long history of India, its unique geography and the absorption of customs, traditions and ideas from some of its neighbours as well as by preserving its ancient heritages, which were formed during the Indus Valley Civilization and evolved further during the Vedic age, rise and decline of Buddhism, Golden age, Muslim conquests and European colonization.

India does not have a strong uniform national culture. India's great diversity of cultural practices, languages, customs, and traditions are examples of this unique co-mingling over the past five millennium. The various religions and traditions of India that were created by these amalgamations have influenced other parts of the world too. Most Indians emphasize the country's cultural diversity, tolerance of difference, and receptiveness to foreign influences.

Religion

India is the birth place of Dharmic religions such as Hinduism, Buddhism, Jainism and Sikhism. Dharmic religions, also known as Indian religions, is a major form of world religions next to the Abrahamic ones. Today, Hinduism and Buddhism are the world's third- and fourth-largest religions respectively, with around 1.4 billion followers altogether.

India is one of the most religiously diverse nations in the world, with some of the most deeply religious societies and cultures. Religion still plays a central and definitive role in the life of most of its people.

The religion of more than 80.4% of the people is Hinduism. Islam is practiced by around 13.4% of all Indians. Sikhism, Jainism and especially Buddhism are influential not only in India but across the world. Christianity, Zoroastrianism, Judaism and the Bahá'í Faith are also influential but their numbers are smaller. Despite the strong role of religion in Indian life, atheism and agnostics also have visible influence along with a self-ascribed tolerance to other faiths.

Society

According to Eugene M. Makar, the traditional Indian culture is defined by relatively strict social hierarchy. He also mentions that from an early age, children are reminded of their roles and places in society. This is reinforced by the fact that many believe gods and spirits have integral and functional role in determining their life. Several differences such as religion divide culture. However, far more powerful division is the traditional Hindu bifurcation into non-polluting and polluting occupations. Strict social taboos have governed these groups for thousands of years. In recent years, particularly in cities, some of these lines have blurred and sometimes even disappeared. Nuclear family is becoming central to Indian culture. Important family relations extend to as far as gotra, the mainly patrilinear lineage or clan assigned to a Hindu at birth. In rural areas it is common that three or four generations of the family live under the same roof. Patriarch often resolves family issues.

Among developing countries, India has low levels of occupational and geographic mobility. People choose same occupations as their parents and rarely move geographically in the society.

Family

India for ages has had a prevailing tradition of the joint family system. It's a system under which even extended members of a family like one's parents, children, the children's spouses and their offspring, etc. live together. The elder-most, usually the male member is the head in the joint Indian family system who makes all important decisions and rules, whereas other family members abide by it. The average nuclear family is relatively small, with only one or two children. Toddlers receive much parental attention. Many children are cared for primarily by their parents in the parental home.

Arranged marriages have the tradition in Indian society for centuries. Even today, overwhelming majority of Indians have their marriages planned by their parents and other respected family-members, with the consent of the bride and groom. Arranged matches were made after taking into account factors such as age, height, personal values and tastes, the backgrounds of their families (wealth, social standing) and their castes and the astrological compatibility of the couples' horoscopes. Monogamy is the only marriage form allowed.

In India, the marriage is thought to be for life and the divorce rate is extremely low — 1.1% compared with about 50% in the United States. The arranged marriages generally have a much lower divorce rate. The divorce rates have risen significantly in recent years: "Opinion is divided over what the phenomenon means: for traditionalists the rising numbers portend the breakdown of society while, for some modernists, they speak of a healthy new empowerment for women."

Although child marriage was outlawed in 1860, it is continued to be practiced in some rural parts of India. According to UNICEF's "State of the World's Children-2009" report, 47% of India's women aged 20–24 were married before the legal age of 18, with 56% in rural areas. The report also showed that 40% of the world's child marriages occur in India.

Indian names are based on a variety of systems and naming conventions, which vary from region to region. Names are also influenced by religion and caste and may come from religion or epics. India's population speaks a wide variety of languages. Although women and men are equal before the law and the trend toward gender equality has been noticeable, women and men still occupy distinct functions in Indian society. Woman's role in the society is often to perform household works and pro bono community work. This low rate of participation has ideological and historical reasons. Women and women's issues appear only 7-14% of the time in news programs. In most Indian families, women do not own any property in their own names, and do not get a share of parental property. Due to weak enforcement of laws protecting them, women continue to have little access to land and property. In many families, especially rural ones, the girls and women face nutritional discrimination within the family, and are anaemic and malnourished. They still lag behind men in terms of income and job status.

Customs

Namaste, Namaskar or Namaskaram is a common spoken greeting or salutation in the Indian subcontinent. Namaskar is considered a slightly more formal version than namaste but both express deep respect. It is commonly used in India and Nepal by Hindus, Jains and Buddhists, and many continue to use this outside the Indian subcontinent. In Indian and Nepali culture, the word is spoken at the beginning of written or verbal communication.

However, the same hands folded gesture is made wordlessly upon departure. In yoga, namaste is said to mean "The light in me honours the light in you," as spoken by both the yoga instructor and yoga students. Taken literally, it means "I bow to you". The word is derived from Sanskrit (namas): to bow, obeisance, reverential salutation, and respectand (te): "to you". When spoken to another person, it is commonly accompanied by a slight bow made with hands pressed together, palms touching and fingers pointed upwards, in front of the chest. The gesture can also be performed wordlessly and carry the same meaning.

Festivals

India, being a multi-cultural and multi-religious society, celebrates holidays and festivals of various religions. The three national holidays in India, the Independence Day, the Republic Day and the Gandhi Jayanti, are celebrated with zeal and enthusiasm across India. In addition, many states and regions have local festivals depending on prevalent religious and linguistic demographics. Popular religious festivals include the Hindu festivals of Diwali, Ganesh Chaturthi, Durga puja, Holi, Rakshabandhan and Dussehra. Several harvest festivals, such as Sankranthi, Pongal and Onam, are also fairly popular. Certain festivals in India are celebrated by multiple religions. Notable examples include Diwali which celebrated by Hindus, Sikhs and Jains and Buddh Purnima which is celebrated by Buddhists and Hindus. Islamic festivals, such Eid ul-Fitr, Eid al-Adha and Ramadan, are celebrated by Muslims across India. Adding colours to the culture of India, the Dree Festival is one of the tribal festivals of India celebrated by the Apatanis of the Ziro valley of Arunachal Pradesh, which is the easternmost state of this country.

Cuisine

The multiple families of Indian cuisine are characterized by their sophisticated and subtle use of many spices and herbs. Each family of this cuisine is characterized by a wide assortment of dishes and cooking techniques. Though a significant portion of Indian food is vegetarian, many traditional Indian dishes also include chicken, goat, lamb, fish, and other meats.

Food is an important part of Indian culture, playing a role in everyday life as well as in festivals. Indian cuisine varies from region to region, reflecting the varied demographics of the ethnically diverse subcontinent. Generally, Indian cuisine can be split into five categories: North, South, East, West Indian and Northeastern India. Despite this diversity, some unifying threads emerge. Varied uses of spices are an integral part of food preparation, and are used to enhance the flavor of a dish and create unique flavors and aromas. Cuisine across India has also been influenced by various cultural groups that entered India throughout history, such as the Persians, Mughals, and European colonists. Though the tandoor originated in Central Asia, Indian tandoori dishes, such as chicken tikka made with Indian ingredients, enjoy widespread popularity. Indian cuisine is one of the most popular cuisines across the globe. Historically,

Indian spices and herbs were one of the most sought after trade commodities. The spice trade between India and Europe led to the rise and dominance of Arab traders to such an extent that European explorers, such as Vasco da Gama and Christopher Columbus, set out to find new trade routes with India leading to the Age of Discovery. The popularity of curry, which originated in India, across Asia has often led to the dish being labeled as the "pan-Asian" dish.

Clothing

Traditional Indian clothing for women are the saris and also Ghaghra Cholis (Lehengas). For men, traditional clothes are the Dhoti, pancha/veshti or Kurta. Bombay, also known as Mumbai, is one of India's fashion capitals. In some village parts of India, traditional clothing mostly will be worn. Delhi, Mumbai, Chennai, Ahmedabad, and Pune are all places for people who like to shop. In southern India the men wear long, white sheets of cloth called dhoti in English and in Tamil. Over the dhoti, men wear shirts, t-shirts, or anything else. Women wear a sari, a long sheet of colourful cloth with patterns. This is draped over a simple or fancy blouse. This is worn by young ladies and woman. Little girls wear a pavada. A pavada is a long skirt worn under a blouse. Both are often gaily patterned. Bindi is part of the women's make-up. Traditionally, the red bindi (or sindhur) was worn only by the married Hindu women, but now it has become a part of women's fashion. Indo-western clothing is the fusion of Western and Subcontinental fashion. Churidar, Dupatta, Gamchha, Kurta, Mundum Neriyathum, Sherwani,uttariya are among other clothes.

Literature

The earliest works of Indian literature were orally transmitted. Sanskrit literature begins with the Rig Veda a collection of sacred hymns dating to the period 1500–1200 BCE. The Sanskrit epics Ramayana and Mahabharata appeared towards the end of the first millennium BCE. Classical Sanskrit literature flourished in the first few centuries of the first millennium CE, as did the Tamil Sangam literature. In the medieval period, literature in Kannada and Telugu appears in the 9th and 11th centuries respectively, followed by the first Malayalam works in the 12th century. During this time, literature in the Bengali, Marathi, and various dialects of Hindi, Persian and Urdu began to appear as well.

Some of the most important authors from India are Rabindranath Tagore, Ramdhari Singh 'Dinkar', Subramania Barathi, Kuvempu, Bankim Chandra Chattopadhyay, Michael Madhusudan Dutt, Munshi Premchand, Muhammad Iqbal, Devaki Nandan Khatri became well known. In contemporary India, among the writers who have received critical acclaim are: Girish Karnad, Agyeya, Nirmal Verma, Kamleshwar, Vaikom Muhammad Basheer, Indira Goswami, Mahasweta Devi, Amrita Pritam, Maasti Venkatesh Ayengar, Qurratulain Hyder and Thakazhi Sivasankara Pillai and others have received critical acclaim.

In contemporary Indian literature, there are two major literary awards; these are the Sahitya Akademi Fellowship and the Jnanpith Award. Seven Jnanpith awards each have been awarded in Kannada, six in Hindi, five in Bengali, four in Malayalam, three each in and Marathi, Gujarati, Urdu and Oriya.

Poetry

India has strong traditions of poetry ever since the Rigveda, as well as prose compositions. Poetry is often closely related to musical traditions, and much of poetry can be attributed to religious movements. Writers and philosophers were often also skilled poets. In modern times, poetry has served as an important non-violent tool of nationalism during the Indian freedom movement. A famous modern example of this tradition can be found in such figures as Rabindranath Tagore and K. S. Narasimhaswamy in modern times and poets such as Basava (vachanas), Kabir and Purandaradasa (padas and devaranamas) in medieval times, as well as the epics of ancient times. Two examples of poetry from Tagore's Gitanjali serve as the national anthems of both India and Bangladesh.

Epics

The Ramayana and Mahabharata are the oldest preserved and still well-known epics of India; some of their versions have been adopted as the epics of Southeast Asian countries like Thailand, Malaysia and Indonesia. In addition, there are five epics in the classical Tamil language -they being Silappadhikaram, Manimegalai, Seevaga-chintamani, Valayaapathi, Kundalakesi. Other regional variations of them as well as unrelated epics include the Tamil Kamba Ramayanam, in Kannada, the Pampa Bharata by Adikavi Pampa, Torave Ramayana by Kumara Valmiki and Karnata Bharata KathaManjari by Kumaravyasa, Hindi Ramacharitamanasa, Malayalam Adhyathmaramayanam.

Music and Dance

The music of India includes multiples varieties of religious, folk, popular, pop, and classical music. The oldest preserved examples of Indian music are the melodies of the Samaveda that are still sung in certain Vedic srauta sacrifices. India's classical music tradition is heavily influenced by Hindu texts. It includes two distinct styles: Carnatic and Hindustani music. It is noted for the use of several Raga, melodic modes. it has a history spanning millennia and it was developed over several eras. It remains instrumental to the religious inspiration, cultural expression and pure entertainment. Purandaradasa is considered the "father of carnatic music" (Karnataka sangeeta pitamaha). He concluded his songs with a salutation to Lord Purandara Vittala and is believed to have composed as many as 475,000songs in the Kannada language. However, only about 1000 are known today. Indian dance too has diverse folk and classical forms. Among the well-known folk dances are the bhangra of the Punjab, the bihu of Assam, the chhau of Jharkhand and Orissa, the ghoomar of Rajasthan, the dandiya and garba of Gujarat, the Yakshagana of Karnataka and lavani of Maharashtra and Dekhnni of Goa. Eight dance forms, many with narrative forms and mythological elements, have been accorded classical dance status by India's National Academy of Music, Dance, and Drama. These are: bharatanatyam of the state of Tamil Nadu, kathak of Uttar Pradesh, kathakali and mohiniattam of Kerala, kuchipudi of Andhra Pradesh, manipuri of Manipur, odissi of the state of Orissa and the sattriya of Assam. Kalarippayattu or Kalari for short is considered one of the world's oldest martial art. It is preserved in texts such as the Mallapurana. Kalari and other later formed martial arts have been assumed by some to have traveled to China, like Buddhism, and eventually developing into Kung-fu. Other later martial arts are Gatka,Pehlwani,and Malla-yuddha. There have been many great practitioners of Indian martial Arts including Bodhidharma who supposedly brought Indian martial arts to China.

Paintings

The earliest Indian paintings were the rock paintings of pre-historic times, the petroglyphs as found in places like Bhimbetka, some of which go back to the Stone Age. Ancient texts outline theories of darragh and anecdotal accounts suggesting that it was common for households to paint their doorways or indoor rooms where guests resided. Cave paintings from Ajanta, Bagh, Ellora and Sittanavasal and temple paintings testify to a love of naturalism. Most early and medieval art in India is Hindu, Buddhist or Jain. A freshly made coloured flour design (Rangoli) is still a common sight outside the doorstep of many (mostly South Indian) Indian homes.

Madhubani painting, Mysore painting, Rajput painting, Tanjore painting, Mughal painting are some notable Genres of Indian Art; while Raja Ravi Varma, Nandalal Bose, Geeta Vadhera, Jamini Roy and B.Venkatappa are some modern painters. Among the present day artists, Atul Dodiya, Bose Krishnamacnahri, Devajyoti Ray and Shibu Natesan represent a new era of Indian art where global art shows direct amalgamation with Indian classical styles. These recent artists have acquired international recognition. Devajyoti Ray's paintings have been acquired by the National Fine Arts Museum in Cuba and so have been the works of some of the new generation artists. Jehangir Art Gallery, Mumbai, Mysore Palace has on display several good Indian paintings.

Sculptures

The first sculptures in India date back to the Indus Valley civilization, where stone and bronze figures have been discovered. Later, as Hinduism, Buddhism, and Jainism developed further, India produced some extremely intricate bronzes as well as temple carvings. Some huge shrines, such as the one at Ellora were not constructed by using blocks but carved out of solid rock. Sculptures produced in the northwest, in stucco, schist, or clay, display a very strong blend of Indian and Classical Hellenistic or possibly even Greco-Roman influence. The pink sandstone sculptures of Mathura evolved almost simultaneously. During the Gupta period (4th to 6th century) sculpture reached a very high standard in execution and delicacy in modelling. These styles and others elsewhere in India evolved leading to classical Indian art that contributed to Buddhist and Hindu sculpture throughout Southeast Central and East Asia.

Architecture

Indian architecture encompasses a multitude of expressions over space and time, constantly absorbing new ideas. The result is an evolving range of architectural production that nonetheless retains a certain amount of continuity across history. Some of its earliest production are found in the Indus Valley Civilization (2600-1900 BCE) which is characterised by well planned cities and houses. Religion and kingship do not seem to have played an important role in the planning and layout of these towns.

During the period of the Maurya and Gupta empires and their successors, several Buddhist architectural complexes, such as the caves of Ajanta and Ellora and the monumental Sanchi Stupa were built. Later on, South India produced several Hindu temples like Chennakesava Temple at Belur, the Hoysaleswara Temple at Halebidu, and the Kesava Temple at Somanathapura, Brihadeeswara Temple, Thanjavur, the Sun Temple, Konark, Sri Ranganathaswamy Temple at Srirangam, and the Buddha stupa (Chinna Lanja dibba and Vikramarka kota dibba) at Bhattiprolu. Angkor Wat, Borobudur and other Buddhist and Hindu temples indicate strong Indian influence on South East Asian architecture, as they are built in styles almost identical to traditional Indian religious buildings.

The traditional system of Vaastu Shastra serves as India's version of Feng Shui, influencing town planning, architecture, and ergonomics. It is unclear which system is older, but they contain certain similarities. Feng Shui is more commonly used throughout the world. Though Vastu is conceptually similar to Feng Shui in that it also tries to harmonize the flow of energy, (also called life-force or Prana in Sanskrit and Chi/Ki in Chinese/ Japanese), through the house, it differs in the details, such as the exact directions in which various objects, rooms, materials, etc. are to be placed. With the advent of Islamic influence from the west, Indian architecture was adapted to allow the traditions of the new religion. Fatehpur Sikri, Taj Mahal, Gol Gumbaz, Qutub Minar, Red Fort of Delhi are creations of this era, and are often used as the stereotypical symbols of India. The colonial rule of the British Empire saw the development of Indo-Saracenic style, and mixing of several other styles, such as European Gothic. The Victoria Memorial or the Victoria Terminus are notable examples.

Indian architecture has influenced eastern and southeastern Asia, due to the spread of Buddhism. A number of Indian architectural features such as the temple mound or stupa, temple spire or sikhara, temple tower or pagoda and temple gate or torana, have become famous symbols of Asian culture, used extensively in East Asia and South East Asia. The central spire is also sometimes called a vimanam. The southern temple gate, or gopuram is noted for its intricacy and majesty.

Contemporary Indian architecture is more cosmopolitan. Cities are extremely compact and densely populated. Mumbai's Nariman Point is famous for its Art Deco buildings. Recent creations such as the Lotus Temple, and the various modern urban developments of India like Chandigarh, are notable.

SERVANTS OF INDIA SOCIETY

The Servants of India Society was formed in Pune, Maharashtra, on June 12, 1905 by Gopal Krishna Gokhale, who left the Deccan Education Society to form this association. Along with him were a small group of educated Indians, as Natesh Appaji Dravid, Gopal Krishna Deodhar and Anant Patwardhan who wanted to promote social and human development and overthrow the British rule in India. The Society organized many campaigns to promote education, sanitation, health care and fight the social evils of untouchability and discrimination, alcoholism, poverty, oppression of women and domestic abuse. The publication of The Hitavada, the organ of the Society in English from Nagpur commenced in 1911. Prominent Indians were its members and leaders. It chose to remain away from political activities and national organizations like the Indian National Congress.

The base of the Society shrank in the 1920s with Gokhale's death and the rise of Mahatma Gandhi's Congress, which launched social reform campaigns on a mass scale throughout the nation and attracted most young Indians. However, it still continues its activities albeit with a small membership. It is based in the city of Mumbai, Maharashtra.

INDIAN VILLAGE SOCIETY, INDIAN VILLAGES

Indian Village Society is the greatest example of the phrase "unity in diversity". The Indian village societies are combined of people following different religious paths and traditions. The formation of the Indian village society largely varies from one region to another. Though there is some similarity in the religious practices and cultural activities in most Indian village societies, their education system or the position of women differ from each other. There are certain other things that can be found in almost every village society in India. People in most of the villages share various common utilities like ponds, grazing grounds, temples and shrines, cremation grounds, schools, sitting spaces under large shade trees, wells, wastelands, etc.

The religious customs and practices in Indian village society vary in different parts of the country, depending upon their cultures and lifestyles. Most of the village societies in India have a Gram Devata (village deity) and consider this deity as the protector of the village. The villagers worship the deity regularly for the well being and prosperity of the village. The villagers usually inhabit a world full of divine and semi-divine beings like the tree spirits (Yakshas), ghosts (Bhootas), Puranic, local, personal and ancestral gods. All of these sprits and gods co-exist in an Indian village society.

Fairs and festivals have always been an integral part of Indian village society. The villagers celebrate different types of festivals like religious, regional, seasonal, or sports festivals together. The style of celebrating festivals also differs from one region to another. Among the religious festivals, the Hindu festivals like Holi, Diwali, Durga Puja, Navaratri, Rakhi Purnima, Baisakhi, Dola Yatra, Mahashivratri, etc. are celebrated in most villages in India. The other religious festivals include the Muslim festivals like Eid-ul-Fitr, Eid-ul-Adha, Muharrum; the Buddhist festivals like Buddha Purnima; the Christian festivals like Christmas and the festivals of other religions like Mahavir Jayanti, Gurupurbas, etc. The villagers share lots of light moments with each other during these festivals and perform different forms of folk music and dance. The festivals act as a great platform for social communication in the Indian village society. Besides religious festivals, there are a few other types of festivals celebrated by people in the Indian village society. These festivals include Poush Mela, Vasanta Utsav, the tribal festivals like Chapchar Kut, Mim Kut, Ningol Chakouba, Heikru Hitongba, etc. The people in an Indian village society also come together in other occasions like marriage ceremonies, or funerals, etc. Marriage ceremonies are considered as major celebrating occasions in Indian villages. The villagers enjoy the marriage party together. They also come together in grief during funerals and mourn for the dead.

The educational scenario in the Indian village society has evolved from the ancient times to the modern times. While, only the members of higher castes used to get education in the ancient period, the people from all castes have a chance to get educated in the contemporary period. The Government of India and the State Governments have established numerous schools and colleges in the Indian villages, in the recent years. As a result, the rural literacy rate in most parts of India has reached an impressive level. Apart from the men, the women in Indian village society are also getting much exposure to modern education, now-a-days.

The position of women in the Indian village society has also changed with time. The women were treated with great respect and honour in the ancient period in Indian villages. They were provided with the opportunity of getting proper education and they used to take active part in the decision making process of their families as well. The scenario changed during the medieval period when the women in Indian village society were restricted within the premises of their houses. There was almost no scope for the women to get education. However, the position of women has changed a lot in the contemporary period. They are now getting enough exposure to modern education and are also getting involved in different kinds of occupation.

An Indian village society represents the real essence of India, "unity in diversity". Most of the Indian villages are characterised by a multiplicity of economic, caste, kinship, occupational and religious groups. The rich diversity in cultural heritage of the village societies in different parts of India attracts people from all over the world. They visit the Indian village society to get the feel of real India and also to experience the cultural richness of India.

INDIAN VILLAGE LIFE

Indian Village Life is a blend of quietness, tranquillity, innocence and serenity. The economy of Indian villages is dependant largely on agriculture. Indian Village life is a mixture of tranquillity, serenity, quietude and innocence. Along with numerous small and big grass fields, several rivers, chirping of birds, swinging of emerald trees, speaking in a low voice the tale of languishment and love to the big and clear blue sky give a mesmerizing, captivating and bewitching effect to the Indian villages. Ever since the country's independence from the British colonial rule in 1947, the economy of the nation has banked upon its agrarian society. A majority of the persons living in India have involved themselves in agriculture and associated industries, and have thus made the country the quickest developing world economy. The country is hope to people of different castes and creeds which rightly demonstrates the principles of 'Unity in Diversity'. Indian village life is fully relied on agriculture and innate all over the land. The lifestyle maintained by the people of Indian villages as well as their working styles are as fascinating as the balance offered by the metropolitan city lifestyles.

The primary occupation of the people living in the India villages is agriculture and is therefore reckoned as an unchangeable part of the Indian village culture. Traditionally, village and caste are regarded as similar to each other and the villages in India also follow the same trend. In Indian village life the presence of all the four castes with the hierarchy of the Brahmin is noticed.

The caste system which originated long back has however remained unchanged in the village life in India. Although, caste system in its original sense has collapsed yet caste identities are very much present there in the village life in India. People belonging to different castes in a village deal with each other in kinship terms, which shows the fictive kinship relationships distinguished within each settlement.

Habitually the Indian villagers manifest a deep loyalty to their villages. A rural family which has its root seated deeply in a specific village does not move easily to another. The uniqueness of the village life in India lies in this deep loyalty which is again marked with a rich culture. The mystic charm and the cultural diversities of the village life in India, make the Indian villages that never never land where beauty never fades away, and dream never cease to exist. The village life in India is idyllic, unchanging with its immense beauty. The villagers of India are normally habituated in sharing and using the common facilities of the village including the village shrines and temples, the village pond, schools, grazing grounds, sitting places, etc. This interdependence of the village life in India perhaps provides a matchless unity amongst the villagers which supports them in surviving amidst thousands of odds. Village unity is therefore the primary concern of the village life in India.

Characteristically, each of the Indian villages recognizes a particular deity as the protector of the concerned village and the people of that village get together to worship the deity. Religion, which is deeply instilled in the village life in India, further supports the villagers to consider this as an essential part of village prosperity. The uninterrupted village life in India entertain themselves amidst the colour of the festivals like Diwali, Holi, Muharram, Dussehra, etc., in the captivating pulse of dance and songs and of course in the emotion of rural theatres.

In the Indian village life, there is a headman who is recognized often to respectfully listen to the village panchayat's decision. The village panchayat comprises of some important men from the major castes of the village. The panchayat in Indian villages are responsible to clarify the disputes within the village boundaries as much as possible, with occasional choices of the interference of police or the court system. In the recent era, the Government supports an elective Panchayat system in the Indian villages.

The Government of India helped the villages with advanced technology for farming implements and presently most of the villages in India have access to modern farming equipments. Now-a-days, the Indian village outskirts boast up with food packaging plants, textile industries, sugar industries and steel plants. These have created for the village youth suitable employment opportunities. Continuous reform is made by the government in order to fashion the country a 'motor' for the economy of the world. Developments in the agrarian infrastructure, public sector reforms, rural development, righted labour norms, etc. have changed the Indian village life. The village life in India blessed with its innocence, purity and uncomplicated saga makes the villages as the quaint, archaic, mystic yet charming places to rediscover nature.

EDUCATION IN INDIAN VILLAGES, INDIAN VILLAGE SOCIETY

Education in Indian villages has witnessed many changes since the ancient period. Education in Indian villages has always been one of the pillars of the society. The Indian people are well aware of the advantages of education since the ancient period and as a result, a proper educational structure was available in most of Indian villages in ancient period. The people used to send their children to schools at an early age and the children received education on different subjects.

In the ancient period, education in Indian villages was in a good state. The backbone of the education system in ancient India was the Gurukul system. The children used to receive education from their Gurus or teachers in the Gurukul. In a Gurukul, the students lived in the house of their Guru. The Gurus taught the students about the religious texts like Vedas, Upanishads and other texts and also gave lessons about archery, sword fighting, gymnastics, etc. The main objective was to make a student fully prepared to face any kind of difficulties in life. The Gurukul system continued to be in existence for a long period and was practised in the medieval period also. The introduction of Madrassa system was an important event in education in Indian villages during the medieval period.

With the inception of colonial rule in India, the Gurukul system started to lose its importance. The British rulers made huge changes in the educational scenario of the Indian villages and they introduced schools that eventually replaced the Gurukuls. They established schools at primary, secondary levels and also established colleges to provide higher education. The subjects taught in the schools were also different from those taught in the Gurukuls. Apart from Sanskrit and Vedic texts, the students started to learn other languages like English. Giving lessons about archery, sword fighting or gymnastics was also demolished with the course of time.

After the independence of India, education in Indian villages witnessed another massive change. The Government of India followed the education system set up by the British to a large extent and established new government schools in the villages. The government viewed rural education as an effective tool for bringing social change through community development. More emphasis was laid on primary education up to the age of 14 years and as a result, many new schools were established in the villages. The children in villages get their primary education from the government primary schools. They are taught various subjects including the languages, mathematics, science subjects, arts subjects, agricultural subjects, housekeeping subjects, etc. The elementary education of eight years has also been made compulsory and free for the children in the villages of India. Apart from that, the government authorities have taken many more steps to further improve the status of education in Indian villages as well.

In the contemporary period, the status of education in the Indian villages has improved a lot in spite of having many obstacles. The rural literacy rate in India is quite impressive and is increasing day by day. The rural literacy has also been taken as a primary agenda by the government and many private organisations are helping the government to serve this purpose better.

4

Family

INDIAN FAMILY LIFE AND VALUES

Even though India is a country made up of numerous religions and communities of people, the basic values and systems of family life remain similar. Even today people don't believe in family planning and treat children as gifts from God. Sons are always more preferred than daughters because daughters are expensive to bring up. They don't earn money for the family and in addition, have to be given a lot of dowry when they get married. Sons normally earn money for the family and support their parents during their old age.

Marriage of daughters traditionally is arranged with boys from the same community. Normally, the parents of the prospective spouses get together either through a common relative or through a matchmaker. The families discuss each other's backgrounds and work out the modalities of the bondage. Traditionally, the boy's family would negotiate with the girl's family for dowry. The higher the amount of dowry the better the proposal. Nowadays, although the dowry system has subsided among the educated people, girls are always sent to their in-laws homes with large sums of money, beautiful saris, jewelry and other valuables. All these things are in effect dowry given with niceties and no negotiation. Children are usually married in order of age i.e. the older child is married off before the younger child. However, when the siblings are a son and a daughter, even though the daughter is younger, the son has to normally wait for the daughter to be married off. Of course, if there is a very vast gap between the ages of the siblings, the son is allowed to marry first. The family usually consists of the man, his wife, their kids, the man's parents and unmarried sisters, if any. The man has to necessarily make his parents live with him and has to look after them. The man's wife, the daughter-in-law of the house treats her parents-in-law as her own parents and calls them "˜Mummy' and "˜Daddy' or "˜Papa'. She has to get along with her unmarried sisters-in-law, if there are any. The man plays a very crucial role in balancing egos and satisfying everyone. He has to please his parents and his wife and tackle any situation of a conflict between the two. The daughter-in-law is often a homemaker and might not be allowed to go out and work. She cooks for the family, supervises the other chores done by a domestic servant and looks after the needs of her parents-in-law. When she has children, she completely immerses herself in looking after them and bringing them up. Meanwhile, her husband is the earning member whose sole duty is to bring the booty home.

Family life has its own advantages and disadvantages. If the parents-in-law don't get along with the daughter-in-law or if the daughter-in-law is not able to get along with her unmarried sisters-in-law, there are lots of emotional tensions and the man has to cope with it skilfully. Also, if there are two brothers, both married and living with their families under the same roof, there is the question of three families getting along - the parents-in-law and the families of the two sons. Usually, in a situation like this, the elder son and his wife are given more respect and importance and have more responsibilities to shoulder.

However, the main advantage of living life in this system is that the children get to learn a lot from their grandparents. Besides, if there are two brothers with their families living together, the cousins i.e. the children of the two brothers grow up together just as real siblings. The children grow up with a strong sense of security and stability. The family system is given a lot of importance in India and has worked more often than not.

Family Ideas

In India, people learn the essential themes of cultural life within the bosom of a family. In most of the country, the basic units of society are the patrilineal family unit and wider kinship groupings. The most widely desired residential unit is the joint family, ideally consisting of three or four patrilineally related generations, all living under one roof, working, eating, worshipping, and cooperating together in mutually beneficial social and economic activities. Patrilineal joint families include men related through the male line, along with their wives and children. Most young women expect to live with their husband's relatives after marriage, but they retain important bonds with their natal families. Despite the continuous and growing impact of urbanization, secularization, and Westernization, the traditional joint household, both in ideal and in practice, remains the primary social force in the lives of most Indians. Loyalty to family is a deeply held ideal for almost everyone.

Large families tend to be flexible and well-suited to modern Indian life, especially for the 67 percent of Indians who are farmers or agricultural workers or work in related activities. As in most primarily agricultural societies, few individuals can hope to achieve economic security without being part of a cooperating group of kinsmen. The joint family is also common in cities, where kinship ties can be crucial to obtaining scarce jobs or financial assistance. Numerous prominent Indian families, such as the Tatas, Birlas, and Sarabhais, retain joint family arrangements even as they work together to control some of the country's largest financial empires.

The joint family is an ancient Indian institution, but it has undergone some change in the late twentieth century. Although several generations living together is the ideal, actual living arrangements vary widely depending on region, social status, and economic circumstance. Many Indians live in joint families that deviate in various ways from the ideal, and many live in nuclear families—a couple with their unmarried children—as is the most common pattern in the West. However, even where the ideal joint family is seldom found (as, for example, in certain regions and among impoverished agricultural labourers and urban squatters), there are often strong networks of kinship ties through which economic assistance and other benefits are obtained. Not infrequently, clusters of relatives live very near each other, easily available to respond to the give and take of kinship obligations. Even when relatives cannot actually live in close proximity, they typically maintain strong bonds of kinship and attempt to provide each other with economic help, emotional support, and other benefits.

As joint families grow ever larger, they inevitably divide into smaller units, passing through a predictable cycle over time. The breakup of a joint family into smaller units does not necessarily represent the rejection of the joint family ideal. Rather, it is usually a response to a variety of conditions, including the need for some members to move from village to city, or from one city to another to take advantage of employment opportunities. Splitting of the family is often blamed on quarrelling women—typically, the wives of coresident brothers. Although women's disputes may, in fact, lead to family division, men's disagreements do so as well. Despite cultural ideals of brotherly harmony, adult brothers frequently quarrel over land and other matters, leading them to decide to live under separate roofs and divide their property. Frequently, a large joint family divides after the demise of elderly parents, when there is no longer a single authority figure to hold the family factions together. After division, each new residential unit, in its turn, usually becomes joint when sons of the family marry and bring their wives to live in the family home.

Variations in Family Structure

Some family types bear special mention because of their unique qualities. In the sub-Himalayan region of Uttar Pradesh, polygyny is commonly practiced. There, among Hindus, a simple polygynous family is composed of a man, his two wives, and their unmarried children. Various other family types occur there, including the supplemented subpolygynous household—a woman whose husband lives elsewhere (perhaps with his other wife), her children, plus other adult relatives. Polygyny is also practiced in other parts of India by a tiny minority of the population, especially in families in which the first wife has not been able to bear children.

Among the Buddhist people of the mountainous Ladakh District of Jammu and Kashmir, who have cultural ties to Tibet, fraternal polyandry is practiced, and a household may include a set of brothers with their common wife or wives. This family type, in which brothers also share land, is almost certainly linked to the extreme scarcity of cultivable land in the Himalayan region, because it discourages fragmentation of holdings.

The peoples of the northeastern hill areas are known for their matriliny, tracing descent and inheritance in the female line rather than the male line. One of the largest of these groups, the Khasis—an ethnic or tribal people in the state of Meghalaya—are divided into matrilineal clans; the youngest daughter receives almost all of the inheritance including the house. A Khasi husband goes to live in his wife's house. Khasis, many of whom have become Christian, have the highest literacy rate in India, and Khasi women maintain notable authority in the family and community.

Perhaps the best known of India's unusual family types is the traditional Nayar *taravad*, or great house. The Nayars are a cluster of castes in Kerala. High-ranking and prosperous, the Nayars maintained matrilineal households in which sisters and brothers and their children were the permanent residents. After an official prepuberty marriage, each woman received a series of visiting husbands in her room in the *taravad* at night. Her children were all legitimate members of the *taravad*. Property, matrilineally inherited, was managed by the eldest brother of the senior woman. This system, the focus of much anthropological interest, has been disintegrating in the twentieth century, and in the 1990s probably fewer than 5 percent of the Nayars live in matrilineal *taravads*. Like the Khasis, Nayar women are known for being well-educated and powerful within the family. Malabar rite Christians, an ancient community in Kerala, adopted many practices of their powerful Nayar neighbours, including naming their sons for matrilineal forebears. Their kinship system, however, is patrilineal. Kerala Christians have a very high literacy rate, as do most Indian Christian groups.

Large Kinship Groups

In most of Hindu India, people belong not only to coresident family groups but to larger aggregates of kin as well. Subsuming the family is the patrilineage (known in northern and central India as the *khandan*, *kutumb*, or *kul*), a locally based set of males who trace their ancestry to a common progenitor a few generations back, plus their wives and unmarried daughters. Larger than the patrilineage is the clan, commonly known as the *gotra* or *got*, a much larger group of patrilineally related males and their wives and daughters, who often trace common ancestry to a mythological figure. In some regions, particularly among the high-ranking Rajputs of western India, clans are hierarchically ordered. Some people also claim membership in larger, more amorphous groupings known as *vansh* and *sakha*.

Hindu lineages and clans are strictly exogamous—that is, a person may not marry or have a sexual alliance with a member of his own lineage or clan; such an arrangement would be considered incestuous. In North India, rules further prohibit marriage between a person and his mother's lineage members as well. Among some high-ranking castes of the north, exogamy is also extended to the mother's, father's mother's, and mother's mother's clans. In contrast, in South India, marriage to a member of the mother's kin group is often encouraged.

Muslims also recognize kinship groupings larger than the family. These include the *khandan*, or patrilineage, and the *azizdar*, or kindred. The *azizdar* group differs slightly for each individual and includes all relatives linked to a person by blood or marriage. Muslims throughout India encourage marriage within the lineage and kindred, and marriages between the children of siblings are common.

Within a village or urban neighbourhood, members of a lineage recognize their kinship in a variety of ways. Mutual assistance in daily work, in emergencies, and in factional struggles is expected. For Hindus, cooperation in specific annual rituals helps define the kin group. For example, in many areas, at the worship of the goddess deemed responsible for the welfare of the lineage, patrilineally related males and their wives join in the rites and consume specially consecrated fried breads or other foods. Unmarried daughters of the lineage are only spectators at the rites and do not share in the special foods. Upon marriage, a woman becomes a member of her husband's lineage and then participates regularly in the worship of her husband's lineage goddess. Lineage bonds are also evident at life-cycle observances, when kin join together in celebrating births, marriages, and religious initiations. Upon the death of a lineage member, other lineage members observe ritual death pollution rules for a prescribed number of days and carry out appropriate funeral rites and feasts.

For some castes, especially in the north, careful records of lineage ties are kept by a professional genealogist, a member of a caste whose traditional task is maintaining genealogical tomes. These itinerant bards make their rounds from village to village over the course of a year or more, recording births, deaths, and glorious accomplishments of the patrilineal descent group. These genealogical services have been especially crucial among Rajputs, Jats, and similar groups whose lineages own land and where power can depend on fine calculations of pedigree and inheritance rights.

Some important kinship linkages are not traced through men but through women. These linkages involve those related to an individual by blood and marriage through a mother, married sisters, or married daughters, and for a man, through his wife. Anthropologist David Mandelbaum has termed these "feminal kin." Key relationships are those between a brother and sister, parents and daughters, and a person and his or her mother's brother. Through bonds with these close kin, a person has links with several households and lineages in many settlements. Throughout most of India, there are continuous visits—some of which may last for months and include the exchange of gifts at visits, life-cycle rites, and holidays, and many other key interactions between such relatives. These relationships are often characterized by deep affection and willingly offered support.

These ties cut across the countryside, linking each person with kin in villages and towns near and far. Almost everywhere a villager goes—especially in the north, where marriage networks cover wide distances—he can find some kind of relative. Moral support, a place to stay, economic assistance, and political backing are all available through these kinship networks. The multitude of kinship ties is further extended through the device of fictive kinship. Residents of a single village usually use kinship terms for one another, and especially strong ties of fictive kinship can be ceremonially created with fellow religious initiates or fellow pilgrims of one's village or neighbourhood. In the villages and cities of the north, on the festival of Raksha Bandhan (the Tying of the Protective Thread, during which sisters tie sacred threads on their brothers' wrists to symbolize the continuing bond between them), a female may tie a thread on the wrist of an otherwise unrelated male and "make him her brother." Fictive kinship bonds cut across caste and class lines and involve obligations of hospitality, gift-giving, and variable levels of cooperation and assistance.

Neighbours and friends may also create fictive kinship ties by informal agreement. Actually, any strong friendship between otherwise unrelated people is typically imbued with kinship-like qualities. In such friendships, kinship terms are adopted for address, and the give and take of kinship may develop. Such bonds commonly evolve between neighbours in urban apartment buildings, between special friends at school, and between close associates at work. The use of kinship terms enhances affection in the relationship. In Gujarat, personal names usually include the word for "sister" and "brother," so that the use of someone's personal name automatically sounds affectionate and caring.

Family Authority and Harmony

In the Indian household, lines of hierarchy and authority are clearly drawn, shaping structurally and psychologically complex family relationships. Ideals of conduct are aimed at creating and maintaining family harmony. All family members are socialized to accept the authority of those ranked above them in the hierarchy. In general, elders rank above juniors, and among people of similar age, males outrank females. Daughters of a family command the formal respect of their brothers' wives, and the mother of a household is in charge of her daughters-in-law. Among adults in a joint family, a newly arrived daughter-in-law has the least authority. Males learn to command others within the household but expect to accept the direction of senior males. Ideally, even a mature adult man living in his father's household acknowledges his father's authority on both minor and major matters.

Women are especially strongly socialized to accept a position subservient to males, to control their sexual impulses, and to subordinate their personal preferences to the needs of the family and kin group. Reciprocally, those in authority accept responsibility for meeting the needs of others in the family group. There is tremendous emphasis on the unity of the family grouping, especially as differentiated from persons outside the kinship circle. Internally, efforts are made to deemphasize ties between spouses and between parents and their own children in order to enhance a wider sense of harmony within the entire household. Husbands and wives are discouraged from openly displaying affection for one another, and in strictly traditional households, they may not even properly speak to one another in the presence of anyone else, even their own children. Young parents are inhibited by "shame" from ostentatiously dandling their own young children but are encouraged to play with the children of siblings.

Psychologically, family members feel an intense emotional interdependence with each other and the family as an almost organic unit. Ego boundaries are permeable to others in the family, and any notion of a separate self is often dominated by a sense of what psychoanalyst Alan Roland has termed a more inclusive "familial self." Interpersonal empathy, closeness, loyalty, and interdependency are all crucial to life within the family.

Family resources, particularly land or businesses, have traditionally been controlled by family males, especially in high-status groups. Customarily, according to traditional schools of Hindu law, women did not inherit land or buildings and were thus beholden to their male kin who controlled these vital resources. Under Muslim customary law, women are entitled to inherit real estate and often do so, but their shares have typically been smaller than those of similarly situated males. Under modern law, all Indian women can inherit land.

THE HISTORY OF THE FAMILY

How the Family Came to Be

The modern family among civilized peoples is based almost universally on the union of one man and one woman. There is good reason to believe that this practice of monogamy was in vogue among primitive human beings, but marriage was unstable and it was only through long experimentation that monogamy proved itself best fitted to survive. At first conjugal affection, which has become intelligent and moral, was merely a sexual desire that led the man to seek a mate and the maid to choose among her suitors. Unbound by long-continued custom or legal and ceremonial restriction, the primitive couple were free to separate if they pleased, but the instinctive feeling that they belonged to each other, the habits of association, adaptation, and cooperation, and jealousy at any attention shown by another tended to preserve the relationship. The presence of offspring sealed the bond as long as the children were dependent, and strengthened the sense of mutual responsibility. The children were peculiarly the mother's children since she gave them birth, but the father instinctively protected the family that was growing up around him, and procured food and shelter for its members, though it is doubtful if he had any realization of his part in giving life to a new generation.

During this period of social development, when the mother's presence constituted the home and the children were regarded as belonging primarily to her, descent was reckoned in the female line, the children were attached to the maternal clan of blood relatives, and such relatives began to move in bands, for the same reason that animals move in packs and herds. Some writers speak of it as a matriarchal period, but it does not appear that women governed; it is more proper to speak of the family as metronymic, for the children bore the mother's name and maternity outweighed paternity in social estimate.

The Patriarchal Household

When population increased and food consequently became more difficult to obtain, the domestication of animals was achieved, and nomadic habits carried the family from pasture to pasture; rival clans wanted the same regions, wars broke out, and physical superiority asserted its claims. The man supplanted the woman as the important member of the household, reduced the others to submission, added to his wives and servants by capture or purchase, and established the patriarchal system. Descent henceforth was reckoned in the paternal line, and society had become patronymic instead of metronymic. It must not be supposed that this change occurred very suddenly. It may have taken many centuries to bring it about, but as the man learned his part in procreation and his power in society, he delighted in his self-importance to lord it over the woman and her children. The marriage relation ceased to be free and reciprocal. The wife no longer had a choice in marriage. Bought or captured, she was no longer wooed for a companion, but was valued according to her economic worth. As population pressed, the domestication of plants followed the taming of animals, but the agricultural settlement of the family only made the woman's lot harder, for she was the burden bearer on the farm.

Polygyny

A better term than polygamy—was the inevitable result of the patriarchal system. Man made the law and the law recognized no restraint upon his sexual and parental instincts. Improvements in living added to the resources of the family and made it possible to maintain large households of wives, children, and slaves. Polygyny had some social utility, because it increased the number of children, and this gave added prestige and power to the family, as slavery had utility because it provided a labour force; but both were weaknesses in ancient society, because they did not tend in the long run to human welfare. Polygyny brutalized men, degraded women, and destroyed that affection and comradeship between parents and their offspring that are the proper heritage of children. Wherever it has survived as a system, polygyny has hindered progress, and wherever it exists in the midst of monogamy it tends to break down civilization.

Another variety of marriage that has been less common than polygyny is polyandry. It is a term that signifies the marriage of one woman to several husbands, and seems to have occurred, as in the interior of Asia, only where subsistence was especially difficult or women comparatively few. Neither polygyny nor polyandry were universal, even where they were a frequent practice. Only the few could afford the indulgence, much the largest percentage of the people remained monogamous.

Conflict and Social Selection

The supreme business of the social group is to adapt itself to the conditions that affect its life. It must learn to get on with its physical environment and with other social groups with which it comes into relation. The methods of adaptation are conflict and cooperation. The primitive savage and his wife learned to work together, and his family and hers very likely kept the peace, until through the increase of population they felt the pinch of hunger when the supply did not equal the demand. Then came conflict. Conflict is an essential element in all progress.

There is conflict between the lower and higher impulses in the human mind, conflict between selfish ambition and the welfare of the group, conflict among individuals and races for a place in the sun. It is conceivable that the baser impulses that provoke much social conflict may give way to more rational and altruistic purpose, but it is difficult to see how all friction can be avoided in social relations. It is certainly to be reckoned with in the history of group life.

The story of human progress shows that in the social conflict those groups survive which have become best adapted to life conditions and so are fitted to cope with their enemies. In the story of the family male leadership proved most useful and was perpetuated, but the practice of polygyny and polyandry proved in the long run to be hurtful to success in the sturdy struggle for existence.

Ancestor-Worship

When a practice or institution is seen to work well it soon becomes indorsed by social custom, law, or religion. The patriarchal system became fortified by ancestor-worship, which helped to keep the family subordinate to its male head. Even the dead hand of the patriarch ruled. The paternal ancestors of the family were believed to have the power to bless or curse their descendants, and they were faithfully placated with gifts and veneration, as has continued to be the custom in China. Among the Romans the household gods were cherished at the hearth long before Jupiter became king of heaven; Æneas must save his ancestral-images if he lost all else in the fall of Troy. At Rome the worship of a common ancestor was the strongest family bond. The marriage ceremony consisted of a solemn transfer of the bride from her duties to her own ancestors over to the adoption of her husband's gods. This transfer of allegiance helped to perpetuate the patriarchal system, and the sanction of religion greatly strengthened the wedded relation, so that divorce and polygyny were unknown in the old Roman period. But the absolute patriarchal control of wife and children made the man selfish and arbitrary and weakened the bond of affection and mutual interests, while Roman political conquest strengthened the pride and power of the imperial masters. Religion lost its prestige and the family bond loosened, until from being one of the purest of social institutions in the early days of the republic, the Roman family became one of the most degenerate. This boded ill for the future of the race and empire.

The Medieval Family

The Roman family seemed in danger of disintegrating, for the matron claimed rights that ran counter to the rights of the man, when two new forces entered Roman society and checked this tendency toward disintegration. The first was Christianity, the second was Teutonic conquest. Christianity taught consideration for women and children, but it taught submission to the man in the home, and so was a constructive force in the conservation of the family. Teutonic custom was similar to the early Roman. When Teutonic enterprise pushed a new race over the goal of race conflict and took in charge the administration of affairs in Roman society, there was a restoration of the rule of force and so of masculine supremacy. In the lord's castle and the peasant's hut the authority of the man continued unquestioned through the Middle Ages, and the church made monogamous marriage a binding sacrament; but sexual infidelity was common, especially of the husband, and divorce was not unknown. In the civilized lands of Christendom monogamy was the only form of marriage recognized by civil law, and with the slow growth toward higher standards of civilization the harshness of patriarchal custom has become softened and the rights of women and children have been increased by law, though not without endangering the solidarity of the family. Similarly, the standards of sex conduct have improved.

Advantages of Monogamy

The advantages of monogamy are so many that in spite of the present restiveness under restraint it seems certain to become the permanent and universal type as reason asserts its right and controls impulse. Nature seems to have predetermined it by maintaining approximately an equal number of the sexes, and nature frowns upon promiscuity by penalizing it with sterility and neglect of the few children that are born, so that in the struggle for existence the fittest survive by a process of natural selection. A study of biology and anthropology gives added evidence that nature favours monogamy, for in the highest grade of animals below man the monogamic relation holds almost without exception, and low-grade human races follow the same practice.

There are moral advantages in monogamy that alone are sufficient to insure its permanence. It is to the advantage of society that altruistic and kindly feelings should outweigh jealousy, anger, and selfishness. Monogamy encourages affection and mutual consideration, and in that atmosphere children learn the graces and virtues that make social life wholesome and attractive. Welcomed in the home, they receive the care and instruction of both parents and become socialized for the larger and later responsibilities of the social order. In the altruism thus developed lie the roots of morals and religion. It is well agreed that the essence of each is the right motive to conduct. Love to men and to God is an accepted definition of religion, and ethics is grounded on that principle. Love is the ruling principle of the monogamic family; from the narrower domestic circle it extends to the community and to all mankind.

Marriage Laws

In spite of the general practice of monogamy as a form of marriage and the noble principles that underlie the monogamic type of family, sex relations need the restraint of law. Human desires are selfish and ideals too often give way before them unless there is some kind of external control. There have been times when the church had such control, and in certain countries individual rulers have determined the law; but since the eighteenth century there has been a steady trend in the direction of popular control of all social relations.

This tendency has been carried farthest in the United States, where public opinion voices its convictions and compels legislative action. It is natural that the people of certain States should be more progressive or radical than others, and therefore in the absence of a national law, there is considerable variety in the marriage and divorce laws, but no other country has higher ideals of the married relation and at the same time as large a measure of freedom. At present marriage laws in the United States agree generally on the following provisions:

(1) Every marriage must be licensed by the State and the act of marriage must be reported to the State and registered.

(2) Marriage is not legal below a certain age, and consent of parents must be obtained usually until the man is twenty-one and the woman eighteen.

(3) Certain persons are forbidden marriage because of near relationship or personal defect. Such marriage if performed may be annulled.

(4) Remarriage may take place after the death of husband or wife, after disappearance for a period varying from three to seven years, or a certain time after divorce.

In the twenty-year period between 1886 and 1906 covered by the United States Census of Marriage and Divorce slow improvements were made in legislation, but a number of States are far behind others in the enactment of suitable laws, and most of the States do not make the provisions that are desirable for law enforcement. Yet there is a limit of strictness beyond which marriage laws cannot safely go, because they hinder marriage and provoke illicit relations. That limit is fixed by the sanction of public opinion. After all, there is less need of better regulation than of the education of public opinion to the sacredness of marriage and to its importance for human welfare. Without the restraints put upon impulse by the education of the understanding and the will, young people often assume family obligations thoughtlessly and even flippantly, when they are ill-mated and often unacquainted with each other's characteristic qualities. Such marriages usually bring distress and divorce instead of growing affection and unity. Without education in the obligation of marriage many well-qualified persons delay it or avoid it altogether, because they are unwilling to bear the burdens of family support, childbearing, and housekeeping. Society suffers loss in both cases.

Reforms and Ideals

Because of all these deficiencies several remedies have been proposed and certain of them adopted. Because of the economic difficulties, it is urged that as far as possible by legislation, illegitimate ways of heaping up wealth for the few at the expense of the many should be checked, and that by vocational training boys should be fitted for a trade and girls prepared for housekeeping.

To meet other difficulties it is proposed that popular instruction be given from press and pulpit, in order that the moral and spiritual plane of married life may be uplifted. The marriage ideal is a well-mated pair, physically and intellectually qualified, who through affection are attracted to marriage and through mutual consideration are ready unselfishly to seek each other's welfare, and who recognize in marriage a divinely ordered provision for human happiness and for the perpetuation of the race. Such a marriage does not plant the seeds of discord and neighbourly scandal or compel a speedy resort to the divorce court.

INDIAN FAMILY STRUCTURE

In India, people learn the essential themes of cultural life within the bosom of a family. In most of the country, the basic units of society are the patrilineal family unit and wider kinship groupings. The most widely desired residential unit is the joint family, ideally consisting of three or four patrilineally related generations, all living under one roof, working, eating, worshiping, and cooperating together in mutually beneficial social and economic activities. Patrilineal joint families include men related through the male line, along with their wives and children. Most young women expect to live with their husband's relatives after marriage, but they retain important bonds with their natal families.

Despite the continuous and growing impact of urbanization, secularization, and Westernization, the traditional joint household, both in ideal and in practice, remains the primary social force in the lives of most Indians. Loyalty to family is a deeply held ideal for almost everyone.

Large families tend to be flexible and well-suited to modern Indian life, especially for the 67 percent of Indians who are farmers or agricultural workers or work in related activities. As in most primarily agricultural societies, few individuals can hope to achieve economic security without being part of a cooperating group of kinsmen. The joint family is also common in cities, where kinship ties can be crucial to obtaining scarce jobs or financial assistance. Numerous prominent Indian families, such as the Tatas, Birlas, and Sarabhais, retain joint family arrangements even as they work together to control some of the country's largest financial empires.

The joint family is an ancient Indian institution, but it has undergone some change in the late twentieth century. Although several generations living together is the ideal, actual living arrangements vary widely depending on region, social status, and economic circumstance. Many Indians live in joint families that deviate in various ways from the ideal, and many live in nuclear families—a couple with their unmarried children—as is the most common pattern in the West. However, even where the ideal joint family is seldom found (as, for example, in certain regions and among impoverished agricultural laborers and urban squatters), there are often strong networks of kinship ties through which economic assistance and other benefits are obtained. Not infrequently, clusters of relatives live very near each other, easily available to respond to the give and take of kinship obligations. Even when relatives cannot actually live in close proximity, they typically maintain strong bonds of kinship and attempt to provide each other with economic help, emotional support, and other benefits.

As joint families grow ever larger, they inevitably divide into smaller units, passing through a predictable cycle over time. The breakup of a joint family into smaller units does not necessarily represent the rejection of the joint family ideal. Rather, it is usually a response to a variety of conditions, including the need for some members to move from village to city, or from one city to another to take advantage of employment opportunities. Splitting of the family is often blamed on quarrelling women—typically, the wives of coresident brothers. Although women's disputes may, in fact, lead to family division, men's disagreements do so as well. Despite cultural ideals of brotherly harmony, adult brothers frequently quarrel over land and other matters, leading them to decide to live under separate roofs and divide their property. Frequently, a large joint family divides after the demise of elderly parents, when there is no longer a single authority figure to hold the family factions together. After division, each new residential unit, in its turn, usually becomes joint when sons of the family marry and bring their wives to live in the family home.

Variations in Indian Family Structure

Some family types bear special mention because of their unique qualities. In the sub-Himalayan region of Uttar Pradesh, polygyny is commonly practiced. There, among Hindus, a simple polygynous family is composed of a man, his two wives, and their unmarried children. Various other family types occur there, including the supplemented subpolygynous household—a woman whose husband lives elsewhere (perhaps with his other wife), her children, plus other adult relatives. Polygyny is also practiced in other parts of India by a tiny minority of the population, especially in families in which the first wife has not been able to bear children.Among the Buddhist people of the mountainous Ladakh District of Jammu and Kashmir, who have cultural ties to Tibet, fraternal polyandry is practiced, and a household may include a set of brothers with their common wife or wives. This family type, in which brothers also share land, is almost certainly linked to the extreme scarcity of cultivable land in the Himalayan region, because it discourages fragmentation of holdings.

The peoples of the northeastern hill areas are known for their matriliny, tracing descent and inheritance in the female line rather than the male line. One of the largest of these groups, the Khasis—an ethnic or tribal people in the state of Meghalaya—are divided into matrilineal clans; the youngest daughter receives almost all of the inheritance including the house. A Khasi husband goes to live in his wife's house. Khasis, many of whom have become Christian, have the highest literacy rate in India, and Khasi women maintain notable authority in the family and community.

Perhaps the best known of India's unusual family types is the traditional Nayar *taravad*, or great house. The Nayars are a cluster of castes in Kerala. High-ranking and prosperous, the Nayars maintained matrilineal households in which sisters and brothers and their children were the permanent residents. After an official prepuberty marriage, each woman received a series of visiting husbands in her room in the *taravad* at night. Her children were all legitimate members of the *taravad*.

Property, matrilineally inherited, was managed by the eldest brother of the senior woman. This system, the focus of much anthropological interest, has been disintegrating in the twentieth century, and in the 1990s probably fewer than 5 percent of the Nayars live in matrilineal *taravads*. Like the Khasis, Nayar women are known for being well-educated and powerful within the family.

Malabar rite Christians, an ancient community in Kerala, adopted many practices of their powerful Nayar neighbours, including naming their sons for matrilineal forebears. Their kinship system, however, is patrilineal. Kerala Christians have a very high literacy rate, as do most Indian Christian groups.

INDIAN FAMILIES AND KINSHIP

One of the great themes pervading Indian life is social interdependence. People are born into groups—families, clans, subcastes, castes, and religious communities—and live with a constant sense of being part of and inseparable from these groups. A corollary is the notion that everything a person does properly involves interaction with other people. A person's greatest dread, perhaps, is the possibility of being left alone, without social support, to face the necessary challenges of life. This sense of interdependence is extended into the theological realm: the very shape of a person's life is seen as being greatly influenced by divine beings with whom an ongoing relationship must be maintained.

Social interaction is regarded as being of the highest priority in Indian families, and social bonds are expected to be long lasting. Even economic activities that might in Western culture involve impersonal interactions are in India deeply imbedded in a social nexus. All social interaction involves constant attention to hierarchy, respect, honour, the feelings of others, rights and obligations, hospitality, and gifts of food, clothing, and other desirable items. Finely tuned rules of etiquette help facilitate each individual's many social relationships.

Western visitors to India are sometimes startled to find that important government and business officials have left their posts—often for many days at a time—to attend a cousin's wedding or participate in religious activities in a distant part of the country. "He is out of station and will be back in a week or two," the absent official's officemates blandly explain to the frustrated visitor. What is going on is not laziness or hedonistic recreation, but is the official's proper recognition of his need to continually maintain his social ties with relatives, caste fellows, other associates, and God. Without being enmeshed in such ties throughout life, a person cannot hope to maintain long-term efficacy in either economic or social endeavors. Social bonds with relatives must be reinforced at family events or at rites crucial to the religious community. If this is not done, people who could offer vital support in many phases of life would be alienated.

In every activity, there is an assumption that social ties can help a person and that their absence can bring failure. Seldom do people carry out even the simplest task on their own. From birth onward, a child learns that his "fate" has been "written" by divine forces and that his life will be shaped by a plan decided by more powerful beings. When a small child eats, his mother puts the mouthfuls of food into his mouth with her own hand. When a boy climbs a tree to pluck mangoes, another stands below with a basket to receive them. When a girl fetches water from the well in pots on her head, someone at her home helps her unload the pots. When a farmer stacks sheaves of grain onto his bullock cart, he stands atop the cart, catching the sheaves tossed up to him by his son.

A student applying to a college hopes that he has an influential relative or family friend who can put in a good word for him with the director of admissions. At the age of marriage, a young person expects that parents will take care of finding the appropriate bride or groom and arranging all the formalities. At the birth of a child, the new mother is assured that the child's kin will help her attend to the infant's needs.

A businessman seeking to arrange a contract relies not only on his own abilities but also on the assistance of well-connected friends and relatives to help finalize the deal. And finally, when facing death, a person is confident that offspring and other relatives will carry out the appropriate funeral rites, including a commemorative feast when, through gifts of clothing and food, continuing social ties are reaffirmed by all in attendance. Indian families locdata 1995

INDIAN FAMILY STRUCTURE, INDIAN SOCIETY

Indian family structure has transformed from a joint family unit to small nuclear units, with the passing decades. Indian family structure is believed to be the unit that teaches the values and worth of an honest living that have been carried down across generations. Since the Puranic ages, Indian family structure was that of a joint family, indicating every person of the same clan living together. However, this idea of elaborate living disintegrated in smaller family units.

In India, people learn the essential themes of cultural life within the bondings of a family. In ancient days, the basic units of society had been the patrilineal family unit with wider kinship groupings. The most widely preferred residential unit is the joint family, ideally consisting of three or four patrilineally related generations, all living under one roof, working, worshiping, eating, and cooperating together in communally beneficial social and economic activities. Patrilineal joint families include men related through the male line, along with their wives and children. The young married women live with their husband's relatives after marriage, but they retain important bonds with their natal families as well. Despite the continuous and growing impact of urbanization, secularization, and Westernization, the conventional joint household of Indian family structure, both in ideal and in practice, remains the chief social force in the lives of Indians. Loyalty to family is a deeply imbibed in every member of the family. Large families eventually faced difficulties to suit with modern Indian life. The modern style of livinf, modern occupations and beliefs are eventually confronting problems to get adjusted. The joint family is now quite unfamiliar in cities. However, the relative ties are maintained within the kinships, since these very ties can prove to be crucial while any kind of emergency. Numerous prominent Indian families, such as the Tatas, Birlas, and Sarabhais, retain joint family arrangements even today and they work together to control some of the country's largest financial empires.

The Indian joint family structure is an ancient phenomenon, but it has undergone some change in the late twentieth century. Living arrangements vary widely depending on region, social status, and economic circumstance. With the passing time, nuclear families have evolved that is a couple living with their unmarried children. There are often strong networks of kinship ties through which economic assistance and other benefits are obtained. Often clusters of relatives live near each other, who are easily available and respond to the give and take of kinship obligations. Even when relatives cannot actually live in close proximity, they typically maintain strong bonds of kinship and attempt to provide each other with economic help, emotional support, and other required benefits.

The Indian joint families grew even larger and finally they divide into smaller units, passing through a expected cycle over time. The breakup of a joint family into smaller units does not necessarily symbolize the rejection of the joint family ideal. Rather, it is usually a reaction to a variety of conditions, including the requirement for some members to move from village to city, or from one city to another to obtain the advantage of employment opportunities.

Splitting of the family is often blamed on quarrelling women, the wives of co-resident brothers and so on. Although women‘s disputes may, in fact, lead to family division, men‘s disagreements are responsible as well. Despite cultural ideals of brotherly harmony, adult brothers often quarrel over land and other matters, leading them to decide to live under separate roofs and split their property. Frequently, a large joint family divides after the death of elderly parents, when there is no longer a solitary authority figure to hold the family factions together. After division, each new housing unit, in its turn, usually comes together when sons of the family marry and bring their wives to live in the family home. Some Indian family structure bears special mention because of their unique qualities. In the sub-Himalayan region of Uttar Pradesh, polygyny is generally practiced. A polygynous family comprises a man, his two wives, and their unmarried children. Various other Indian family structures occur there, including the supplemented subpolygynous household, where a woman whose husband lives elsewhere, stays with her children and other adult relatives. Among the Buddhist people of the mountainous Ladakh District of Jammu and Kashmir, fraternal polyandry is practiced; a household may include a set of brothers with their common wife or wives. This family type, in which brothers also share land, is almost certainly linked to the extreme scarcity of cultivable land in the Himalayan region, because it discourages disintegration of holdings.

The inhabitants of the northeastern hill areas are known for their matriliny order that distinguish the decent and inheritance of a family in the female line rather than the male line. One of the largest of these groups, the Khasis of Meghalaya is divided into matrilineal clans. Here, the youngest daughter receives almost all of the inheritance including the house. A Khasi husband lives in his wife's house.

Perhaps the strangest Indian family structure form is the traditional Nayar taravad, or great house. The Nayars are a cluster of castes in Kerala who are high-ranking and prosperous. The Nayars maintained matrilineal households in which sisters and brothers and their children remain as the permanent residents. After an official childhood marriage, each woman received a series of visiting husbands in the taravad. Her children were all considered as the legitimate members of the taravad. The eldest brother of the senior woman managed property, matrilineally inherited. This kind of Indian family structure has been eleminated in the twentieth century, and in the 1990s probably fewer than 5 percent of the Nayars still live in matrilineal taravads. Like the Khasis, Nayar women are well educated and powerful within the family.

Malabar rite Christians, an ancient community in Kerala, adopted many Indian family structure practices alike their powerful Nayar neighbours, including naming their sons for matrilineal descent. Their relationship system, however, is patrilineal.

Thus, Indian family structure has been varied in varied periods of time and in different regions of the nation. The society structure and regulations have the highest influence on such formations of Indian family structures.

AMID CONTINUITY AND CHANGE

Chennai is a quaint mix of the old and the new. Though the English legacy is undeniable, beauty and peace permeate this city of many faces where cultures and social mores mingle to form a rare harmony. M R Venkatesh finds himself enveloped in its enigmatic fold.

A single rose hardly makes a garden. As the blue screen before the mind's eye livened, juxtaposing four spatially proximate but fleeting images, it was some comfort for collective memory. It is 7 pm on a stop-clock on frame one. The mellowed, venerable bungalow on Dr Sarvapalli Radhakrishnan Salai, housing the famous New Woodlands Hotel, lights up to a garrulous variety of guests.

People are already waiting in queue for its sofa-like seats in the midst of a rishi's kutir-like ambience. From the metaphysics of rebirth and the latest matrimonial hits to fuzzy family prattle, the young and the old happily find their wavelengths, just as their salwar-kameez and jeans do not dilute the impressiveness of traditional dhoti and gleaming Kancheepuram silks.

Founded by the legendary K Krishna Rao, who set up the first 'Udupi hotel' in Chennai on arterial Mount Road (now Anna Salai) in the mid-1920's, synonymous with quality from day one, old-timers say that it was on the lawns of Woodlands – later New Woodlands — that Congress leader Rajaji hosted tea to celebrate India's birth to freedom in 1947.

Offering a variety of North and South Indian cuisines, its hotelwares are, interestingly, sourced from S Selladurai Nadar, a merchant from a well accomplished community by that name, who may have a tip or two in retailing for Walmart. A budget tourists' paradise, Woodlands, now a three-star hotel, keeps alive Krishna Rao's legend.

Dart another 200 m west, your soul has already jumped the gastronomical barrier. Sway into another world, the Music Academy here, as this mother of classicism gets ready for another glorious December Season. In its hallowed precincts where many legendary musicians from 'Tiger' Varadachari to M S Subbulakshmi have been ambassadors of the divine, the best of classical Indian music and dance vie for God's infinity.

Diversities Galore

Waft out of its musical clime, cross the road under one of Chennai's best flyovers that even the irrepressible Jayalalithaa cannot fault, you would run into a cornerstone another 200 meters away. A plaque there announces that it was once Tilak Bhavan, where Mahatma Gandhi first met Rajaji and spent the restless historic night of March 18, 1919, "when the sad tidings of the (British) passing the humiliating Rowlatt Bills enveloped him." It was there the idea of an all-India hartal to protest the Rowlatt Act dawned on Gandhiji in a dream-like consciousness. Now the place has given way to a five-star hotel, but still remains a hallowed ground for satyagrahis.

And then the fourth frame crosses past, as a slice of post-independent history manifests on the quiet streets of Gopalapuram, right behind the main road. A quaint Lord Krishna Temple in the heart of the city diagonally faces the street-side house of the DMK patriarch, M Karunanidhi, reminiscent of an agrahara in a typical Thanjavur village.

The atheist politician may not care for prayers. But as he gets into his car, the rationalist leader reflexively ducks his head at the sight of the Venugopala Krishna deity. "Are you silently thanking God daily?" he was once teasingly asked. "Yes, I daily thank my personal physician, Dr Gopal," Karunanidhi quipped, turning to his accompanying doctor by that name.

These are not just images, but the quintessential warp and woof that weaves any contemporary sociology of Chennai. They are windows to how cities are as organic as their people. No wonder, Ludwig Wittgenstein, one of 20th century's greatest thinkers, likened language to an ancient city.

"A maze of little streets and squares, of old and new houses, and of houses with additions from various periods, and this, surrounded by a multitude of new boroughs, with straight regular streets and uniform houses," as he put it. The more you walk through it, the more the diversity.

Wittgenstein used this analogy to show how a language is as incomplete as a city, dancing to the vicissitudes of time, the fortunes of a few and the toil of the many. But, as I tossed this metaphor to my friend-teacher while in Calcutta recently, its ancientness was hardly embraced with vigour.

"It (Calcutta) is now more a dilapidated city," was his smiling crystalline reply to convey that one never knew when a building would crumble. And property development is stymied by layers of sentiments and litigation. "Oh! How succinctly a city's past and present is bridged?" I mused. It lingered for several days as one rustled through the ethnography of modern Chennai.

Looking Back

Founded on August 22, 1639, Madras, that is now Chennai, then began its tryst with destiny. Francis Day, a Captain of the English East India Company, looking for a better trading post along India's East coast, was granted some privileges by Venkatappa Nayaka, a Noble under the fugitive Vijayanagara ruler of Chandragiri and controlling this region then known as Madrasapatnam, 'for trading and fortifying'. A new history began to unfold. As documents in the Fort Museum inside Fort St George — the seat of Government here for over 350 years now until the new State Assembly-cum-Secretariat complex on arterial Anna Salai gets fully functional — reveal, a long romantic, but tough journey of the British from London to Madras had many twists and turns to finally make it the place where the Raj all began.

Ironically, after the East India Company was given a royal charter to travel to the east on December 31, 1600, their first ship anchored in Indian waters at Surat on August 24, 1608. They also built their first factory there by 1612. But the high quality painted clothe and cotton fabrics — a craze across Europe those days — in which the company was keen on trading, was being made in the present day Andhra Pradesh and northern coast of Tamil Nadu. Hence, the Company was forced to look to India's east coast.

Moving first to what the documents say was a 'fugitive lodgement' near modern Nizamapatnam, and then to Masulipatnam along the east coast, the British traders, to their grave discomfort, found the Dutch poaching their territory. So Francis Day began to sail south in search of calmer waters, with the backing of Andrew Cogan, who was then the Company's agent at Masulipatnam.

That was how the duo zeroed in on Madrasapatnam (later Madras) as they landed here with about 50 early settlers. "They were unlikely to have realised that the voyage is going to be remembered in history, as it not only laid the foundation for the mega-city of Madras (now Chennai), but also for a great empire," records a document at the Fort Museum.

New Identity

The shifting of the Company's trading post itself and the construction of the fort here were mired in controversy. But, with the inception of the fort, their trade flourished. New support structures, including the first Army base that would later play a big role in the Company's territorial consolidation in the south, blossomed.

The Saint Mary's Church, built in 1680 and which still is the jewel of Fort St George, is the oldest surviving Anglican Church outside England. At the other end, under the governorship of Elihu Yale, after whom the world renowned Yale University was named in the US later, the Corporation of Madras, the first institution of its kind in India, was inaugurated in 1688. As years rolled by, Madras, as the Company's pivotal base, had firmly come to stay. From then, several educational and scientific institutions began to be established in Madras that contributed to "shape the institutions of Modern India," notes another exhibit at the Fort St George Museum.

With so much history behind it, Madras then heralded a theatre of politics, art, culture et al for a new generation seeking newer avenues. This dynamics was anchored in a positive idea of Indian self-esteem and Nationalist ethos, shaped by English education and self-rule ideals. Yet, for all the impact of the rationalist ideology of the 'Dravidian Movement' and the cynicism of post-modernist Tamil writers, an eased fidelity and respect for tradition on the one hand, and a measured flexibility in accepting changes on the other, continue to be the hallmark of Chennai's life-world.

But as time moves on, the obverse and seamy side of Chennai are on the ascendant — be it architecture, housing, music, fine arts or lifestyle — contesting its identity even if it never really radically breaks with its past.

From the Pallava-style Sri Parthasarathy Temple, one of the fine survivors of an early architectural style, Chennai has a whole range of it, including the Greek style with big pillars, to the finest specimens of the Indo-Saracenic (mix of the Hindu, Islamic and Gothic revival styles) that dominated the British colonial period with most public buildings designed in that style, says the diligent culture historian V Sriram. The 'art deco buildings' reflecting the modernist style in the large bungalows of old Madras is discerned from the 1930's, he said. From the more modern smaller houses of the 1970's, the trend radically changed in the 1990's with pressure on urban space giving way to huge multi-storied complexes, more so as the urban sprawl moved south-westwards with the new economy IT boom, points out Sriram. "But we still don't have a sense of history or heritage. We are totally rotten in preserving our architecture and rapidly losing what little we have," regretted Sriram.

Composite Culture

Leaf through the trends in classical or popular film music, you will notice a sparkling rainbow of talent dazzling across the sky. The relatively younger group, be it Sudha Raghunathan, Nithyashree Mahadevan, Krishna, or Gayathri Kamakoti in the Carnatic world, and an A R Rahman or Harris Jayaraj in tinsel town, all are ably adding to Chennai's composite culture.

"They are all very smart, well informed, hard working and manage their stage very well," reflects noted Carnatic musician and teacher, Radha Ramji, a disciple of the lot revered gurus G K Govinda Rao and Semmangudi Srinivasa Iyer.

There are now many sabhas and a lot more concerts in the December Season all across the city, besides the Tamizh Isai Sangam enriching Tamil music in the Nagarathar's (the traditional bankers community from Chettinad) inimitable style.

Chennai's outdoors has seen a lot more opening up. "In the last 15 years there has been a sea change in our social mores, whether it is socialising on the Marina Beach, cinema theatres or in pubs and bars in up-end hotels," says senior Tamil journalist D Sekar who keeps track of culture trends. "Young couples dating is the in thing while pubs buzz with more women these days," says Sekar, adding, everything from pulp fiction, biking and tattooing to sporting bindis has changed.

"Girls should have freedom, but we should avoid aping the west; our tradition is equally important," sums up Anusha Raghu, a middle-level banking sector executive. How Chennai will respond to this new identity crisis and roll on in the coming years is anybody's guess

CITY AND VILLAGE: CONTINUITY AND CHANGE IN SOCIAL MOBILITY

More striking than new opportunities for group mobility within the traditional status hierarchy has been the appearance in recent decades of new status hierarchies-new arenas for status competition. They have emerged from the impact of urbanization and westernization but are not independent of the traditional social organization in which they are based. Urbanism is nothing new in India but rapid urbanization is new. The emergency of industrial employment, of easy communication over long distances, of increasingly efficient distribution of goods and services and of more effective centralized administration has made urban living a more accessible alternative to more people in India than ever before.

Urban life affords a measure of independence from the ties and constraints of membership in rural based social groups by granting a degree of individual anonymity and mobility quite unattainable in rural communities. Caste, religion, ritual, tradition and the social controls implicit therein are not as rigid or pervasive in the city. People are increasingly able to seek status and other rewards on an individual or small family basis largely independent of caste or the other larger social entities of which they are also a part. They do this primarily by going to the city although the values of the city also extend into the country-side and have loosened the hold of tradition even there.

To a great extent urban Indians can achieve status as a result of behaviours and attributes rather than simply as a result of birth. According to Harold Gould industrialization brought about the transfer of specialized occupations of all kinds from the context of the kin groups to factories organized on bureaucratic principles. This meant that occupational role and role occupant would be in principle separated and that the preponderant criteria for determining occupations would be performance qualities and that economic rewards and social mobility would constitute the principle standards for evaluating the worth or the status of any given role. Traditional status -caste status does not disappear in the city. It remains important in the most private contexts; the family and neighbourhood. Some neighborhoods essentially reproduce the village setting in personnel as well as social structure; others do not.

A very large proportion of city dwellers are in close touch with their native villages. Tradition and ascription are important in the city in those relationships upon which the day to day functioning and future composition of the family depends of which the epitome is marriage. In the city primary relationships occupy a diminishing proportion of most people's time, attention and energies. Much of the individual's interaction takes place on the basis of particular or even fragmented roles. He can often behave in a way consistent with the requirements of the situation without reference to his group membership. He is even able to pass if that is his desire by learning the superficial symbols of the status such as that of white collar worker, student, middle class householder or professional. In these statuses skill in handling the language, in pursuing the occupation or success in acquiring money or an appropriate life style may be socially recognized and rewarded irrespective of caste and family.

Contemporary urban life has available more means to mobility and suggests to those who seek it a greater likelihood of success that the highly structured closely controlled traditional village setting. Mobility occurs in all settings. Some low status groups have been victims of technological displacement with the result that their economic, political and social statuses have declined. They drift either into the status of rural landless laborers or into unskilled urban employment, both of which are overpopulated and underpaid. The result is underemployment, unemployment, poverty and lack of opportunity for improvement. For examples: water carriers comprise a caste whose members have been displaced in many parts of Northern India with the advent of handpumps. In some instances new occupations have been created and with them opportunities for enhancement of economic and social status thus allowing certain mobility.

FAMILY FUNCTIONS FOR SOCIALIZATION

Family means a group of people living together having blood relationship, their mentality may be same or different but they share same kitchen. Family is the oldest institution among all institution. The family is the social institution where one can look for personal psychological peace & security.

Definition: MacIver & pages said, "A family is a group defined by sex relation, sufficiently precise & enduring to provide for the procreation & upbringing of children".

Functions of a family:

1. Division of labour
2. Reproduction & upbringing of children
3. Socialization
4. Residence
5. Economic function
6. Social care
7. Regulate sex relation.

Division of Labour

In a family the power must be distributed between its members according to their role & status within the family & society. It should be accepted by everyone that a female is working within the house as cooking, taking care of children, look after her husband & total family member, worship, collect firewood & drag water from well whereas a male is working for production. He is working at outside home to maintain the family.

Reproduction and Upbringing of Children

The reproduction & bringing of children is one of the most important function of every Indian family. Children is the first desire of every family. So family is called as the centre of production & reproduction. As the production is essential to live a better & satisfactory life, reproduction is a basic need of every family to run a family in a better way.

Socialization

When a baby take birth she/he observe & learn many things as morality, ethics, value of life, respect, love & affection from the family & society. Family is the oldest institution from which a child learn many things & make a place within the family and society.

Residence

Residence is a permanent place where a person live. A family provide residence & security to all family members. A family provides name of its own to all its member according to which one can get prestige within a family & in society.

Economic Function

A family is consists of its member whose prior function is to provide economic support to the family. The male & female both have the duty to provide minimum finance to the family.

Social Care

Family is consisting of its members who have blood relationship & who are a part of society. Who learn how to care, look-after other members within a family. They learn that things from the family & society. Giving equal status to all its members & protecting its member from insult, crisis & social problem.

Regulate Sex-relation

Family is a primary & oldest association where upbringing of children & sex relation is a primary concern. But unlike the animals human being have a limit sex relation. A family regulate the sex-relation.

Other functions as:

- Biological Function
- Psychological Function
- Social Function
- Socialization
- Formation of personality trades.

5

Caste, Class and Tribes

THE CASTE SYSTEM IN INDIA

India's caste system : India has a hierarchical caste system in the society. Within Indian culture, whether in the north or the south, Hindu or Muslim, urban or village, virtually all things, people, and groups of people are ranked according to various essential qualities. If one is attuned to the theme of hierarchy in India, one can discern it everywhere. Although India is a political democracy, in daily life there is little advocacy of or adherence to notions of equality. Castes systems in India and caste like groups—those quintessential groups with which almost all Indians are associated—are ranked. Within most villages or towns, everyone knows the relative rankings of each locally represented caste, and people's behaviour toward one another is constantly shaped by this knowledge. Between the extremes of the very high and very low castes, however, there is sometimes disagreement on the exact relative ranking of castes clustered in the middle.

Castes system in India are primarily associated with Hinduism but also exist among other Indian religious groups. Muslims sometimes expressly deny that they have castes—they state that all Muslims are brothers under God—but observation of Muslim life in various parts of India reveals the existence of castelike groups and clear concern with social hierarchy. Among Indian Christians, too, differences in caste are acknowledged and maintained. Throughout India, individuals are also ranked according to their wealth and power. For example, there are "big men" (*bare admi*, in Hindi) and "little men" (*chhote admi*) everywhere. "Big men" sit confidently on chairs, while "little men" come before them to make requests, either standing or crouching down on their haunches, certainly not presuming to sit beside a man of high status as an equal. Even men of nearly equal status who might share a string cot to sit on take their places carefully—the higher-ranking man at the head of the cot, the lower-ranking man at the foot.

Within families and kinship groupings, there are many distinctions of hierarchy. Men outrank women of the same or similar age, and senior relatives outrank junior relatives. Several other kinship relations involve formal respect. For example, in northern India, a daughter-in-law of a household shows deference to a daughter of a household. Even among young siblings in a household, there is constant acknowledgment of age differences: younger siblings never address an older sibling by name, but rather by respectful terms for elder brother or elder sister. However, an older sibling may address the younger by name. Even in a business or academic setting, where colleagues may not openly espouse traditional observance of caste or class ranking behaviour, they may set up fictive kinship relations, addressing one another by kinship terms reflecting family or village-style hierarchy. For example, a younger colleague might respectfully address an older colleague as *chachaji* (respected father's younger brother), gracefully acknowledging the superior position of the older colleague.

HISTORY OF THE INDIAN CASTE SYSTEM

The history of the Indian caste system dates back to the Vedic period.

Origin

The origin of the caste system as it is today is still obscure. A 2001 genetic study, led by Michael Bamshad of University of Utah, found that the genetic affinity of Indians making their way to Europeans is proportionate to caste rank, the upper castes being most similar to Europeans, whereas lower castes are more like Asians. The researchers believe that the Indo-European speakers entered India from the Northwest, admixing with or displacing the proto-Dravidian speakers. Subsequently they may have established a caste system and placed themselves primarily in higher castes. The study concludes that the Indian castes "are most likely to be of proto-Asian origin with West Eurasian admixture resulting in rank-related and sex-specific differences in the genetic affinities of castes to Asians and Europeans.". Because the Indian samples for this study were taken from a single geographical area, it remains to be investigated whether its findings can be safely generalized. However the findings of this study is considered controversial since the study was limited to one state, Andhra Pradesh, in India during the regime of a Chief Minister who was reprimanded several times by the Indian courts for Anti-Hindu activities. At the end of this article, the acknowledgments state that it incorporates contributions from an anonymous reviewer and because of its financial support, it has to be classified as an *advertisement. The publication costs of this article were defrayed in part by payment of page charges. This article must therefore be hereby marked "advertisement" in accordance with 18 USC section 1734 solely to indicate this fact.* The findings of this article is also in contradiction to later Human Genetic studies conducted with larger samples.

An earlier 1995 study by Joanna L. Mountain et al. of Stanford University had concluded that there was "no clear separation into three genetically distinct groups along caste lines", although "an inferred tree revealed some clustering according to caste affiliation".

A 2002-03 study by T. Kivisild et al. concluded that the "Indian tribal and caste populations derive largely from the same genetic heritage of Pleistocene southern and western Asians and have received limited gene flow from external regions since the Holocene." A 2006 genetic study by the National Institute of Biologicals in India, testing a sample of men from 32 tribal and 45 caste groups, concluded that the Indians have acquired very few genes from Indo-European speakers.

According to a 2006 study by Ismail Thanseem et al. of Centre for Cellular and Molecular Biology (India) "the vast majority (>98%) of the Indian maternal gene pool, consisting of Indo-European and Dravidian speakers, is genetically more or less uniform", while the invasions after the late Pleistocene settlement might have been mostly male-mediated. The study concluded that the "lower caste groups might have originated with the hierarchical divisions that arose within the tribal groups with the spread of Neolithic agriculturalists, much earlier than the arrival of Aryan speakers", and "the Indo-Europeans established themselves as upper castes among this already developed caste-like class structure within the tribes." The study indicated that the Indian caste system may have its roots much before the arrival of the Indo-Aryan immigrants; a rudimentary version of the caste system may have emerged with the shift towards cultivation and settlements, and the divisions may have become more well-defined and intensified with the arrival of Indo-Aryans. More recent studies have also debunked the British claims that so-called "Aryans" and "Dravidians" have a "racial divide". A study conducted by the Centre for Cellular and Molecular Biology in 2009 (in collaboration with Harvard Medical School, Harvard School of Public Health and the Broad Institute of Harvard and MIT) analyzed half a million genetic markers across the genomes of 132 individuals from 25 ethnic groups from 13 states in India across multiple caste groups. The study establishes, based on the impossibility of identifying any genetic indicators across caste lines, that castes in South Asia grew out of traditional tribal organizations during the formation of Indian society, and was not the product of any mythical "Aryan Invasion" and "subjugation" of Dravidian people.

Hindu Scriptures

Although the Hindu scriptures contain some passages that can be interpreted to sanction the caste system, they also contain indications that the caste system is not an essential part of the Hindu religion, and both sides in the debate are able to find sections in scriptures that support their views. The most ancient scriptures—the *Shruti* texts, or Vedas, place very little importance on the caste system, mentioning caste only rarely and in a cursory manner. A hymn from the Rig Veda seems to indicate that one's caste is not necessarily determined by that of one's family: Rig Veda 9.112.3 —*I am a bard, my father is a physician, my mother's job is to grind the corn.*

In the Vedic period, there also seems to no discrimination against the Shudras (which later became an ensemble of the so-called low-castes) on the issue of hearing the sacred words of the Vedas and fully participating in all religious rights, something which became totally banned in the later times. Later scriptures such as *Bhagavad Gita* and *Manusmriti* state that the four varnas are created by God. However, at the same time, the Gita says that one's varna is to be understood from one's personal qualities and one's *karma* (work), not one's birth. Some scholars believe that, in its initial period, the caste system was flexible and it was merit and job based. One could migrate from one caste to other caste by changing one's profession. This view is supported by records of sages who became Brahmins. For example, the sage Vishwamitra belonged to a Kshatriya caste, and only later became recognized as a great Brahmin sage, indicating that his caste was not determined by birth. Similarly, Valmiki, once a low-caste robber, became a great sage. Veda Vyasa, another sage, was the son of a fisherwoman. Vasishtha was a shudra and he became sage later.

Manusmriti, dated between 200 B.C.E. and 100 A.D., contains some laws that codified the caste system. Varna is mentioned as caste equivalent in Manusmriti. Manusmriti and some other shastras mention four varnas: The Brahmins (teachers, scholars and priests), the Kshatriyas (kings and warriors), the Vaishyas (traders, landowners and some artisan groups), and Shudras (agriculturists, service providers, and some artisan groups). Another group of untouchables excluded from the main society was called Parjanya or Antyaja. A varna can be viewed as a group of castes or a social division that consists of various sub-castes called *jâtis*. Passages in Manusmriti and other scriptures suggest that the Indian caste system was originally non-hereditary:

ManuSmriti X:65 — *As the son of Shudra can attain the rank of a Brahman, the son of Brahman can attain rank of a Shudra. Even so with him who is born of a Vaishya or a Kshatriya*

The various smritis, like the Yagnavalkyasmriti and the Manusmriti strongly disapprove of marrying outside one's caste. The smritis also argue that new, despicable castes are formed out of such cases. According to these smritis, the chamars were born out of the union of a vaideha and a nishada, the chandals were born out of the sexual relations between a Brahmin and a Shudra.

Emergence of Rigid Caste Structures

Megasthenes, the Greek ambassador to Chandragupta Maurya's court in India classified people of India into seven classes: philosophers, peasants, herdsmen, craftsmen and traders, soldiers, government officials and councillors.

In its later stages, the caste system is said to have become rigid, and caste began to be inherited rather than acquired by merit. In the past, members of different castes would not partake in various activities, such as dining and religious gatherings, together. In addition, the performance of religious rites and rituals were restricted to Brahmins, who were the designated priesthood. The "Pandaram" priests are an example of an order of Dravidian tamil priests, based in Nepal and South India. The Pandaram maintain the same tradition as the Brahmin priests, including the use of the Sanskrit language (traditionally reserved for the Brahmins) for the rituals. While they are not generally as well trained as the Brahmin priests, they are highly respected within their community and are addressed with reverence.

According to the Manusmriti, every caste belongs to one of the four varnas (Brahmin, Kshtriya, Vaishya, and Shudra). However, there have been many disputes about the varna of many castes, such as castes being considered Kshatriya by some scholars, while described as Shudra by others. While texts such as the Manusmriti attempted to rationalize ambiguous castes by placing them in varna-sankaras (i.e. mixed varna), the fact remains that Indian society was, and is, composed of numerous geographically diversified but endogamous groups. With many occupational groups practicing endogamy within a particular region, as well as numerous sub-divisions within the four main castes, a more complex system of subcastes and jâtis is evident. The jatis have broken up into clans like Agarwal, Iyer, etc.

Mobility Across the Castes

The view of the caste system as "static and unchanging" has been disputed by many scholars. For instance, sociolgists such as Bernard Buber and Marriott McKim describe how the perception of the caste system as a static and textual stratification has given way to the perception of the caste system as a more processual, empirical and contextual stratification. Other sociologists such as Y.B Damle have applied theoretical models to explain mobility and flexibility in the caste system in India.. According to these scholars, groups of lower-caste individuals could seek to elevate the status of their caste by attempting to emulate the practices of higher castes.

Some scholars believe that the relative ranking of other castes was fluid or differed from one place to another prior to the arrival of the British. The distinctions, particularly between the Brahmans and the other castes, were in theory sharper, but in practice it now appears that social restrictions were not so rigid. Brahmans often lived off the land and founded dynasties. Most of the groups claiming Kshatriya status had only recently acquired it. The conscious reference to being Kshatriya, a characteristic among Rajputs, is a noticeable feature in post-Gupta politics. The fact that many of these dynasties were of obscure origin suggests some social mobility: a person of any caste, having once acquired political power, could also acquire a genealogy connecting him with the traditional lineages and conferring Kshatriya status. A number of new castes, such as the Kayasthas (scribes) and Khatris (traders), are mentioned in the sources of this period. According to the Brahmanic sources, they originated from intercaste marriages, but this is clearly an attempt at rationalizing their rank in the hierarchy. Many of these new castes played a major role in society. The hierarchy of castes did not have a uniform distribution throughout the country.

Flexibility in caste laws permitted very low-caste religious clerics such as Valmiki to compose the Ramayana, which became a central work of Hindu scripture. According to some psychologists, mobility across broad caste lines may have been "minimal", though sub-castes (jatis) may change their social status over the generations by fission, re-location, and adoption of new rituals..

Sociologist M. N. Srinivas has also debated the question of rigidity in Caste. In an ethnographic study of the Coorgs of Karnataka, he observed considerable flexibility and mobility in their caste hierarchies. He asserts that the caste system is far from a rigid system in which the position of each component caste is fixed for all time.

Movement has always been possible, and especially in the middle regions of the hierarchy. It was always possible for groups born into a lower caste to "rise to a higher position by adopting vegetarianism and teetotalism" i.e adopt the customs of the higher castes. While theoretically "forbidden", the process was not uncommon in practice.

The concept of sanskritization, or the adoption of upper-caste norms by the lower castes, addressed the actual complexity and fluidity of caste relations.

Historical examples of mobility in the Indian Caste System among Hindus have been researched. There is also precedent of certain Shudra families within the temples of the Shrivaishava sect in South India elevating their caste.

Historical Advantages of the Caste System

Historically, the caste system offered several advantages to the population of the Indian subcontinent. While Caste is nowadays seen by instances that render it anachronistic, in its original form the caste system served as an important instrument of order in a society in which mutual consent rather than compulsion ruled; where the ritual rights as well as the economic obligations of members of one caste or sub-caste were strictly circumscribed in relation to those of any other caste or sub-caste; where one was born into one's caste and retained one's station in society for life; where merit was inherited, where equality existed within the caste, but inter-caste relations were unequal and hierarchical.

A well-defined system of mutual interdependence through a division of labour created security within a community.

1. Preservation of order in society through the use of institutional stratification of social groups.
2. Integration of foreigners and invading forces into Indian culture by assigning a caste to them (a process that historian Jawaharlal Nehru referred to as "Indianization"): India has faced repeated invasions from outside the region, dating back to the Macedonian invasion by Alexander the Great. Most invaders were swiftly assimilated into ancient Indian society by assigning them specific castes. Examples include the Kambojas, believed to be of Indo-Scythian descent, who

were retroactively assigned a social position in the Manusmriti.

3. The Varna system, with its normative interpretation as a division of labour, had and continues to have a heavy bias towards spiritual evolution. The deep religious proclivities and the urge for spiritual uplift had induced the people to search for simpler and effective ways to achieve the spiritual goal which led to innovations like the Bhakti movement which had a powerful impact on the socio-cultural-spiritual life of the people even at mass level without distinctions of caste or class or other social differences. It is these deeply run cultural roots which caused an abiding following for Hinduism even in the face of unrelenting assaults by other religions and had in fact continued to influence the lives of people even after their conversion to other faiths. Thus, the caste system can be said to have preserved ancient cultural values in Indian society.
4. The caste system played an influential role in shaping economic activities. The caste system functioned much like medieval European guilds, ensuring the division of labour, providing for the training of apprentices and, in some cases, allowing manufacturers to achieve narrow specialisation. For instance, in certain regions, producing each variety of cloth was the speciality of a particular sub-caste.
5. Philosophers argue that the majority of people would be comfortable in stratified endogamous groups and have been in ancient times. Membership in a particular caste, with its associated narrative, history and genealogy would instill in its members a sense of group accomplishment and cultural pride. Such sentiments are routinely expressed by the Marathas, for instance.

CHANGES IN THE CASTE SYSTEM

Despite many problems, the caste system has operated successfully for centuries, providing goods and services to India's many millions of citizens. The system continues to operate, but changes are occurring. India's constitution guarantees basic rights to all its citizens, including the right to equality and equal protection before the law. The practice of untouchability, as well as discrimination on the basis of caste, race, sex, or religion, has been legally abolished. All citizens have the right to vote, and political competition is lively. Voters from every stratum of society have formed interest groups, overlapping and crosscutting castes, creating an evolving new style of integrating Indian society.

Castes themselves, however, far from being abolished, have certain rights under Indian law. As described by anthropologist Owen M. Lynch and other scholars, in the expanding political arena caste groups are becoming more politicized and forced to compete with other interest groups for social and economic benefits. In the growing cities, traditional intercaste interdependencies are negligible. Independent India has built on earlier British efforts to remedy problems suffered by Dalits by granting them some benefits of protective discrimination. Scheduled Castes are entitled to reserved electoral offices, reserved jobs in central and state governments, and special educational benefits. The constitution mandates that one-seventh of state and national legislative seats be reserved for members of Scheduled Castes in order to guarantee their voice in government. Reserving seats has proven useful because few, if any, Scheduled Caste candidates have ever been elected in nonreserved constituencies.

Educationally, Dalit students have benefited from scholarships, and Scheduled Caste literacy increased (from 10.3 percent in 1961 to 21.4 percent in 1981, the last year for which such figures are available), although not as rapidly as among the general population. Improved access to education has resulted in the emergence of a substantial group of educated Dalits able to take up white-collar occupations and fight for their rights.

There has been tremendous resistance among non-Dalits to this protective discrimination for the Scheduled Castes, who constitute some 16 percent of the total population, and efforts have been made to provide similar advantages to the so-called Backward Classes, who constitute an estimated 52 percent of the population. In August 1990, Prime Minister Vishwanath Pratap (V.P.) Singh announced his intention to enforce the recommendations of the Backward Classes Commission, issued in December 1980 and largely ignored for a decade. The report, which urged special advantages for obtaining civil service positions and admission to higher education for the Backward Classes, resulted in riots and self-immolations and contributed to the fall of the prime minister. The upper castes have been particularly adamant against these policies because unemployment is a major problem in India, and many feel that they are being unjustly excluded from posts for which they are better qualified than lower-caste applicants.

As an act of protest, many Dalits have rejected Hinduism with its rigid ranking system. Following the example of their revered leader, Dr. Ambedkar, who converted to Buddhism four years before his death in 1956, millions of Dalits have embraced the faith of the Buddha. Over the past few centuries, many Dalits have also converted to Christianity and have often by this means raised their socioeconomic status. However, Christians of Dalit origin still often suffer from discrimination by Christians—and others—of higher caste backgrounds.

Despite improvements in some aspects of Dalit status, 90 percent of them live in rural areas in the mid-1990s, where an increasing proportion—more than 50 percent—work as landless agricultural labourers. State and national governments have attempted to secure more just distribution of land by creating land ceilings and abolishing absentee landlordism, but evasive tactics by landowners have successfully prevented more than minimal redistribution of land to tenant farmers and labourers.

In contemporary India, field hands face increased competition from tractors and harvesting machines. Similarly, artisans are being challenged by expanding commercial markets in mass-produced factory goods, undercutting traditional mutual obligations between patrons and clients. The spread of the Green Revolution has tended to increase the gap between the prosperous and the poor—most of whom are low-caste.

The growth of urbanization (an estimated 26 percent of the population now lives in cities) is having a far-reaching effect on caste practices, not only in cities but in villages. Among anonymous crowds in urban public spaces and on public transportation, caste affiliations are unknown, and observance of purity and pollution rules is negligible. Distinctive caste costumes have all but vanished, and low-caste names have been modified, although castes remain endogamous, and access to employment often occurs through intracaste connections. Restrictions on interactions with other castes are becoming more relaxed, and, at the same time, observance of other pollution rules is declining—especially those concerning birth, death, and menstruation.

Several growing Hindu sects draw members from many castes and regions, and communication between cities and villages is expanding dramatically. Kin in town and country visit one another frequently, and television programs available to huge numbers of villagers vividly portray new lifestyles. As new occupations open up in urban areas, the correlation of caste with occupation is declining.

Caste associations have expanded their areas of concern beyond traditional elite emulation and local politics into the wider political arenas of state and national politics. Finding power in numbers within India's democratic system, caste groups are pulling together closely allied subcastes in their quest for political influence. In efforts to solidify caste bonds, some caste associations have organized marriage fairs where families can make matches for their children. Traditional hierarchical concerns are being minimized in favour of strengthening horizontal unity. Thus, while pollution observances are declining, caste consciousness is not.

Education and election to political office have advanced the status of many Dalits, but the overall picture remains one of great inequity. In recent decades, Dalit anger has been expressed in writings, demonstrations, strikes, and the activities of such groups as the Dalit Panthers, a radical political party demanding revolutionary change. A wider Dalit movement, including political parties, educational activities, self-help centres, and labour organizations, has spread to many areas of the country.

In a 1982 Dalit publication, Dilip Hiro wrote, "It is one of the great modern Indian tragedies and dangers that even well meaning Indians still find it so difficult to accept Untouchable mobility as being legitimate in fact as well as in theory...." Still, against all odds, a small intelligentsia has worked for many years toward the goal of freeing India of caste consciousness.

CASTE IN VARNA SYSTEM

The Caste System or varna-ashrama has been one of the most misrepresented, misinformed, misunderstood, misused and the most maligned aspects of Hinduism. If one wants to understand the truth, the original purpose behind the caste system, one must go to antiquity to study the evolution of the caste system. Caste System, which is said to be the mainstay of the Hindu social order, has no sanction in the Vedas. The ancient culture of India was based upon a system of social diversification according to SPIRITUAL development, not by birth, but by his karma. This system became hereditary and over the course of many centuries degenerated as a result of exploitation by some priests, and other socioeconomic elements of society.

However, as Alain Danielou, son of French aristocracy, author of numerous books on philosophy, religion, history and arts of India, says: "Caste system has enabled Hindu civilization to survive all invasions and to develop without revolutions or important changes, throughout more than four millennia, with a continuity that is unique in history. Caste system may appear rigid to our eyes because for more than a thousand years Hindu society withdrew itself from successive domination by Muslims and Europeans. Yet, the greatest poets and the most venerated saints such as Sura Dasa, Kabir, Tukaram, Thiruvalluvar and Ram Dasa; came from the humblest class of society." In the words of Sarvepalli Radhakrishnan, " In spite of the divisions, there is an inner cohesion among the Hindu society from the Himalayas to the Cape Comorin."

Caste system has been exploited against the Hindus, for the last two centuries by the British, Christian Missionaries, Secular historians, Communists, Muslims, Pre and Post-Independence Indian politicians and Journalists for their own ends. One way to discredit any system is to highlight its excesses, and this only adds to the sense of inferiority that many Indians feel about their own culture.

Caste system is often portrayed as the ultimate horror, in the media, yet social inequities continue to persist in theoretically Egalitarian Western Societies. The Caste system is judged offensive by the Western norms, yet racial groups have been isolated, crowded into reserves like the American Indians or Australian Aborigines, where they can only atrophy and disappear.

This chapter is not a justification of the abuse of caste system, rather it is a collection of interesting information. Caste system has enabled Hindu civilization to survive all invasions and made Indian society stronger. Caste system served a purpose, performed certain functions, and met the needs appropriate to the times in history. India's caste norms may once have had a rationale; but the norms are outlived today. Caste system is not stagnant and is undergoing changes under the impact of modernization. Caste system should undergo reforms in the social arena so that unjustified discrimination and abuse is eliminated.

Further, according to the scriptures, there is no hierarchy at all inherent in the varna system. All parts are of equal importance and equal worth. A good example is to imagine a human body. The brain which thinks, plans and guides represents the Brahmin caste. The hands and arms which fight, protect and work represent the Kshatriya caste. The stomach which serves as the source of energy and "transactions" represents the vaishya caste, and the legs/feet which do the necessary running around in the service of the rest of the body represent the shudra caste. No one can say the brain is better than the legs or that hands are superior to feet. Each is equally important for the overall functioning of the body system. They just serve different roles. " Look at Bhagwan Ram and Bhagwan Krishna. Both show the example of taking their food from even people of the lowest caste and going to the homes of the lower caste people. It is devotion, purity and commitment which make us great or small, not our caste.

M V Nadkarni writes: "It is necessary to demolish the myth that caste system is an intrinsic part of Hinduism. This myth is believed by orthodox elements within Hinduism and also is propagated by elements outside Hinduism with the mischievous intent of proselytising. Even Vedic and classical Hinduism-not only does not support the caste system, but has taken lots of pains to oppose it both in principle and practice, making it obvious that caste system is not an intrinsic part of Hindu canon, philosophy and even practice.

It is only in the dharmashastras (dharma sutras and smritis) that we find support to the caste system, and not in other canon. However, dharmashastras never had the same status as other canon known as shruti (Vedas and Upanishads) and it is laid down that whenever there is a conflict between the shruti and smriti literature, it is the former that prevails. It is Manusmriti, which is particularly supportive of caste system but where it conflicts with Vedas and Upanishads, the latter would prevail. Though Bhagawad Gita (Gita) is not regarded as a part of shruti, Gita is highly regarded as sacred and is very much a part of classical Hinduism. As we shall just see even the Gita is against caste system based on birth, and not supportive to it. Thus, to the extent that dharmashastras conflict with shruti and the Gita, the latter prevails. Apasthambha dharmasutra may have supported untouchability, but it seems to be read more by those who like to attack Hinduism with it than by its followers! It is hardly regarded as canon, even if any Hindu has heard of it. Vedanta philosophy declares that there is divinity in every lecture. Rig Veda emphasises equality of all human beings. It goes to the extent of saying, which sounds quite modern: 'No one is superior, none inferior. All are brothers marching forward to prosperity' "

John Burdon Sanderson Haldane (1892-1964) the world-renowned geneticist. In 1922, he joined Cambridge University to take up research in biochemistry. Among his significant contributions is an estimate of the rate of mutation of a human gene. Some of his famous books are The Causes of Evolution, New Paths in Genetics and Biochemistry of Genetics.

He immigrated to India and soon found himself attracted to Hindu culture. Himself a rationalist, Haldane told his colleagues, "I do not think that a Rationalist and Humanist need necessarily break with Hinduism." He watched with disdain the way the socialist government machinery rooted in sycophancy and corruption, was developing a stranglehold on the budding Indian science. The stranglehold on the progress of India, as Haldane observed was of a socialist government's making and not that of the Dharma. He wrote: "The old caste system had this merit, that the richest merchant or Zamindar could not buy the status of Brahmin for his son, even if the son was learned and pious. Whatever the defects of that system-

and I think that they were and are grievous-it was not subservient to wealth. The new caste system, which the university administrative authorities, with the connivance of many government officials, are trying with some success to impose upon India, has no such excuse.... In India today the unworthy successors of Durvasa and Vishvamitra actually invite governors, vice-chancellors, and the like, to address them. This may be a relic of British Rule. If so, it is a regrettable one."

Gerald Heard American thinker and writer who has studied the Indian social system, has called it "organic democracy", and suggests in his work, Man the Master, that it is the type of democracy the world as a whole needs today. Heard defines "organic democracy" as "the rule of the people who have organized themselves in a living and not a mechanical relationship; where instead of all men being said to be equal, which is a lie, all men are known to be of equal value, could we but find the position in which their potential contribution could be released and their essential growth so pursued." He calls the four varnas by the names "seers" (Brahmins), "politicians (Kshatriyas), "technicians" (vaishyas) and "coherers" (Shudras). "These four classes are distinguished by unmistakable psychological characteristics which suit them to their particular purpose, function and place." It is this organization that made Indian society stable, efficient and strong. It produced in India great scholars, warriors, administrators, and producers of wealth.

The caste system has been the most misunderstood, the most vilified subject of Hindu society at the hands of Western scholars and even today by "secular" Indians. The Hindu caste system has often been described as " the most cruel apartheid, imposed by the barbaric white Aryan invaders on the gentle dark-skinned natives."

The earliest reference to the four classes is in the Purusa Sukta of the Rig Veda, where they are described as having sprung from the body of the creative spirit, from his head, arms, thighs, and feet. This indicates that just as in a human body, the different organs perform different functions so also in human society different people must perform different functions, according to their predominant traits or temperament. Man is not only himself, but is in solidarity with all of his kind.

Man is not an abstract individual. He belongs to a certain social group by virtue of his character, behaviour, and function in the community. The fourfold classification is conceived in the interests of world progress.

Sir Sidney Low (1857-1932) in his book, A Vision of India: with a frontispiece says: "There is no doubt that it (caste) is the main cause of the fundamental stability and contentment by which Indian society has been braced for centuries against the shocks of politics and the cataclysms of Nature. It provides every man with his place, his career, his occupations, his circle of friends. It makes him, at the outset, a member of a corporate body; it protects him through life from the canker of social jealousy and unfulfilled aspirations; it ensures him companionship and a sense of community with others in like case with himself. The caste organization is to the Hindu his club, his trade union, his benefit society, his philanthropic society. There are no work houses in India, and none are as yet needed. The obligation to provide for kinsfolk and friends in distress is universally acknowledged; nor can it be questioned that this is due to the recognition of the strength of family ties and of the bonds created by associations and common pursuits which is fostered by the caste principle. An India without caste, as things stand at present, it is not quite easy to imagine." Nirad C. Chaudhari, (1897-1999) prominent Indian author and scholar, who rejected Western culture in an independent India, has defended the caste system on the grounds that the successive waves of migrant tribes or invaders probably made a class society inevitable in India, and that caste still has a useful function:

> *"The Caste system has only organized the disparities created by historical forces and movements. By doing so, it has done great good by reducing the competition of the diversities, by freezing them within certain limits, and by making each not only legitimate but even moral.....It canalized competitions and helped the coexistence of elements which otherwise would have been at war. It was a social system specially suited to a country like India, which history has made into a warehouse of civilizations, and a couloir and cul-de-sac of diverse people and cultures." He emphasized that if he considered the caste system in any danger-which he does not-he would add, "Please do not pulverize a society which has no other force of cohesion, into amorphous dust."*

Alain Danielou (1907-1994) author of several books, including History of India and Virtue, Success, Pleasure, & Liberation: The Four Aims of Life in the Tradition of Ancient India, writes: "It is easy to see that despite all the national and linguistic barriers, even modern Western society is fundamentally, like all societies, a caste system. The problem of Western society derive from the fact that while proclaiming the equality of men, it is entirely graded on a hierarchical system as far as the professions are concerned. Under the pretext of equality, Western lawmakers do not let the various groups cooperate among themselves while keeping their different habits, ethics, and social life. Jews, Mormons, Muslims, Celts, Basques, Albigemsoams, Pygmies, Blacks or Inuits are accorded a relative equality only on condition that they conform to our customs, losing most of their social, national, and religious characteristics and in fact abandoning their own personality."

Hindu Society is 'caste-ridden' while modern democratic society reveals the presence of 'classes', sociologist explain. They acclaim 'class' and condemn 'caste'. Caste, according to them, has its roots in Hindu (Brahmannical) religion, while 'class' has its roots in economic disparities. Mark Tully was the BBC correspondent in New Delhi and author of several books including No Full Stops in India and The Heart of India.

He points out: "The alienation of many young people in the West and the loneliness of the old show the suffering that egalitarianism inflicts on those who do not win, the superficiality of an egalitarianism which in effect means equal opportunities for all to win and then ignores the inevitable losers. For all that, the elite of India have become so spellbound by egalitarianism that they are unable to see any good in the only institution which does provide a sense of identity and dignity to those who are robbed from birth of the opportunity to compete on an equal footing-CASTE. Caste is obnoxious to the egalitarian West, so it is obnoxious to the Indian elite too."

> *"The very fact that the institution of caste has survived about 3,000 years is a clear proof of the services which it must have rendered to the Hindu society in different periods of history. It is the caste system that has been largely responsible for the preservation of Hindu religion and culture. The caste brotherhoods, on account of their policy of exclusiveness, did not mix with the foreigners. So*

the Greeks, Huns or Muslims could not conquer Hindu culture. On the contrary, most of these foreigners were themselves absorbed into the Hindu fold."

"The caste system is based on the sound economic principle of division of labour which ensures efficiency of production. A person from his birth knew what profession he was to follow later on. So from the start, he devoted all his energy to the one profession of his forefathers. It was because of this reason that in every period of Indian history, there was no dearth of highly-skilled workers and scholars. Megasthenes, Hieun Tsang, Alberuni, Ibn Batuta, Babar and even the early Britishers were impressed by the talents and artistic skill of the Indians in every art and craft."

Note: Mark Tully has spoken in defense of the caste system and denounced the spread of consumerism in the subcontinent. The BBC pushed him out because of his excessive identification with Indian culture.

Michael Pym wrote: "Caste is the secret of that amazing stability which is characteristic of the Indian social structure. It is the strength of Hinduism. Naturally, it can be abused. The moment a Brahmin treats a sweeper cruelly because he is a sweeper, he departs from his Brahminhood. He becomes a usurper and a social danger. And in due course, he will have to pay for this mistake. Because men are imperfect, and because power is a deadly intoxicant, such abuses may and do occur, but they are not inherent in the institution-they are contrary to its principles, though they may be inherent in the make up of the individual.

Caste in itself is also a protection for the individual, because it permits group action. The reason why a Hindu dreads being outcaste is analogous to the reason why, in England say, a worker would dread being thrown out of his trade union.

While Marxists and other anti-Hindu intellectuals calling themselves Secularists never miss an opportunity to denounce it, the fact of the matter is that the Indian civilization survived nearly a thousand year onslaught of Islam. Several other ancient civilizations-like those of Iran (Zorastrian), the Byzantine Empire (Christian) and Central Asia (Buddhist) broke down under the same force over a much shortest period. This shows that they must have lacked a social order capable of protecting their societies.

The so called 'egalitarian' Buddhist society lacked the social organization which enabled the Hindu society to survive. It was the same story in Egypt, Syria, and Turkey which were part of the Christian Byzamtine Empire. They lacked the strength and resilience of the Hindu society and succumbed to the Islamic invasion.

Dr. Koenraad Elst (1959-) Dutch historian, born in Leuven, Belgium, on 7 August 1959, into a Flemish (i.e. Dutch-speaking Belgian) Catholic family. He graduated in Philosophy, Chinese Studies and Indo-Iranian Studies at the Catholic University of Leuven. He is the author of several books including The Saffron Swastika, Decolonising The Hindu Mind-Ideological Development of Hindu Revivalism and Negationism in India: Concealing the Record of Islam. The caste system is often portrayed as the ultimate horror. Inborn inequality is indeed unacceptable to us moderns, but this does not preclude that the system has also had its merits.

Caste is perceived as an "exclusion-from," but first of all it is a form of "belonging-to," a natural structure of solidarity. For this reason, Christian and Muslim missionaries found it very difficult to lure Hindus away from their communities. Sometimes castes were collectively converted to Islam, and Pope Gregory XV (1621-23) decreed that the missionaries could tolerate caste distinction among Christian converts; but by and large, caste remained an effective hurdle to the destruction of Hinduism through conversion. That is why the missionaries started attacking the institution of caste and in particular the Brahmin caste. This propaganda has bloomed into a full-fledged anti-Brahminism, the Indian equivalent of anti-Semitism.

T. M. P. Mahadevan wrote about the castes: "The origin of caste is lost in obscurity. It purpose however, seems to have been the same as that of Plato's division of the State into three classes, castes, or professions, viz. philosophers-rulers, warriors and masses. The underlying principle is division of labour. Originally the castes were professional and subsequently became hereditary. The Brahmins were custodians of the spiritual culture of the race. He was friend, philosopher, guide to humanity. The Kshatriya is the guardian of society, its protector and preserver. The Vaishya is the expert in economics. His was the duty of arranging for the production and distribution of wealth. The Śudra was the worker or manual labourer. By his manual labour he places the entire community under a debt of gratitude. The system was evolved to keep the social fabric in a harmonious condition; but in later years it became a divisive force. The original designers built the edifice of caste on the secure foundations of obligations; the lesser men who came after them produced a caricature on the shifting sands of rights.

The four classes were not meant to be warring communities but complementary classes. Mahatma Gandhi said: "It is a law of spiritual economics" "It has nothing to do with superiority or inferiority". And as the system of caste is purely a social adjustment, there is nothing that can stand in the way of its revision and readjustment except a sense of pride and obstinacy and a demand to preserve the status quo on the part of some of its members." When Julius Caesar occupied the Celtic West of Europe, he found that the Druid class was the backbone of this society (the parallel with the Brahmins in the perception of the missionaries is quite exact): therefore, he persecuted the Druids.

Huston Smith (1919-) born in China to Methodist missionaries, a philosopher, most eloquent writer, world-famous religion scholar who practices Hatha Yoga. He has written various books, The World's Religions. He says: Men and women that are lining the bathing ghats are all Hindus, but how different they are. But India looked past their bodies into their minds where she found the prolificness of the infinite exploding like a Roman cantle.

No other civilization saw, appreciated, and classified so precisely the full spectrum of human personality types...an achievement that has earned for India-the title of the world's introspective psychologist. "India identified four such types and once again honoured all of them. Likening society to an organism, she pictured Brahmins-its head, Brahmins are intellectuals, their chief delight in art, ideas, and things of spirit generally.

Dr. Koenraad Elst has written: "Increasingly, Hinduism is identified by the international public with the caste system and nothing but the caste system. The caste system, in turn, is painted in the ugliest colours: as a racist Apartheid system designed to oppress the native population. These notions are eagerly welcomed and amplified by outside forces such as Christian missionary centres, followed by their Islamic counterparts. Till recently, American foreign policy agencies made no secret of their designs on India's unity. When she was US ambassador to the UN, Mrs. Jean Kirkpatrick once said that "the break-up of India is one of the goals of the American foreign policy." Patrick Moynihan, who had held the same job, said more recently, "After the break-up of the Soviet Union, the artificial state India is also bound to break up."

Ronald B. Inden has pointed out: "Caste, the Western scholars held, is the type of society characteristic of India, the institution that distinguishes it from the other civilization dominated by caste from the West. The representation of India as a civilization dominated by caste are legion. Caste, considered the essence of Indian civilization, has often been treated as though it were the unchanging agent of the civilization, from the rise of the Indus Valley culture and the arrival of the Aryans down to the present day of regionalism and caste in electoral politics. It is, thus, deeply embedded in Indological discourse. Many of the more recent accounts of caste have dropped the racialist discourse, but they have not broken with the notion that caste is a unique type of society, one that displaces the economically oriented politics of the West. Accounts of caste can and have been used as a foil to build up the West's image of itself."

> *"It would lead to a greater respect for India's culture, and indeed a better understanding of it, if it were recognized that the caste system has never been totally static, that it is adapting itself to today's changing circumstances and that it has positive as well as negative aspects. The caste system provides security and a community for millions of Indians. It gives them an identity that neither Western Science nor Western thought has yet provided, because caste is not just a matter of being a Brahmin or a Harijan: it is also a kinship system. The system provides a wider support group than a family: a group which has a social life in which all its members participate."*

In the September 1989 issue of Seminar magazine, Madhu Kishwar, one of India leading feminists, wrote, "The caste system provides for relatively greater stability and dignity to the individuals than they would have as atomized individuals. This is part explains why the Indian poor retain a strong sense of self-respect. It is that self-respect which the thoughtless insistence on egalitarianism destroys."

Caste system is often perceived to be an integral part of Hindu religion. This erroneous perception arises when people mix the ancient social tradition (caste system) with Hindu religious philosophy.

According to V. A. Smith, most of the misunderstanding on the subject of caste system has arisen from the persistent mistranslation of Manu's term "Varna" as caste, whereas it should be rendered class or order or by some equivalent term.

CLASSES IN INDIA

In village India, where nearly 74 percent of the population resides, caste and class affiliations overlap. According to anthropologist Miriam Sharma, "Large landholders who employ hired labour are overwhelmingly from the upper castes, while the agricultural workers themselves come from the ranks of the lowest—predominantly Untouchable—castes." She also points out that household-labour-using proprietors come from the ranks of the middle agricultural castes. Distribution of other resources and access to political control follow the same pattern of caste-cum-class distinctions. Although this congruence is strong, there is a tendency for class formation to occur despite the importance of caste, especially in the cities, but also in rural areas.

In an analysis of class formation in India, anthropologist Harold A. Gould points out that a three-level system of stratification is taking shape across rural India. He calls the three levels Forward Classes (higher castes), Backward Classes in India (middle and lower castes), and Harijans (very low castes). Members of these groups share common concerns because they stand in approximately the same relationship to land and production—that is, they are large-scale farmers, small-scale farmers, and landless laborers. Some of these groups are drawing together within regions across caste lines in order to work for political power and access to desirable resources. For example, since the late 1960s, some of the middle-ranking cultivating castes of northern India have increasingly cooperated in the political arena in order to advance their common agrarian and market-oriented interests. Their efforts have been spurred by competition with higher-caste landed elites.

In cities other groups have vested interests that crosscut caste boundaries, suggesting the possibility of forming classes in the future. These groups include prosperous industrialists and entrepreneurs, who have made successful efforts to push the central government toward a probusiness stance; bureaucrats, who depend upon higher education rather than land to preserve their positions as civil servants; political officeholders, who enjoy good salaries and perquisites of all kinds; and the military, who constitute one of the most powerful armed forces in the developing world.

Economically far below such groups are members of the menial underclass, which is taking shape in both villages and urban areas. As the privileged elites move ahead, low-ranking menial workers remain economically insecure. Were they to join together to mobilize politically across lines of class and religion in recognition of their common interests, Gould observes, they might find power in their sheer numbers.

India's rapidly expanding economy has provided the basis for a fundamental change—the emergence of what eminent journalist Suman Dubey calls a "new vanguard" increasingly dictating India's political and economic direction. This group is India's new middle class—mobile, driven, consumer-oriented, and, to some extent, forward-looking. Hard to define precisely, it is not a single stratum of society, but straddles town and countryside, making its voice heard everywhere. It encompasses prosperous farmers, white-collar workers, business people, military personnel, and myriad others, all actively working toward a prosperous life. Ownership of cars, televisions, and other consumer goods, reasonable earnings, substantial savings, and educated children (often fluent in English) typify this diverse group. Many have ties to kinsmen living abroad who have done very well. The new middle class is booming, at least partially in response to a doubling of the salaries of some 4 million central government employees in 1986, followed by similar increases for state and district officers. Unprecedented liberalization and opening up of the economy in the 1980s and

1990s have been part of the picture. There is no single set of criteria defining the middle class, and estimates of its numbers vary widely. The mid-range of figures presented in a 1992 survey article by analyst Suman Dubey is approximately 150 to 175 million—some 20 percent of the population—although other observers suggest alternative figures. The middle class appears to be increasing rapidly. Once primarily urban and largely Hindu, the phenomenon of the consuming middle class is burgeoning among Muslims and prosperous villagers as well. According to V.A. Pai Panandikar, director of the Centre for Policy Research, New Delhi, cited by Dubey, by the end of the twentieth century 30 percent—some 300 million—of India's population will be middle class.

The middle class is bracketed on either side by the upper and lower echelons. Members of the upper class—around 1 percent of the population—are owners of large properties, members of exclusive clubs, and vacationers in foreign lands, and include industrialists, former maharajas, and top executives. Below the middle class is perhaps a third of the population—ordinary farmers, tradespeople, artisans, and workers. At the bottom of the economic scale are the poor—estimated at 320 million, some 45 percent of the population in 1988—who live in inadequate homes without adequate food, work for pittances, have undereducated and often sickly children, and are the victims of numerous social inequities.

INTERCASTE RELATIONS

In a village, members of different castes are often linked in what has been called the *jajmani* system, after the word *jajman*, which in some regions means patron. Members of various service castes perform tasks for their patrons, usually members of the dominant, that is, most powerful landowning caste of the village (commonly castes of the Kshatriya *varna*). Households of service castes are linked through hereditary bonds to a household of patrons, with the lower-caste members providing services according to traditional occupational specializations. Thus, client families of launderers, barbers, shoemakers, carpenters, potters, tailors, and priests provide customary services to their patrons, in return for which they receive customary seasonal payments of grain, clothing, and money. Ideally, from generation to generation, clients owe their patrons political allegiance in addition to their labors, while patrons owe their clients protection and security.

The harmonious qualities of the *jajmani* system have been overidealized and variations of the system overlooked by many observers. Further, the economic interdependence of the system has weakened since the 1960s. Nevertheless, it is clear that members of different castes customarily perform a number of functions for one another in rural India that emphasize cooperation rather than competition. This cooperation is revealed in economic arrangements, in visits to farmers' threshing floors by service caste members to claim traditional payments, and in rituals emphasizing interdependence at life crises and calendrical festivals all over South Asia. For example, in rural Karnataka, in an event described by anthropologist Suzanne Hanchett, the annual procession of the village temple cart bearing images of the deities responsible for the welfare of the village cannot go forward without the combined efforts of representatives of all castes. It is believed that the sacred cart will literally not move unless all work together to move it, some pushing and some pulling.

Some observers feel that the caste system must be viewed as a system of exploitation of poor low-ranking groups by more prosperous high-ranking groups. In many parts of India, land is largely held by dominant castes—high-ranking owners of property—that economically exploit low-ranking landless laborers and poor artisans, all the while degrading them with ritual emphases on their so-called god-given inferior status. In the early 1990s, blatant subjugation of low-caste labourers in the northern state of Bihar and in eastern Uttar Pradesh was the subject of many news reports. In this region, scores of Dalits who have attempted to unite to protest low wages have been the victims of lynchings and mass killings by high-caste landowners and their hired assassins.

In 1991 the news magazine *India Today* reported that in an ostensibly prosperous village about 160 kilometers southeast of Delhi, when it became known that a rural Dalit labourer dared to have a love affair with the daughter of a high-caste landlord, the lovers and their Dalit go-between were tortured, publicly hanged, and burnt by agents of the girl's family in the presence of some 500 villagers. A similar incident occurred in 1994, when a Dalit musician who had secretly married a woman of the Kurmi cultivating caste was beaten to death by outraged Kurmis, possibly instigated by the young woman's family. The terrified bride was stripped and branded as punishment for her transgression. Dalit women also have been the victims of gang rapes by the police. Many other atrocities, as well as urban riots resulting in the deaths of Dalits, have occurred in recent years. Such extreme injustices are infrequent enough to be reported in outraged articles in the Indian press, while much more common daily discrimination and exploitation are considered virtually routine.

CLASS ANALYSIS

A useful heuristic device for studying class is Katznelson's (1986) view to analyse it at four "levels" (which are perhaps better understood as aspects), each of which takes a different perspective: first, class as part of the structure of capitalist economic development; second, class as life patterns within particular social formations (class as an experience dealing with patterns of life and social relations with respect to work and residence); third, class as shared dispositions resulting from subjectively lived experiences of "objective" positions and limits to action; and fourth, class as conscious collective action to affect society and the position of the class within it. With their customary focus on human interaction, culture, power, and community, anthropologists could contribute to the latter two aspects, while historians, sociologists, and economists usually center analyses at the first two levels. Interestingly many of the latter specialists have turned to anthropological insights in their efforts to understand class and capitalism. The question of class formation is best understood as "concerned with the conditional (but not random) process of connection between the four levels of class".

One anthropologist's approach to social reproduction and economic anthropology could be read as emphasizing exactly such a connection between these aspects of class analysis. "Cultural particularities are part of the class structure because they are crucial to the structure of exploitation and they might or might not be pertinent to class consciousness and the meaningful organization of class identity". Culture is not merely part of a superstructure that is independent of or determined by the infrastructure. Rather, culture is part of the structure of society since it structures the crucial social process of exploitation. Most interesting here is that culture as structure goes into the making of class in the sense that Marxists have repeatedly emphasized, that "classes should be defined in terms of what people (in some sense) have to do, not by what they actually do". Finally, it is possible that these aspects of class could be viewed as mutually dependent or even as constituting each other. Not all forms of class action are possible, given the class structure of a society, and not all class dispositions can be compatible with particular forms of class action. Such considerations are appropriate for studying a place like India, a country that has much in common with less advanced capitalist countries, but which is also unmatched for its class formations and the role of the still relatively autonomous state, even in the age of privatization and liberalization. One would thus not assume priori that the trajectory of class formation in India would follow a model based on England, or that class-consciousness of Indian workers would be signaled in ways similar to English workers. Smith (1984:467) observes that... if anthropology has contributed anything to the discussion of class, it is a recognition that societies are differentially "inserted" into the world system, that the cultural or ideological dimension of class relations (if that is what they are) is more important than is often assumed, less easy to understand, and has a transformative capacity that complements and often exceeds that of technological change.

THE CHHATTISGARH POTTER CASTE COMMUNITY

The late 1960s saw the birth of an organization called the Chhattisgarh Potter Caste Community (1) in three districts of the central Indian state of Chhattisgarh. (2) This organization claims to represent about 40,000 people, all of whom belong to the Jhariya Potters caste and the overwhelming majority of whom are traditional potters. (3) Almost all potters produce utilitarian items such as pots and pans, roof tiles made on the potter's wheel, and ritual items linked to the local agricultural and Hindu festival cycle. In this region, men work the potter's wheel while women gather firewood and do the marketing. Children may help with preparing the clay and firing items in the kiln.

The leaders who formed the CPCC are not potters, although all of them come from families who were potters a generation or more ago. Numbering no more than 100, these Potters are employed as (or retired) factory or clerical workers in industry or government, teachers, lawyers, or are small businessmen in retailing or restaurants. There also are other, smaller Potter castes in this region that have either migrated from other states such as Rajasthan and Madhya Pradesh or reside in those districts within Chhattisgarh and are not represented by the CPCC. While a few of these Potter castes are potters, most of them are entirely divorced from pottery and engage in petty trade and businesses like those from Rajasthan, while others are brick-makers.

In 1971, the leaders of the CPCC tried to unite all castes of Potters as the Chhattisgarh Potter Organization (CPO) to represent all Potters in the region. But only the leaders of the various caste organizations currently belong to the CPO. The CPO in turn operates as a branch of the All India Potters Organization (AIPO), a national organization headquartered in Delhi that is the ideological inspiration for Potter organizations in various states. The conventional characterization of groups that attempt to form collectives of endogamous caste-groups by establishing horizontal and vertical links in modern India is that they are a federation of castes.

But why should artisans like potters in today's India choose to politically represent themselves in the form of a Potter Organization rather than a potter trade union? Related to the question of the form of collective action of group workers is that of the class character of the CPCC, the CPO, and the AIPO. The easy answer to both questions would take the form of arguing that the CPO and AIPO are examples of class alliances or blocs, since one class (potters, who are petty commodity producers in household economies) is part of a coalition with other classes (a mix of factory workers and petty bourgeoisie, such as clerical workers, teachers, and petty merchants, with the caveat that they all claim to be Potters) in which the latter classes take the lead for the Potter organization on the basis of caste unity. Yet, such a conclusion does not illuminate the process of class formation in India. It cannot shed light on how, for example, class takes root as a lived category of experience, if it does so at all in India. For it cannot be simply assumed that potters consider themselves as a different class than their leaders who are Potters but not potters. Pursuing this line of thinking will eventually lead to what Mitra (1994:52) has called the "sterile debate" of studying class and caste "as if caste had no economy, and class no culture."

ANALYSING THE PROBLEM OF VARIOUS CLASSES

The various classes within the caste of Potters identify only what Wright (1990) calls the class locations of individuals, but fail to determine whether the leaders and the potters in the Potter organizations are linked to each other as two classes in a class relation; i.e., a social relation of production in which there is an unequal distribution of rights and powers over productive resources, control over the labour process, and the products of labour. It is only when such locations are placed within class relations that it is possible to view a class structure of society as the sum total of class relations.

This requires taking into account the fact that potter-artisans have a diversity of work experiences and relations with capital. While all potters subsist on making utilitarian and ritual pottery for the market, many potter households depend on one or more members working in agriculture during the agricultural season, (4) as wage labour making bricks, in construction, or as contract workers making roof tiles. Some have their most direct contact with capital working part of the year for a government financed cooperative while others, having joined the chronically unemployed, have lost faith in their traditional occupation. More important, they have been deprived of access to clay or firewood due to the usurping of their land by brickmakers or through discriminatory policies of the Forest Department that favour paper manufacturers over the traditional rights of potters. Finally, almost every potter's residence in a village or town has some of its members owning or working in teashops, cigarette stalls, or small groceries. Both class and caste in India articulate with a process that has increasingly become a key form of collective action for groups seeking to shape relations with the state and the market in their own perceived interests. This is the process of forming communities, and it provides an important lesson: that politics can produce a particular consciousness, rather than the other way around.

Questioning the basis of community is critical because it challenges prevalent assumptions of culture as shared, rather than as used by and on behalf of capital to disorganize classes. As Narotzky (1997) emphasizes, the task is to use the terms "culture" and "community" seriously and go past the fragmentation that pervades new narratives of capitalist society. What follows here is an ethnographic example that brings out the connections between aspects of class: structure, conditions, dispositions (Bourdieu 1977), and action in the context of community-making.

TRIBE

A tribe, viewed historically or developmentally, consists of a social group existing before the development of, or outside of, states. Many anthropologists use the term to refer to societies organized largely on the basis of kinship, especially corporate descent groups. Some theorists hold that tribes represent a stage in social evolution intermediate between bands and states. Other theorists argue that tribes developed after, and must be understood in terms of their relationship to, states.

ETYMOLOGY

The English word *tribe* occurs in 13th century Middle English literature as referring to one of the Twelve Tribes of Israel. The word is from Old French *tribu*, in turn from Latin *tribus*, the name of the tripartite ethnic divisions of the original Roman state Tites, Ramnes, and Luceres, corresponding, perhaps, to the Latins, Sabines, and Etruscans). The term's ultimate etymology is uncertain, perhaps from the PIE roots **tri-*"three" and **bhew-*"to be". From 242-240 BC, the Tribal Assembly (*comitia tributa*) in the Roman Republic was organized in 35 Tribes (4 "Urban Tribes" and 31 "Rural Tribes"). The Latin word as used in the Bible translates as Greek *phyle* "race, tribe, clan". In the historical sense, "tribe", "race" or "clan" can be used interchangeably.

Definition

Considerable debate takes place over how best to characterize tribes. Some of this debate stems from perceived differences between pre-state tribes and contemporary tribes; some of this debate reflects more general controversy over cultural evolution and colonialism. In the popular imagination, tribes reflect a way of life that predates, and is more " natural", than that in modern states. Tribes also privilege primordial social ties, are clearly bounded, homogeneous, parochial, and stable. Thus, many believed that tribes organize links between families (including clans and lineages), and provide them with a social and ideological basis for solidarity that is in some way more limited than that of an "ethnic group" or of a "nation". Anthropological and ethnohistorical research has challenged all of these notions.

Anthropologist Elman Service presented a system of classification for societies in all human cultures based on the evolution of social inequality and the role of the state. This system of classification contains four categories:

1. Hunter-gatherer bands, which are generally egalitarian.
2. Tribal societies in which there are some limited instances of social rank and prestige.
3. Stratified tribal societies led by chieftains.
4. Civilizations, with complex social hierarchies and organized, institutional governments.

In his 1972 study, *The Notion of the Tribe*, anthropologist Morton H. Fried provided numerous examples of tribes the members of which spoke different languages and practised different rituals, or that shared languages and rituals with members of other tribes. Similarly, he provided examples of tribes where people followed different political leaders, or followed the same leaders as members of other tribes. He concluded that tribes in general are characterized by fluid boundaries and heterogeneity, are not parochial, and are dynamic.

Fried, however, proposed that most contemporary tribes do not have their origin in pre-state tribes, but rather in pre-state bands. Such "secondary" tribes, he suggested, actually came about as modern products of state expansion. Bands comprise small, mobile, and fluid social formations with weak leadership, that do not generate surpluses, pay no taxes and support no standing army. Fried argued that secondary tribes develop in one of two ways. First, states could set them up as means to extend administrative and economic influence in their hinterland, where direct political control costs too much. States would encourage (or require) people on their frontiers to form more clearly bounded and centralized polities, because such polities could begin producing surpluses and taxes, and would have a leadership responsive to the needs of neighbouring states (the so-called "scheduled" tribes of the United States or of British India provide good examples of this). Second, bands could form "secondary" tribes as a means to defend themselves against state expansion. Members of bands would form more clearly bounded and centralized polities, because such polities could begin producing surpluses that could support a standing army that could fight against states, and they would have a leadership that could coordinate economic production and military activities.

Archeologists continue to explore the development of pre-state tribes. Current research suggests that tribal structures constituted one type of adaptation to situations providing plentiful yet unpredictable resources. Such structures proved flexible enough to coordinate production and distribution of food in times of scarcity, without limiting or constraining people during times of surplus.

The Constitution of India does not define Scheduled Tribes as such. Article 366(25) refers to scheduled tribes as those communities who are scheduled in accordance with Article 342 of the Constitution. According to Article 342 of the Constitution, the Scheduled Tribes are the tribes or tribal communities or part of or groups within these tribes and tribal communities which have been declared as such by the President through a public notification. As per the 1991 Census, the Scheduled Tribes account for 67.76 million representing 8.08 percent of the country's population. Scheduled Tribes are spread across the country mainly in forest and hilly regions

The essential characteristics of these communities are:

- Primitive Traits

- Geographical isolation
- Distinct culture
- Shy of contact with community at large
- Economically backward.

The 1991 Census figures reveal that 42.02 percent of the Scheduled Tribes populations were main workers of whom 54.50 percent were cultivators and 32.69 per cent agricultural labourers. Thus, about 87 percent of the main workers from these communities were engaged in primary sector activities. The literacy rate of Scheduled Tribes is around 29.60 percent, as against the national average of 52 percent.

More than three-quarters of Scheduled Tribes women are illiterate. These disparities are compounded by higher dropout rates in formal education resulting in disproportionately low representation in higher education. Not surprisingly, the cumulative effect has been that the proportion of Scheduled Tribes below the poverty line is substantially higher than the national average. The estimate of poverty made by Planning Commission for the year 1993-94 shows that 51.92 percent rural and 41.4 percent urban Scheduled Tribes were still living below the poverty line.

The Constitution of India incorporates several special provisions for the promotion of educational and economic interest of Scheduled Tribes and their protection from social injustice and all forms of exploitation.

These objectives are sought to be achieved through a strategy known as the Tribal Sub-Plan strategy, which was adopted at the beginning of the Fifth Five Year Plan. The strategy seeks to ensure adequate flow of funds for tribal development form the State Plan allocations, schemes/programmes of Central Ministries/Departments, financial and Developmental Institutions. The cornerstone of this strategy has been to ensure earmarking of funds for TSP by States/UTs in proportion to the ST population in those State/Uts. Besides the efforts of the States/UTs and the Central Ministries/Departments to formulate and implement Tribal Sub-Plan for achieving socio-economic development of STs, the Ministry of Tribal Affairs is implementing several schemes and programmes for the benefits of STs.

The progress over the years on the literacy front may be seen from the following:

	1961	1971	1981	1991
Total literate population	24	29.4	36.2	52.2
Scheduled Tribes (STs) population	8.5	11.3	16.3	29.6
Total female population	12.9	18.6	29.8	39.3
Total Scheduled Tribes (STs) female population	3.2	4.8	8.0	18.2

There are now 194 Integrated Tribal Development Projects (ITDPs) in the country, where the ST population is more than 50% of the total population of the blocks or groups of block. During the Sixth Plan, pockets outside ITDP areas, having a total population of 10,000 with at least 5,000 scheduled tribes were covered under the Tribal Sub-Plan under Modified Area Development Approach (MADA). So far 252 MADA pockets have been identified in the country. In addition, 79 clusters with a total population of 5,000 of which 50 per cent are schedule tribes have been identified. In order to give more focused attention to the development of Scheduled Tribes, a separate Ministry, known as the Ministry of Tribal Affairs was constituted in October 1999. The new Ministry carved out of the Ministry of Social Justice and Empowerment, is the nodal Ministry for overall policy, planning and coordination of programmes and schemes for the development of Scheduled Tribes.

The mandate of the Ministry includes social security and social insurance with respect to the Scheduled Tribes, tribal welfare planning, project formulation research and training, promotion and development of voluntary efforts on tribal welfare and certain matters relating to administration of the Scheduled Areas. In regard to sectoral programmes and development of these communities, the policy, planning, monitoring, evaluation as also their coordination is the responsibility of the concerned central Ministries/Departments, State Governments and UT Administrations. Each Central Ministry/Department will be the nodal Ministry of Department concerning its sector. Ministry of Tribal Affairs supports and supplements the efforts of State Governments/U.T. Administrations and the various Central Ministries/Departments for the holistic development of these communities.

SCHEDULED TRIBES

The term 'Scheduled Tribes' first appeared in the Constitution of India. Article 366 (25) defined scheduled tribes as "such tribes or tribal communities or parts of or groups within such tribes or tribal communities as are deemed under Article 342 to be Scheduled Tribes for the purposes of this constitution". Article 342, which is reproduced below, prescribes procedure to be followed in the matter of specification of scheduled tribes.

Article 342 Scheduled Tribes

- The President may, with respect to any State or Union territory, and where it is a state, after consultation with the Governor there of by public notification, specify the tribes or tribal communities or parts of or groups within tribes or tribal communities which shall, for the purposes of this constitution, is deemed to be scheduled tribes in relation to that state or Union Territory, as the case may be.
- Parliament may by law include in or exclude from the list of Scheduled tribes specified in a notification issued under clause (1) any tribe or tribal community or part of or group within any tribe or tribal community, but save as aforesaid, a notification issued under the said clause shall not be varied by any subsequent notification.

Thus, the first specification of Scheduled Tribes in relation to a particular State/Union Territory is by a notified order of the President, after consultation with the State governments concerned. These orders can be modified subsequently only through an Act of Parliament. The above Article also provides for listing of scheduled tribes State/Union Territory wise and not on an all India basis.

The criterion followed for specification of a community, as scheduled tribes are indications of primitive traits, distinctive culture, geographical isolation, shyness of contact with the community at large, and backwardness. This criterion is not spelt out in the Constitution but has become well established. It subsumes the definitions contained in 1931 Census, the reports of first Backward Classes Commission 1955, the Advisory Committee (Kalelkar), on Revision of SC/ST lists

(Lokur Committee), 1965 and the Joint Committee of Parliament on the Scheduled Castes and Scheduled Tribes orders (Amendment) Bill 1967 (Chanda Committee), 1969.

In exercise of the powers conferred by Clause (1) of Article 342 of the Constitution of India, the President, after Consultation with the State Governments concerned have promulgated so far 9 orders specifying the Scheduled Tribes in relation to the state and union territories. Out of these, eight are in operation at present in their original or amended form. One order namely the Constitution (Goa, Daman & Diu) Scheduled Tribes order 1968 has become defunct on account of reorganization of Goa, Daman & Diu in 1987. Under the Goa, Daman & Diu reorganization Act 1987 (18 of 1987) the list of Scheduled Tribes of Goa has been transferred to part XIX of the Schedule to the Constitution (Scheduled Tribes) Order, 1950 and that of Daman & Diu II of the Schedule of the Constitution (Scheduled Tribes) (Union Territories) Order, 1951.

State wise Scheduled Tribes.

(a) General

Where a person claims to belong to a Scheduled Tribe by birth it should be verified:

(i) That the person and his parents actually belong to the community claimed;

(ii) That the community is included in the Presidential Order specifying the Scheduled Tribes in relation to the concerned State.

(iii) That the person belongs to that State and to the area within that State in respect of which the community has been scheduled.

(iv) He may profess any religion.

(v) That he should be permanent resident on the date of notification of the Presidential Order applicable in his case.

(vi) person who is temporarily away from his permanent place of adobe at the time of the notification of the Presidential order applicable in his case, say for example to earn a living or seek education, etc. can also be regarded as a scheduled tribe, if his tribe has been specified in that order in relation to his state/union territory. But he cannot be treated as such in relation to the place of his temporary residence notwithstanding the fact that the name of his tribe has been scheduled in respect of that are areain any Presidential Order.

In the case of persons born after the date of notification of the relevant Presidential Order, the place of residence for the purpose of acquiring Scheduled Tribe Status, is the place of permanent abode of their parents at the time of the notification of the presidential order under which they claim to belong to such a tribe.

(b) Scheduled Tribe claims on migration

(i) Where a person migrates from the portion of the state in respect of which his community is scheduled to another part of the same state in respect of which community is not scheduled, he will continue to be deemed to be a member of the Scheduled Tribe, in relation to that State;

(ii) Where a person migrates from one state to another, he can claim to belong to a scheduled tribe, only in relation to the State to which he originally belonged and not in respect of the state to which he has migrated.

(c) Scheduled Tribe claims through marriages

The guiding principle is that no person who was not a Scheduled Tribes by birth will be deemed to be a member of Scheduled Tribe merely because he or she has married a person belonging to a Scheduled Tribe. Similarly a person who is a member of a schedule tribe would continue to be a member of that scheduled Tribe, even after his or her marriage with a person who does not belong to a Scheduled Tribe.

(d) Issue of Scheduled Tribe Certificates

The candidates belonging to Scheduled Tribes may be issued Scheduled Tribe Certificates, in the prescribed form (Annexure-III) from one of the prescribed authorities in support of their claim.

(e) Punishments for officials issuing Scheduled Tribe Certificates without proper verification

(f) Liberalization of procedure for the issue of Scheduled Tribe certificates to migrants from other States/Union Territories.

Person belonging to Scheduled Tribes, who have migrated from one State to another for the purpose of employment, education etc. experience great difficulty in obtaining tribe certificate from the State from which they have migrated.

In order to remove this difficulty, it has been decided that the prescribed authority of a State government/Union Territory Administration may issue the Scheduled Tribe certificate to a person who has migrated from another state, on the production of the genuine certificate issued to his father/mother's origin except where the prescribed authority feels that detailed inquiry is necessary through the State of origin before issue of the certificate. The certificate will be issued irrespective of whether the tribe in question is scheduled or not in relation to the State/ Union Territory to which the person has migrated. However, they would not be entitled to ST benefits in the migrated State.

TRIBAL DEVELOPMENT IN INDIA

The Scheduled Tribes (STs) according to the 1991 Census account for 67.76 millions representing 8.08 per cent of the country's population. They are spread across the country mainly in the forest and hilly regions. More than 70 per cent of the ST population is concentrated in Madhya Pradesh, Maharashtra, Orissa, Bihar, Andhra Pradesh, West Bengal and Gujarat. The essential characteristics of these communities are primitive traits, geographical isolation, distinctive culture, shyness of contact with communiies at large and backwardness.

The founding fathers of the Indian constitution were aware of their problems. Therefore, they made special provisions for their protection and development. The main safeguards include promotion of educational and economic interests and their protection from social injustices and all forms of exploitation. The constitution protects the general rights of all Indian citizens to move freely, settle anywhere and acquire property. It also permits the States to make reservation in public services in case of inadequate representation and requiring them to consider their claims in appointments to public services. The constitution provides special representation for the STs in the Lok Sabha and State legislative assemblies till 25th January, 2010 (Arts, 330, 332 and 334) and enjoins the setting up of separate departments in the States and National Commission at the Centre to promote their welfare and safeguard their interests (Arts 164 and 338). Special provision for administration and control of Schedule Areas and Tribal Areas (Art. 224, Fifth and Sixth Schedules) and grant-in-aid to the States to meet the cost of such schemes of development as may be undertaken by them for promoting the welfare of the Schedule Tribes or raising the level of Schedule Areas (Art. 275 (1) are also guaranteed. Later on with a view to effectively deal with the crimes against the Scheduled Tribes two special laws, viz., Protection of Civil Rights Act, 1955 and the Scheduled Castes, Scheduled Tribes (Prevention of Atrocities) Act 1989 were enacted.

Special economic development of the Scheduled Tribes and protection against their exploitation has been an important agenda of the Government. To ensure that the constitutional mandates listed above and translated into various policies and programmes and put into effective action, high priority for the welfare and development of Scheduled Tribes right from the beginning of the First Five Year Plan (1952-57 is being accorded. Recognising their special problems the principles of *Panchsheel* have been adopted in the welfare and development of these communities so as to ensure an understanding of their culture and traditions and an appreciation of the social, psychological and economic problems with which they are faced. An important landmark was opening of 43 Special Multipurpose Tribal Blocks (SMPTBs) during the Second Five Year Plan, later called Tribal Development Blocks (TDBs), each having about 25000 people as against 65000 in a normal block. An amount of Rs.15.0 lakh per SMPTB was contributed by the Central Government.

Further, an important step in this direction was taken during the Fourth Five Year Plan when six pilot projects in Andhra Pradesh, Bihar, Madhya Pradesh and Orissa were set up in the Central sector. A separate Tribal Development Agency was established for each project and an amount of Rs.2.0 crore was allotted to these agencies. Commissions and Committees appointed by the Government to review the tribal situation brought to its notice that the percolation theory had not helped the tribals in getting their due share and the backward classes sector had substituted general sectors instead of supplementing them and viewed that much more was still needed to be done to bring up the STs on par with the general population of the country.

TRIBAL SUB-PLAN

The Fifth Five Year Plan marked a shift in the approach when the Tribal Sub Plan (TSP) for direct benefit of the STs was launched. The Tribal Sub-Plan for the Scheduled Tribes was designed to channelise the flow of outlays and benefits from the general sectors in the plans of the States and Union Territories (UTs) and Central Ministries in proportion to their population both in physical and financial terms. It is an umbrella under which all schemes implemented by the States and Central Governments are dovetailed for addressing different needs of the Scheduled Tribes.

It is basically an area development programme with focus on tribals under which infrastructural development and family-oriented programmes are undertaken. The strategy has been successful in garnering larger flow of funds for the development of Scheduled Tribes from Rs. 759 crore during the Fifth Five Year Plan to about Rs. 16902.66 crore by the end of the Eighth Five Year Plan (1992-97).

The Ministry of Tribal Affairs, besides providing Special Central Assistance, which is an additive to the Tribal Sub Plan of the States and UTs and grants under Article 275 (1) of the Constitution for raising the level of infrastructure in the Scheduled Areas and economic development of the Scheduled Tribes to the level of general population, is also implementing various Centrally-sponsored and Central sector schemes under which financial assistance ranging from 50 per cent to 100 per cent is given to the States and UTs for construction of hostels and coaching of ST students for competitive examinations, upgradation of their merit, research and training, setting up of *ashram* schools, vocational training centres, village grain banks, educational complexes for ST girls in low literacy pockets and development of primitive tribal groups. Besides, non-governmental organisations (NGOs) have also been involved in the development of STs. Their developmental and financial needs are being taken care of over and above the credit available through priority sector lending of banks and other institutions by the NSFDC.

With the prime objective of providing marketing assistance and remunerative prices to tribals for their minor forest produce (MFP) and surplus agricultural produce (SAP) and to wean them away from exploitative private traders and middlemen, the Tribal Cooperative Marketing Development Federation (TRIFED) was set up by the Government in the year 1987. The TRIFED has ensured remunerative prices for the MFP to tribals.

While these achievements are a matter of some satisfaction as various development plans, policies and programmes have brought forth a perceptible improvement in the socioeconomic status of the Scheduled Tribes a lot more needs to be done with concerted focus on the issues crucial to improve their status on par with the rest of the population. These are: prevention of land alienation from tribal to no-tribal, review of National Forest Policy and Forest (Conservation) Act 1980, taking into consideration symbiotic relationship the tribals are having with forest, provision of clean drinking water and medical facilities, effective rehabilitatiion of the tribals displaced on account of setting up of development projects and legal measures to crub the activities of money lenders and traders by effective implementation of laws and regulations. Women play a significant role in tribal society: their empowerment with upgradation of their skills is one of the issues to be addressed urgently. To look into these issues and further focus attention on the development of tribals the Government has set up separate Ministry under the charge of a Cabinet Minister. The Government is working hard towards a new social order based on social equality and social harmony.

RESOLUTION ON TRIBAL PROBLEMS

The 18th congress of the Communist Party of India (Marxist) reaffirms its firm pledge to organise ceaseless struggles of people of the scheduled tribes against all forms of exploitation, social oppression and discrimination, which have intensified in the neo-liberal regime. The NDA government, far from addressing the real problems of the tribals, had implemented the provision contained in the Forest Act of 1980 to evict them from their own traditional habitat. The Forest Act provisions, which are anti-tribal, have to be withdrawn. In response to the militant revolts of the tribal people, colonial rule was forced to enact legislation to prevent the alienation of tribal people from their land. However, this legislation proved altogether ineffective and that legacy continues today. The fraudulent transfer of the land of tribal people to non-tribals has intensified after the mining sector has been opened up to corporate plunder.

There has been massive eviction of tribal people from their land in order to handover the land to private corporations, Indian and foreign. There are more than 84 million people of the scheduled tribes in India today; more than 15 per cent of them have been displaced without any comprehensive programme of rehabilitation in order to make way for development projects such as dams, manufacturing industries, and mines. The traditional access of the tribal people to forest and minor forest resources has made them victims of the contractor-forest official nexus. These circumstances have forced many Adivasi people into contract labour gangs and even to bonded labour and many atrocities are being committed on them.

Illiteracy, poverty, ill-health, malnutrition, hunger and starvation continue to be higher among the scheduled tribes than among any other section of the population. The designation of criminal tribes by the British of certain communities, though formally annulled in 1952, continues to be used by the police administration, who treat these communities as 'habitual criminals'. The identities of the scheduled tribes of India – their culture and languages – and the status of tribal women today are under serious threat. Only the Left-ruled states stand as an exception — be it with regard to the question of land, or, those of culture, language, regional autonomy and extension of the Scheduled Areas Act. If not for the intervention of CPI(M) members of parliament, *Santhali* would never have been included in the Eighth Schedule of the Constitution.

The tribal problem of the North-East is of a somewhat different nature. Successive central governments have ignored the development needs of the region, particularly with respect to the building of infrastructure. Due to the spread of education in North East states, a good number of educated unemployed tribal youth are not getting any avenue for future employment and are thereby frustrated. These frustrated youth are becoming victims of certain divisive forces who are channelising them towards insurgency in the region. In many cases, they are aided and abetted by the agencies connected with imperialist forces, which are very active in destabilising our country.

The capacity of our Party to emerge as the party of the toiling scheduled tribes is illustrated nowhere so well as in Tripura and West Bengal. Against heavy odds in Tripura this year, the CPI(M) and its allies won all the 28 seats in the Tribal Area Autonomous District Council, winning 72 per cent of the popular vote. In West Bengal, in all Adivasi-dominated areas, the CPI(M) has won the overwhelming majority of seats at every level of representation – parliament, assembly, zilla parishad, block and gram panchayat.

6

Indian State

NATURE OF INDIAN STATE

To study the nature of any particular state, it is necessary to analyse to relation between state, power, and social classes and the purpose of the state. The reason being, modern states are generally divided into two broad forms. – liberal democratic form and totalitarian form, while the former stands on the foundation of democracy, the later is anti – thesis of the formal where power lies at the hand of few.

The other view, which also has to be analysed is the Marxists view, which analyses the state as an instrument of class. In Studying Indian state, therefore we have to analyse the above mentioned aspects.

Liberal Democratic Form

The nature of Indian state can be studied from a liberal, Marxists, and Gandhi's view. The constitution of Indian declares it as a sovereign socialist republic democratic country. Thus, Indian state is characterized as a liberal democratic model regarding the state which the powers lie the hands of people. Moreover India is a representative form of government, where elections are held on the basis of universal adult franchise, characterized by independent judiciary, rule of law and separations of powers.

Totalitarian Form

We have also analysed the relationship between the state and society. Though India has a federal system, it may be in relation to economic development or social change. It consists of a "Dominant political centre"

Though India is a welfare state, it is often characterized by interventionist nature. Thus in one hand, it gives freedom and in the other hand it takes away.

The Marxist view of Indian State

The Marxist view sees the Indian state as a bourgeois state – where the benefits are only with the big industrialists and rich farmers. Though this nature does not completely dominates the state it exercises a powerful influence over the Indian state.

Even someone says that India has no autonomy of its own. It is completely subservient to the elite class. The leaders in India are mostly from the elite group and they make a elitist state.

Form of Gandhi's State

Sovereign state: Gandhi would like the state to be absolutely free from foreign rule, domination or interference. Federal state: Gandhi was against the concentration and centralization of political power, because is regarded power as a corrupting force. Therefore, he wanted federal and Panchayats.

Secular state: The state should be free from religious matters. Democratic state: Gandhi's state means Government by the participation of the people. He agreed with Abraham Lincoln that a truly democratic government is a "Government of the people, by the people, for the people."

However, Gandhi's state is not an end in itself, but only means to the realization of a stateless society.

Criticism

India has a highly plural society marked by various ethnic groups of different language and different religion. After independence India has experienced difficulty to maintain its unity. But growth of violence, regionalism, poverty, slow development of economy has questioned the working of Indian state and its nature.

Consequently the nature of Indian state has suffered a lot of criticism. In practice, democracy has not been able to meet the challenge of the poor and lower castes. These characters make the Indian state very oppressive in nature.

From the above analysis we see that the nature of Indian state has become a matter of controversy in contemporary discussions. However the agreed point is that the nature of Indian state has changed over this time.

The impact of social rule is visible in India. Recently, faith in democratic, institution, redistributions, justice and secularism seems to be eroded in Indian state. However, the state continues to solve conflicting interest and development problem.

Thus today's India stands as a political and economic paradox of a rich – poor nation with a weak – strong state.

NATURE OF THE INDIAN CONSTITUTION

The Constitution of India is not an end but a means to an end, not mere democracy as a political project but a socio-juridical process which opens up through a humanist, radical social order, the opportunity to unfold the full personhood of every citizen. The Indian Federalism is unique in nature and is tailored according to the specific needs of the country. Federalism is a basic feature of the Constitution of India in which the Union of India is permanent and indestructible. Both the Centre and the States are co-operating and coordinating institutions having independence and ought to exercise their respective powers with mutual adjustment, respect, understanding and accommodation.

Tension and conflict of the interests of the Centre and the respective units is an integral part of federalism. Prevention as well as amelioration of conflicts is necessary. Thus, the Indian federalism was devised with a strong Centre. Federalism with a strong Centre was inevitable as the framers of the Indian Constitution were aware that there were economic disparities as several areas of India were economically as well as industrially far behind in comparison to others. The nation was committed to a socio economic revolution not only to secure the basic needs of the common man and economic unity of the country but also to bring about a fundamental change in the structure of Indian society in accordance with the egalitarian principles. With these considerations in mind the Constitution makers devised the Indian federation with a strong

Union.Federalism Defined Federalism constitutes a complex governmental mechanism for the governance of a country.

It seeks to draw a balance between the forces working in favour of concentration of power in the Centre and those urging a dispersal of it in a number of units. A federal Constitution envisages a demarcation of governmental functions and powers between the Centre and the regions by the sanction of the Constitution, which is a written document.

From this follows two necessary consequences- (i) That the invasion by one level of government on the area assigned to the other level of the government is a breach of the Constitution.(ii) That any breach of the Constitution is a justifiable issue to be determined by the Courts as each level of government functions within the area assigned to it by the Constitution. K.C. Wheare defines federal government as an association of states, which has been formed for certain common purposes, but in which the member states retain a large measure of their original independence. A federal government exists when the powers of the government for a community are divided substantially according to a principle that there is a single independent authority for the whole area in respect of some matters and there are independent regional authorities for other matters, each set of authorities being co-ordinate to and subordinate to the others within its own sphere.

The framers of the Indian Constitution attempted to avoid the difficulties faced by the federal Constitutions of U.S.A, Canada and Australia and incorporate certain unique features in the working of the Indian Constitution. Thus, our Constitution contains certain novel provisions suited to the Indian conditions. The doubt which emerges about the federal nature of the Indian Constitution is the powers of intervention in the affairs of the states given to the Central Government by the Constitution According to Wheare, in practice the Constitution of India is quasi-federal in nature and not strictly federal. Sir Ivor Jennings was of the view that India has a federation with a strong centralizing policy.

In the words of D.D.Basu The Constitution of India is neither purely federal nor unitary, but is a combination of both. It is a union or a composite of a novel type. The Indian Constitution is not only regarded as Federal or Unitary in the strict sense of the terms. It is often defined to be quasi-federal in nature also. Throughout the Constitution, emphasis is laid on the fact that India is a single united nation. India is described as a Union of States and is constituted into a sovereign, secular, socialist, democratic republic. As opposed to this is the opinion of some scholars who regard the Indian Constitution to be unitary in nature. It has been argued that the Indian Constitution does not satisfy certain essential tests of federalism, namely- the right of the units to make their own Constitution and provision of double citizenship.

Further, in the three-fold distribution of powers, the most important subjects have been included in the Union list, which is the longest of the three lists containing 97 items. Even regarding the Concurrent list, Parliament enjoys an overriding authority over the State Legislatures. Article 253 empowers the Union Parliament to make laws implementing any treaty, agreement or convention with another country or any decision made at any international conference, association, or other body. Some of the other Constitutional provisions, which are often quoted in favour of the Unitary status of the Indian Constitution are- emergency powers of the president to declare national emergency or declaring emergency in a state in the event of failure of Constitutional machinery, the appointment of governors, unification of judiciary and the dependence of the States on the Centre for finance. The power of the Union to alter the names and territory of the states, to carry out Constitutional amendments and to affect co-ordination among the States and settle their mutual disputes is also regarded as an indicator of the unitary character of the Indian Constitution. It should be remembered that the aforementioned provisions in the Constitution are aimed at establishing a working balance between the requirements of national unity and autonomy of the States. Dr Ambedkar, one of the architects of the Indian Constitution, rightly prophesied: Our Constitution would be both unitary as well as federal according to the requirements of time and circumstances. Constitutional Intent being aware that not withstanding a common cultural heritage, without political unity, the country would disintegrate under the pressure of fissiparous forces, the Constituent Assembly addressed itself to the immensely complex task of devising a

Union with a strong Centre. In devising the pattern of the Centre State relations they were influenced by the Constitutions of Canada and Australia which have a Parliamentary form of government and America which has a Presidential form of government. The Government of India Act, 1935 was also relied upon with significant changes. The Constitution cannot be called "federal" or "unitary" in the ideal sense of the terms. It is stipulated in the Constitution that India will be a Union of States (Art.1).

The Constitution, thus postulated India as a Union of States and consequently, the existence of federal structure of governance for this Union of States becomes a basic structure of the Union of India. Dr. Ambedkar, the principal architect of the Constitution observed-........ the use of the word Union is deliberate. The Drafting Committee wanted to make it clear that though India was to be a federation, the federation was not a result of an agreement by the States to join in the federation and that the federation not being the result of an agreement no state has a right to secede from it. Though the country and the people may be divided into different states for convenience of administration the whole country is one integral whole, its people a single people living under a single imperium derived from a single source. The Constitution makes a distribution of powers between the Union and the States, the jurisdiction of each being demarcated by the Union, State and Concurrent lists.

In case of a conflict between the two legislatures over a matter in the Concurrent list the will of the Parliament prevails. The supremacy of the Constitution- the hallmark of a federation- is an important feature of the Indian polity. Neither the Central government nor the State Governments can override or contravene the provisions of the Constitution. Another pre-requisite of a federation, namely, an independent judiciary - an interpreter and guardian of the Constitution - is also present in the Indian Federation. The Supreme Court can declare any law passed by the Union Parliament or a State legislature ultra vires if it contravenes any of the provisions of the Constitution. Judicial Interpretation. The debate whether India has a 'Federal Constitution' and 'Federal Government' has been grappling the Apex court in India because of the theoretical label given to the Constitution of India, namely, federal, quasi-federal, unitary. The first significant case where this issue was discussed at length by the apex Court was State of West Bengal V. Union of India. The main issue involved in this case was the exercise of sovereign powers by the Indian states.

The legislative competence of the Parliament to enact a law for compulsory acquisition by the Union of land and other properties vested in or owned by the state and the sovereign authority of states as distinct entities was also examined. The apex court held that the Indian Constitution did not propound a principle of absolute federalism. Though the authority was decentralized this was mainly due to the arduous task of governing the large territory. The court outlined the characteristics, which highlight the fact that the Indian Constitution is not a "traditional federal Constitution".

Firstly, there is no separate Constitution for each State as is required in a federal state. The Constitution is the supreme document, which governs all the states.

Secondly, the Constitution is liable to be altered by the Union Parliament alone and the units of the country i.e. the States have no power to alter it.

Thirdly, the distribution of powers is to facilitate local governance by the states and national policies to be decided by the Centre.

Lastly, as against a federal Constitution, which contains internal checks and balances, the Indian Constitution renders supreme power upon the courts to invalidate any action violative of the Constitution.

The Supreme Court further held that both the legislative and executive power of the States are subject to the respective supreme powers of the Union. Legal sovereignty of the Indian nation is vested in the people of India. The political sovereignty is distributed between the Union and the States with greater weight age in favor of the Union. Another reason which militates against the theory of the supremacy of States is that there is no dual citizenship in India. Thus, the learned judges concluded that the structure of the Indian Union as provided by the Constitution one is centralized, with the States occupying a secondary position vis-à-vis the Centre, hence the Centre possessed the requisite powers to acquire properties belonging to States. As against this opinion, was the judgment rendered by Justice Subba Rao, the great champion of State rights. Justice Subba Rao was of the opinion that under the scheme of the Indian Constitution, sovereign powers are distributed between the Union and the States within their respective spheres. As the legislative field of the union is much wider than that of the State legislative assemblies, the laws passed by the Parliament prevail over the State laws in case of any conflict.

In a few cases of legislation where inter-State disputes are involved, sanction of the President is made mandatory for the validity of those laws. Further, every State has its judiciary with the State High Court at the apex. This, in the opinion of the learned judge does not affect the federal principle. He gives the parallel of Australia, where appeals against certain decisions of the High Courts of the Commonwealth of Australia lie with the Privy Council. Thus the Indian federation cannot be negated on this account. In financial matters the Union has more resources at its disposal as compared to the states. Thus, the Union being in charge of the purse strings, can always, persuade the States to abide by its advice. The powers vested in the union in case of national emergencies, internal disturbance or external aggression, financial crisis, and failure of the Constitutional machinery of the State are all extraordinary powers in the nature of safety valves to protect the country's future. The power granted to the Union to alter the boundaries of the States is also an extraordinary power to meet future contingencies.

In their respective spheres, both executive and legislative, the States are supreme. The minority view expressed by Justice Subba Rao has consistency with the federal scheme under the Indian Constitution. The Indian Constitution accepts the federal concept and distributes the sovereign powers between the coordinate Constitutional entities, namely, the Union and the States. The next landmark case where the nature of the Indian Constitution was discussed at length was State of Rajasthan V. Union of India. The learned judges embarked upon a discussion of the abstract principles of federalism in the face of the express provisions of the Constitution. It was stated that even if it is possible to see a federal structure behind the establishment of separate executive, legislative and judicial organs in the States, it is apparent from the provision illustrated in Article 356 that the Union Government is entitled to enforce its own views regarding the administration and granting of power in the States. The extent of federalism of the Indian Union is largely watered down by the needs of progress, development and making the nation integrated, politically and economically co-ordinated, and socially and spiritually uplifted. The Court then proceeded to list out some of the Constitutional provisions which establish the supremacy of the Parliament over the State legislatures. In conclusion the apex Court held that it was the 'prerogative' of the Union Parliament to issue directives if they were for the benefit of the people of the State and were aimed at achieving the objectives set out in the Preamble. The issue of federalism was carried forward in S.R.Bommai V. Union of India.

Four opinions were rendered, expressing varying views. Justice Ahmadi opined that in order to understand the true nature of the Indian Constitution, it is essential to comprehend the concept of federalism. The essence of the federation is the existence of the Union and the States and the distribution of powers between them. The significant absence of expressions like 'federal' or 'federation' in the Constitution, the powers of the Parliament under Articles 2 and 3, the extraordinary powers conferred to meet emergency situations, residuary powers, powers to issue directions to the States, concept of single citizenship and the system of integrated judiciary create doubts about the federal nature of the Indian Constitution. Thus, it would be more appropriate to describe the Constitution of India as quasi- federal or unitary rather than a federal Constitution in the true nature of the term. As opposed to this, Justice Sawant and Justice Kuldip Singh regarded democracy and federalism as essential features of the Indian Constitution.

The overriding powers of the Centre in the event of emergency do not destroy the federal character of the Indian Constitution. The learned judges elaborated upon the scope and justified use of the power conferred on the president by Article 356 which will not restrict the scope of the independent powers of the respective States for "......every State is constituent political unit and has to have an exclusive Executive and

Legislature elected and constituted by the same process as the Union Government." In the opinion of Justice Ramaswamy, the units of the federation had no roots in the past and hence the Constitution does not provide mechanisms to uphold the territorial integrity of the States above the powers of the Parliament. The end sought to be achieved by the Constitution makers was to place the whole country under the control of a unified Central Government, while the States were allowed to exercise their sovereign powers within their legislative, executive and administrative powers. The essence of federalism lies in the distribution of powers between the Centre and the State. Justice Ramawamy declared the Indian structure as organic federalism, designed to suit the parliamentary form of Government and the diverse conditions prevailing in India. Justice Jeevan Reddy and Justice Agarwal opined that the expression federal or federal form of government has no fixed meaning.

The Constitution is also distinct in character, a federation with a bias in favour of the Centre. But this factor does not reduce the States to mere appendages of the Centre. Within the sphere allotted to them the states are supreme. We can henceforth see that the Indian judiciary had interpreted the Constitution to declare India a unitary nation. This view of the apex court has lately undergone a change. The Court has recognized the fact that the framers of the Indian Constitution intended to provide a federal structure with a strong Centre, which would prevent the nation from disintegration. In a subsequent case Chief Justice P.B.Gajendragadkar, emphasized upon the federal nature of the Constitution and the Judiciary as the sole interpreter of the Constitution which could not be changed by the process of ordinary legislation. In the basic structure thesis case Keshavananda Bharti V. State of Kerala some of the judges in the full Constitutional Bench expressed federalism as one of the basic features of the Indian Constitution.

In another case Justice Bhagwati, described Indian Constitution as a federal or quasi- federal Constitution. In Sat Pal V. State of Punjab, the Supreme Court again held that Ours is a Constitution where there is a combination of federal structure with unitary features....... In Pradeep Jain V. Union of India, the Apex Court expressed a non-traditionalistic yet pragmatic opinion while explaining the federal concept in the context of the unified legal system in India- India is not a federal State in the traditional sense of that term. It is not a compact of sovereign State which have come together to form a federation by ceding undoubtedly federal features.

In Ganga Ram Moolchandani v. State of Rajasthan the Supreme Court reiterated: Indian Constitution is basically federal in form and is marked by the traditional characteristics of a federal system, namely supremacy of the Constitution, division of power between the Union and States and existence independent judiciary. The apex Court in ITC LTD v Agricultural Produce Market Committee expressed a similar opinion.The finer federal facet has often been misinterpreted by the central operators. So the battle for federal affirmation and restoration of democratic decentralization has gained momentum over the decade. Important Commissions like Rajamannar and Sarkaria Commission have stressed on the federal soul of the Constitution. In the opinion of Amal Ray, the Indian Constitution is a product of two conflicting cultures one representing the national leader's normative concern for India's unique personality and the other over-emphasizing the concern for national unity, security, etc. And as a result, the founding fathers opted for a semi-hegemonic federal structure where the balance is in favour of the Centre.

This concept is aptly described in the insight offered by Dr. Ambedkar: the Indian Constitution would work as a federal system in 'normal times' but in times of 'emergency' it could be worked as though it were a unitary system. The critics of the Indian Federal system must not ignore the fact that not only the Federal Government in India has been made deliberately strong, there is also a centralizing tendency in the other federal states of the world such as Switzerland, Australia, Canada and the United States.In an attempt to assert their independence the States have, at various points of time tried to flout the Centre's orders. An example was the disobedience of Karnataka to confirm to the Centre's directives regarding release of water to Tamil Nadu. Such actions have generated wide spread opposition from interested parties. A similar situation arose when Punjab Termination of Agreements Bill, 2004, was flouted by the State of Punjab recently.

The unilateral termination of a tripartite agreement raised a controversy in which the authority of the State to commit such an act is being questioned. Annulling the very basis on which the Supreme Court had pressured the State to implement the river water-sharing agreement of 1981, the Bill has created an unprecedented Constitutional crisis. In a response to the increasing number of water disputes the United Progressive Alliance Government has proposed to set up two Commissions to look into the Centre- State relations, including river water-sharing, and to examine administrative reforms. In the light of the past experiences of misuse of power certain amendments should be effected which will strengthen the federal nature of our Constitution.

Firstly, there should be devolution of more financial resources and powers on the States so that they do not have to depend on the Centre for financial assistance.

Secondly number of statutory grants to which the States are entitled should increase.

Thirdly, the States should also be given greater autonomy to undertake developmental programmes.

Lastly, there should be some inbuilt safeguards against the blatant misuse of Article 356 by successive central Governments. It is time to undertake a study of Indian Federalism with a view to valuate the trends, frictions and difficulties which have developed in the area of inter-governmental relations and to seek to evolve ways and means to meet the challenging task of making the Indian federation a more robust, strong and workable system so that the country may meet the tasks of self-improvement and development. The responsibility lies on not only the jurists and policy framers, but also the citizens of the country to work in a harmonious manner for the development of the country.

THE NATURE OF INDIAN INEQUALITY

Inequality might not always be bad. Some inequality is a necessary push factor which prompts people to be productive. Often "the urge to keep up with the Joneses" may be a source of dynamism in an economy. On the other hand inequality which has nothing to do with "inequality in productivity" might dim incentives to increase productive powers. A middleman who increases his total share in the sales revenue at the expense of the producing peasant seriously dents the peasant's incentive to produce more. There also might be cases in which government policies might bypass vast sections of the population giving rise to huge differences in human capital and therefore productivity. In these and other cases income inequality might be large enough to lead to social unrest. Such large degrees of income inequality might be undesirable.

The table given above indicates that after 1991 the Indian economy became much more open to external influences. The increase in openness to external influences is what we term as "liberalization" in this paper. Compared to 1985, the year 1991 saw a much higher export to GDP, import to GDP and, therefore, foreign trade (exports plus imports) to GDP ratio. The period 1991-2003 marked a continuation of this trend with an increase in trade, exports and imports as a proportion of GDP. In 2003 trade accounted for as much as 31.55% of GDP, out of which exports and imports accounted for 15.48% and 16.07% respectively. Net foreign direct investment was almost non-existent in 1991 and attained a level of 0.87% of GDP in 1997. That percentage level was almost maintained in 2003 when it was 0.76% of a much larger GDP. Thus, there was an almost continuous liberalization of the economy with the relative importance of the external sector in the economy increasing continuously over time.

As explained below, this obviously had some implications for inequality. The rate of growth of per capita income increased from 3.28% p.a. in the period 1987-92 to 4.5% in the period 1993-98 and 4.34% in 1999-2004, suggesting that liberalization possibly had a positive impact on growth. Some increase in inequality was to be expected as it was just the formal economy which was involved directly in external dealings. The large subsistence agricultural and informal sector in India only benefited indirectly through demand linkages and labour absorption. This paper tries to arrive at a more detailed understanding of this increase in inequality and its potential as a source of social unrest.

Another channel through which liberalization affected the distribution of income was through its differential impact on skilled and unskilled labour. The Hecksher-Ohlin model implies that trade should benefit unskilled labour in a developing economy more than skilled labour because such an economy is characterized by an abundance of unskilled labour and it exports goods which are intensive in that factor. In reality, liberalization has often implied the greatest reduction in protection for industries marked by the highest intensity of unskilled labour. Consequently the fortunes of unskilled labour relative to skilled labour have dipped. Liberalization also implies reduction in tariffs on capital goods imports. This is also marked by a rise in the fortunes of skilled labour which is a complementary factor to such capital goods. The factor rewards earned by skilled labour in developing countries under autarky are less than those in developed countries. These imply that on the opening up of trade, entrepreneurs in developed countries often outsource many skill-intensive production processes to skilled labour in developing countries at a wage rate which is higher than their autarkic wage rate but is lower than that in the developed countries. Thus, the conventional theoretical prediction of shrinking inequality between skilled and unskilled labour does not often hold in practice.

National inequality might be decomposed in a large number of ways. A decomposition at the national level would focus on the rural urban divide at the national level and the inequality within urban and rural income distributions at the national level. A decomposition at the state level focuses on inter-state inequality, intra-state income distributions for rural and urban areas taken separately and the state-wise rural urban divides.

While inequality characterized by Gini coefficients greater than 0.45 can possibly lead to social unrest, the nature of inequality surely matters. Inequality among people who live in close proximity to each other can often be more serious than inequality among distant provinces or among distant towns and cities. It is in this sense that the need for decomposition assumes importance.

Inequality at the All-India Level

Inequality at the household level in India is analyzed usually in terms of monthly expenditure data, pertaining to households, collected by the National Sample Survey Organization (NSSO) all over the country at different points of time. Similar time series data on income distribution among households are not available. This implies that any picture about income distribution among households has to be gauged from data on consumption expenditure of households.

In order to gauge the inequality in distribution of consumption expenditure among Indian households we make use of data from the 48th, 50th, 55th and 61st rounds of the NSS. The overall picture for inter-household inequality at the All India level, as reflected by Gini coefficients, shows a decrease in inequality in the period, 1987-93 and a marked reversal of this trend in 1993-1999 and 1999-2004. As the first and the next two phases can be seen to be falling in two different regimes, pre-liberalization and post-liberalization, it would be tempting to come to the conclusion that liberalization led to a rapid increase in inequality among households in India. Two reasons, however, call for a deeper analysis. One is that the data reported are for expenditure inequality and not income inequality. We, therefore, have to investigate through indirect means as to whether the trends in income inequality mirror those in expenditure inequality. Second, the social effect of increasing inequality depends on whether it increases with relation to agents who are near each other. For example, an inequality increase among residents of the Harlem neighbourhood in New York City has far more dangerous implications for social unrest than an increase in the gap in per capita incomes between Harlem and Bel Air in Los Angeles. Thus, it is very important to look at state level income distributions.

What about the rural and urban national level income distributions taken separately? In both cases there is a decline in inequality from 1987-88 to 1993-94 (the preliberalization period). Thereafter, both Gini coefficients keep on increasing over time implying that liberalization is associated with an increase in inequality.

Intra-state Rural and Urban Inequality

Trends in intra-state urban and rural inequality for monthly per capita expenditure. The number of states exhibiting a decrease in inequality in the pre-liberalization period, 1987-93 is 13 in the case of both rural and urban areas, with the rest of the states showing an increase in inequality. In the post-liberalization periods, 1993-99 and 1993-2004, the corresponding number for urban areas is 7 and 1 respectively. Thus, the pre-liberalization phenomenon of inequality decrease is reversed in the urban areas of many of the states. The rural case shows that the pre-liberalization trend of inequality reduction is maintained for the post-liberalization period of 1993-99. However, if we consider the larger post liberalization period, 1993-2004, there is only one state which shows a reduction in inequality. Thus, if we take recent experience into account we can conclude that liberalization has been associated with an accentuation of inequalities.

The above conclusions follow from a casual inspection of the data. The results from panel regressions confirm the impression formed by casual inspection. In the case of urban inequality the time trend is statistically significantly negative in the period 1987-93 (pre-liberalization) and statistically insignificant and positively significant in the two post liberalization periods, 1993-99 and 1999-2004 respectively. In the case of rural inequality there is a negatively significant trend in the periods 1987-93 (pre-liberalization) and 1993-99 (post liberalization) but a positively significant trend in the period 1993-2004 (post liberalization) signifying that the recent liberalization experience has not yielded good results for inequality within states.

Examination of Inter-state Inequalities

If we look at the monthly per capita expenditures of various states we find that for the rural and urban areas, the gap between the poorest and the richer states increased at a faster rate in the post-liberalization period. In urban areas the gap actually reduces in the pre-liberalization period but increases greatly in the post-liberalization periods. If we consider the combined rural and urban area of each state the overall picture is of a deceleration in the increase in the gap between the poorest state and the richer states in the immediate post-liberalization period, 1993-99. But if we consider the recent period 1993-2004, the net increase in gap is indeed very large. This makes for the impression that recent liberalization experience has contributed to a widening of disparities between the poorest and the richer states. If however, we consider the gap between the states in the upper half of the interstate income distribution (those above the 60th percentile) there seems to be a reversal in the recent-post liberalization period, 1999-2004, of previous trends in widening of such gaps. Thus, the overall impression is that with liberalization most states seem to be coming closer together in terms of per capita consumption expenditure. However, there are a few laggard states which are falling further and further behind the rest.

If we consider the inter-state coefficient of variation we see that the period 19992004 has seen a reduction in inter-state inequality in rural areas whereas the two preceding periods, one in the pre-liberalization and the other in the post-liberalization era (1987-93 and 1993-99) are actually characterized by an increase in inequality. The situation is however, not the same for urban areas where liberalization has resulted in a reversal of previous decline in inequality.

If we consider the coefficient of variation among states in overall per capita consumption expenditure there is a continuous trend of increase over time. However, the increase over time seems to be of a greater magnitude in the post liberalization periods. Thus, the coefficient of variation (CV) increased by .028 in the period 1987-93, by .032 in the period 1993-99 and by .0327 in 99-2004. If we consider the CV in per capita incomes this variable too increases continuously over time, irrespective of whether we are dealing with pre-liberalization or post-liberalization periods. However, inequality has increased at a much slower rate over time in the postliberalization period. An examination of gaps between the state with the lowest per capita income and richer states at higher percentiles shows that the widening of gaps decelerated with liberalization. In the period 1999-2004 some of the gaps actually narrowed. This result is again opposite to that for per capita consumption expenditure, suggesting the importance of savings behaviour.

Thus, we can conclude that the trend in change in inequality in per capita consumption expenditure among states does not mirror that in per capita income. While consumption inequality among states seems to accelerate from the first period to the second period income inequality decelerates in the post-liberalization period. This can only be explained through a sudden spurt in the propensity to consume of the richer states. In other words, it seems that the richer states saved a smaller proportion of their income in the second period as compared to the first, whereas the poorer states were compelled by the need to satisfy their basic requirements to maintain their propensities to consume at the earlier high level.

In this case what is true of states must be true of individuals as state per capita incomes and expenditures are the result of aggregation of individual incomes and expenditures respectively. In other words state A has a higher per capita income than state B if the proportion of rich persons in the population of state A is higher than that of state B. Now imagine that all the rich persons revise their propensity to consume upwards. Because state A has a higher proportion of rich people the gap in per capita consumption expenditure between the two states will widen as the rise in per capita expenditure for A will exceed the rise for B.

It is obvious that this is what has happened in the Indian case as it is the only way in which one can reconcile the differing secular trends in per capita income and consumption expenditure. Affluent people saved a very high proportion of their income in the pre-liberalization days when product variety and imported good availability was low. However, their propensity to consume increased vastly when the situation changed after liberalization. This implied that inequality in consumption expenditure changed vastly after liberalization even without a rapid increase in income inequality.

One similarity in consumption expenditure and income trends for states. Over time the inequality among states in the upper half of the expenditure or income distribution has reduced. This implies that even though the divide between less developed and more developed states is glaring, within the latter group the levels of affluence enjoyed are becoming more similar.

This paper looks at the implications of the liberalization process for the magnitude and nature of inequality in India and its possible ramifications for social harmony. It is seen that liberalization has contributed to an accentuation of intra-state rural and urban inequalities. This accentuation did not start immediately after the liberalization process but around 1999, eight years after what is formally acknowledged as the start of the liberalization process in India. Surprisingly, there was no further accentuation of the high urban biases that characterized India in the pre-liberalization period. However, the gaps among the poorest and the richer states did increase with liberalization. A positive development though was that states in the upper half of the inter-state income distribution did come closer.

Researchers have suggested (Aghion, Burgess, Redding and Zilbotti, 2003) that states with better/more flexible institutions had firms closer to the production possibility frontier. These states were better able to cope with the competition introduced by international trade than others. This might be considered a reason for the widening of inter-state equality.

Another important conclusion of this paper is that consumption expenditure data overstate inequalities among states as well as individuals. The per capita income data for states show a deceleration of inequality increase from the last pre-liberalization period to the first post-liberalization period whereas the consumption expenditure data show a reduction in inequality in the former period and a sharp increase in the latter. This can only be explained if the propensity to consume of richer states and individuals increased after liberalization which definitely improved product and service variety.

A HISTORY OF LIBERALISM IN INDIA

1757 - 1947: The Effect of British Liberal Ideas

The strengthening of British influence in Bengal with the battle of Plassey in 1757 coincided with significant developments of thought in England (John Locke in the 1680s, Adam Smith with his monumental book in 1776, and Edmund Burke) and in the USA (Thomas Jefferson, John Adams and Alexander Hamilton, among others). The English language came to India in 1603 in Akbar's time but there was then no pressing economic reason for Indian people to learn English. It was only after the consolidation of Bengal by Robert Clive and the extension of the East India Company into the Indian political landscape, that the demand for learning English began to grow. By 1835,

Indians were paying serious money to be taught English, as it gave them job openings in the Company. As Thomas Babington Macaulay noted in his famous Minute: "the natives" had become "desirous to be taught English" and were no longer "desirous to be taught Sanscrit or Arabic". Further, those who wished to, seemed to picked up English very well: "it is unusual to find, even in the literary circles of the Continent, any foreigner who can express himself in English with so much facility and correctness as we find in many Hindoos."

Those who learnt English quickly became aware of its literature, including the rapid evolution of Western political thought. This greater awareness of the advances in freedom laid the seeds for the demand for self-rule.

While people like Raja Ram Mohan Roy (1772-1833) were beginning to articulate elements of these political arguments, no one was in a position to explore and articulate new insights. However they did catch up with key liberal ideas and began implementing some of these advances thought through their new demands for greater freedom in India. While the West was firmly embedding its new political institutions, or contesting the growing forces of socialism (which had overpowered parts of the feudal and aristocratic West), the Indian intelligentsia was grappling with the challenge of the first major task ahead of it, namely independence.

As well as Raja Ram Mohan Roy, other contributors to political thought on freedom in 19th century India included Dadabhai Naoroji (1825-1917), Mahadeo Govind Ranade (1842-1901), Gopal Krishna Gokhale (1866-1915) and Pherozeshah Mehta (1845-1915). Theory led to an independence movement in India. Gandhi demonstrated through a humane, non-violent, and dignified protest, that all humans were equal and should be treated equally, including their being given the opportunity to govern themselves. This was a major advance in the theory and practice of freedom and can be argued to have had a major effect in ending the age of imperialism and the age of racial discrimination.

Nehru, who was very well-educated and fully aware of the history of liberalism, seems to have had surprisingly little faith in an individual's ability to think and take responsibility for himself or herself. Nehru did not emphasise the importance of each individual undertaking self reflection and choosing among ethical alternatives. Possibly, in his view, making these ethical choices was too difficult for the common man. He definitely believed that these choices were best directed through state level dictates laid down by governing elites. Through planning. In any event, he veered toward collectivist and socialist thinking where decision making power is concentrated in the state. Decentralisation, where power and freedom vests with people at the lowest levels, was anathema to Nehru. He stated in his Autobiography : "socialism is... for me not merely an economic doctrine which I favour; it is a vital creed which I hold with all my head and heart." Indian industrialists (with their Bombay Plan) also sided with Nehru on a socialist pattern based on the Russian 5-year plan model.

Despite the environment in which socialist thought was flourishing, India was fortunate to enjoy at least a few liberties even before independence. The advances made in political institutions in England as a result of liberalism were imported and embedded into India over the decades by British rulers. Things like the right of assembly and protest under reasonable circumstances, the right to property, and freedom of expression % with a relatively free press, became a part and parcel of Indian political landscape before independence.

Post Independence Liberalism

The 1949 Indian Constitution gave to Indians some of the liberal rights that the British and Americans had come to expect by then. In addition, India extended franchise to everyone: all adults had the right to vote in the Indian Republic. That was earlier than even most developed countries had provided to their citizens at that time. But on most political issues, India adopted Nehru's socialist model, that included a significant dilution in property rights, among others. The government entered businesses as its primary activity, to help it achieve the 'commanding heights of the economy.' Government factories sprung up quickly and began churning out shirts, watches, fridges, scooters, bicycles, milk, bread, and cheese.

While Rajaji and Masani, and economists like B.R. Shenoy advocate the greater freedom, they were unable to over-ride the Indian fascination with socialism. Chakravarthi Rajagopalachari, the second Governor-General of India, and a Bharat Ratna, was a close colleague of Nehru during the independence movement. But soon after independence he quickly began to see the risks to India of letting Nehru's fervour with socialism go unchallenged. Despite having fought for independence by Nehru's side, and without regard for his own advanced age (Rajaji was 80 by then), Rajaji decided to act to block Nehru's onslaught on freedom. He formed the Freedom (Swatantra) Party, to oppose Nehru's policies.

For the next 14 years till his death in 1972 he waged a battle with Nehru's Congress to advance freedom. But as Nehru was extremely popular at that time, and also had the resources of the government at his command, Rajaji's was inevitably a losing battle. He wrote about his Party in 1960:

"The Swatantra Party stands for the protection of the individual citizen against the increasing trespasses of the State. It is an answer to the challenge of the so-called Socialism of the Indian Congress party. It is founded on the conviction that social justice and welfare can be attained through the fostering of individual interest and individual enterprise in all fields better than through State ownership and Government control. It is based on the truth that bureaucratic management leads to loss of incentive and waste of resources. When the State trespasses beyond what is legitimately within its province, it just hands over the management from those who are interested in frugal and efficient management to bureaucracy which is untrained and uninterested except in its own survival.

"The Swatantra Party is founded on the claim that individual citizens should be free to hold their property and carry on their professions freely and through binding mutual agreements among themselves and that the State should assist and encourage in every possible way the individual in this freedom, but not seek to replace him."

Rajaji's opposition arguably helped India minimize the excesses of socialism. His party held 44 seats in Parliament in the Fourth Lok Sabha (1967-71). Swatantra was also part of the opposition to the Nath Pai Bill that advocated primacy for the Directive Principles of State Policy over Fundamental

Rights. There were many other occasions when Swatantra acted as the voice of reason in a very unreasonable time. Making use of the free press and democracy, Swatantra pressed on for freedom, regardless of the difficulties it faced, but ran out of steam in 1973.

Since then, many new thinkers such as S.Raju, Sharad Joshi, Barun Mitra, Parth Shah, Gurcharan Das, Sauvik Chakraverti, and many others have emerged on the Indian liberal scene, contributing to the debate on freedom in India, and advancing classical liberalism.

Liberalism in Indian Politics

The Indian National Congress, the flag-ship of Indian Independence Movement, was founded by liberal nationalist, like Gopal Krishna Gokhale. Almost the entire leadership of the Congress till mid-1920s was liberal in its stance. Sometime in the 1920s, the Congress leadership was taken over by socialists like Jawaharlal Nehru and Subhash Chandra Bose, forcing liberals to move into a separate platform. Gandhi however retained liberal leanings and never supported socialism. He was opposed to government taking over ownership of property. He wanted to bring responsible business (trusteeship) and local self-government.

After Independence, Swatantra Party was founded as India's Liberal Party in 1959. It was founded by Rajaji, but merged with B.K.D. led by Charan Singh. It has been India's only genuinely liberal political group so far, with a large number of seats in Parliament. This effort ended in 1973.

In January 2004 Indian liberals attempted to revive the spirit of the Swatantra Party by forming the Swantantra Bharat Party (SBP). SBP now has one seat in Parliament, namely of its President, Sharad Joshi.

A minor but distinctly liberal effort, the Liberal Party of India (LPI), based on economic and political liberalism, was floated in 12 April 2005 independent to the Swatantra Bharat Party. The need for a separate party arose over a significant difference of opinion regarding the level of transparency needed in a liberal party. However, LPI wound up within a few months given only a few active members.

The Lok Satta Party launched in 2006 claims to be rooted in liberalism, but its strategy and policies are awaited.

The Jago Party launched in 2008 is a serious political party based on principles of liberalism and it openly supports free market economy for India. It contested on 17 seats in Lok Sabha elections in 2009 and got around 0.5% votes.

In the meanwhile, Indians are able to take advantage of economic liberalism now on offer from a number of 'mainstream' parties, which, however, are not grounded in philosophical liberalism.

Liberalism in Indian Economy

After Independence, India adopted the Socialist model of development. This led to creation of Licence Raj, the elaborate licences, regulations and the accompanying red tape that were required to set up business in India.

The economic liberalisation of 1991, initiated by then Indian prime minister P. V. Narasimha Rao and his finance minister Manmohan Singh in response to a balance-of-payments crisis, did away with the Licence Raj and ended many public monopolies, allowing automatic approval of foreign direct investment in many sectors.

Since 1990, India has emerged as one of the fastest growing economies in the developing world; during this period, the economy has grown constantly with only a few major setbacks. This has been accompanied by increases in life expectancy, literacy rates and food security. However, India had also shown fast growth in 1980's while its rating in the Economic Freedom of Nations (EFN) had actually fallen. Agriculture which still employs 60% people had shown faster growth in the 1980s than the 1990s. In fact, post-liberalization, the productivity growth in agriculture has fallen behind the growth in population.

THE DECEPTION OF THE INDIAN LIBERAL DISCOURSE ON KASHMIR

After two months of almost continuous clampdowns and lockdowns, 50 systematic killings, and hundreds of incarcerations, the debate in India about protests in Kashmir has continued to hover between bleeding-heart liberal talk and state attempts at dissimulation. While state deception, and the

Hindu right racket, is obvious, expected, and nothing new, the increased space for liberal discourse has given a false impression that there is a change in heart. The liberal discourse in India on the question of Kashmir is not open, fair, or objective, but often borders on, and oftentimes overlaps, the more popular, explicitly nationalist polemics.

From news shows to newspaper articles every death in Kashmir is slyly or openly justified. Since the day some protestors in Pampore and Srinagar burnt a few police jeeps and a couple of decrepit old, low-level government office structures, fit not even to be cowsheds, the Indian media suggested that people are shot because they attack public property. They tried to conceal the fact that most of the victims were killed before those structures were burnt down. But then even before the Pampore incidents big media in India tried to create a moral equivalence between intentional murders of dozens of unarmed Kashmiri protestors and Indian paramilitary soldiers not getting enough rest, or their jeeps getting a few bumps.

India's "Kashmir experts" (some of them from Kashmir as well), who fall over each other to get a place on noisy and bogus talk shows in Delhi, have been bandying about that the current series of protests began with the June 11 killing of Tufail Mattoo. The fake encounter killings of three young men in Machil and of a 70-year-old man in Kupwara, the fatal shooting of another man in Keller forests, the wanton killings of Zahid and Wamiq in Srinagar, and numerous others preceded Tufail's death. Not only were these other killings deliberately forced to recede from the public view, but the immense suffering, the daily grind, humiliation and torture that marks life in Kashmir under military occupation continues to be glossed over. The gloss often is the much-abused fabrication that Kashmiris live off Indian taxpayers' money. Somehow it is assumed that Kashmiris don't pay taxes, or that Kashmir doesn't have an economy of its own beyond the government dole. The fact deliberately obscured is that the very thin slice of Kashmiri society that does benefit from Indian handouts is the one the Indian state has actively promoted as a class of collaborators in Kashmir. These are mostly the people who appear on TV shows in Delhi, and their view is projected as the countervailing view to the Indian hawks, who saturate the public sphere in Delhi newsrooms. The problem is that these same people openly announce that common Kashmiris will lynch them if they went out of their security cocoons.

Then there are the nauseating media pundits who, on one side, show injured young children with bullet marks on their chests and, on the other, bring heavy mustached ex-military generals to offer their views on why children get shot. They implicitly announce that if Kashmiri children have to live, their parents better keep them inside their homes. This is the liberal Indian media. On the more popular platforms, like Rediff News or Times of India, respondents openly call for genocide of Kashmiris. It is crucial to read the low ethical barometer of this Delhi based media since it directly generates much Indian public opinion about Kashmir. How do societies become so pachydermic to gulp down with eager credulity such moral depravity? Even in the left–liberal big media, the systematic nature of deceit is clearly visible to the point that it has become farcical. The Hindu published an editorial that unscrupulously tried to make a case for curtailing Internet services to Kashmiris, one of the few places where the Indian government has not been completely successful in muzzling dissent. So disgruntled was this calumnious piece's author that he created fictitious names to smear all the protest Kashmiris express online.

For long the existence of Kashmiri protest was shrugged off as directed by Pakistan. Now after those theories have fallen flat, attempts are made to mystify what Kashmiris want. Isn't it truly baffling that, while the rest of the world clearly know what Kashmiris want, India's liberal experts have a hard time comprehending this resounding reality? For the last 20 years these experts have repeatedly asked the question: "But what do Kashmiris want?" Kashmiris have declared what they want in clear, succinct slogans (always in English, and in Hindustani) over microphones, on banners, and in protests, by raising fists, throwing stones, and firing guns, through their tears, cries, and wails, through burnt homes, imprisoned lives, and wounded, life-deprive bodies.

The ones, who have finally managed to read the writing on the bloodied wall, fulminate in self-righteous anger that India will never give azadi to Kashmiris. This rejection of

Kashmir's freedom takes supercilious forms. They tell us Kashmiris to see 'reason.' Free Kashmir is not viable. In return, we ask them, if unfree, occupied Kashmir is viable for Kashmiris? They tell us Kashmir will become another playground for Great Power politics, and we ask them if India's denial of Kashmir's right to self-determination has not already turned Kashmir into one. Some of them warn us that independent Kashmir will be taken over by the U.S. But we ask them, have India and Pakistan not been 'taken over' by the U.S. already? Didn't India eagerly, and without being asked, offer the U.S. its bases to attack Afghanistan? Don't India and Pakistan race to Washington to get a little smile, a nod, a shoulder brush, an acknowledgement from Americans? They even tell Kashmiris that we will not survive, because we are landlocked, as if through history, which we successfully survived, we weren't landlocked. (Are there no landlocked countries in the world?) And when these arguments sound all speculative, they tell us that Muslims in India will come under great threat from the majority Hindus if Kashmir separates from India. And, in the same breath they hasten to add that Indians are a tolerant, pluralist nation.

Only in the end they tell us that we need to see the "harsh reality" of India's power. Well, this is an argument that is shorn of fake sympathy for Kashmiris, of moral self-righteousness, and of the supercilious concern for the viability of an independent Kashmir. This is an argument, which one can grant a degree of objectivity, if not morality. The argument that uses the rationale of India's superior military power against the logic of the Kashmiri struggle for freedom, however, also lays bare the irreconcilable interests of the present nature of the Indian state and those of the Kashmiri people. To that question, however, we ask them, who more than Kashmiris has faced, and knows about, the "harsh reality" of India's power? According to their argument it is clear that Kashmiris should live with the occupation, if they must at all. Some even point out that gradually the "perception" of military occupation will go away.

For instance, in a number of circles in India, it has falsely been argued that killings happen in reaction to protests, rather than the other way round. It is claimed that if protests were to stop, the so-called "cycle of death" will stop as well—a thesis

India's prime minister also delineated while asking Kashmiris to end protest. The fact is that the killings, protest or no protest, are intimately tied to the grating reality of the military occupation. This occupation, which lets half a million military personnel, along with a chain-link network of dark operatives of intelligence agencies, sit atop a dissenting population as a force for suppressive pacification, has uses for these regular killings. Regular killings, maiming, rapes and molestations, random raids and arrests, merciless beatings, forced labour, daily dishonor, are all employed to destroy our social bonds, to pulverize our sense of self, to create utter disillusionment and despondency, to demolish the basis for any claim to self-respect, and ultimately to tear apart being political from being Kashmiri and achieving the death of these feelings of belonging. Or better, kill politics and turn us Kashmiris into artifacts of our presumed culture. Is this in the Kashmiri national interest, one may ask those who justify it all in the name of "Indian national interest"?

Occupation is a vicious process. It has gradually entered, and continues to enter, all aspects of Kashmiri life. Mass protests are outbursts, impassioned attempts to wriggle free. Freedom from this occupation is not just an aspiration, a wish, or a longing for a pipedream, but a desperate need. The struggle for life in Kashmir is the struggle for freedom. The protests surely intensify the occupation, but they also render the beast more visible, and easier to grasp. Ending protest will definitely not end the occupation, only it will be a sure, if slow route to a form of death down the road. The liberal discourse covers up all the contradictions present in the forced relations between India and Kashmir, and sells the dream of the Great Indian Democracy, a dream which large number of Indians themselves hardly believe in any more. This liberal discourse, which is too close to power, doesn't mediate between Kashmiris and the Indian state. It is often just a face of the latter, even if a more slippery one.

A STRUCTURALIST CRITIQUE OF THE LIBERAL POINT OF VIEW

Structuralism seeks to critique and change the inequality and exploitation of the working class that capitalist and liberal viewpoints produce. Karl Marx tried to understand the nature of this inequality. He believed the bourgeoisie, who owned all the capital and means of production, sought to exploit the proletariat, or the working class. "Critical for Marx is the fundamental imbalance of power between the classes" (74). While a liberal believes the bourgeoisie and proletariat are capable of forming a mutually advantageous relationship, Marx believed "the bourgeoisie and the proletariat are trapped in a decidedly one-sided relationship, with an 'unemployed army' of workers frustrating the ability of the labour force to organize itself...giving the capitalists the upper hand in all negotiations". Even though "Marx believes that capitalism is fundamentally flawed", he still believed that it was a necessary stage toward socialism because it builds wealth, technology, and raises living standards. To understand why the capitalist and liberal viewpoints produce exploitation of the laboring class, we must analyse "the market economy as a system, rather than piece by piece".

Structuralists focus "on the production structure inherent in capitalism". This structure leads to classes, leading to class struggles that create crises. These crises lead to revolution. Lliberals "have a tendency to view individual actions as cooperative and constructive, not competitive and destructive". According to the liberal perspective, the state seeks to be abusive of the liberties of the individual. This leads to tension between the state and the market. Thus, to solve this problem, the liberals believe the government must only "perform the limited number of tasks that individuals cannot perform by themselves, such as establish a basic legal system, assure national defense, and coin money". This was actually one of Adam Smith's central ideas; the government should do the work that private interests won't. Because classic liberals see the state as destructive to the market, they seek no governmental interference in the market outside of the tasks that people cannot do themselves. This is a piece-by-piece viewpoint of the market economy. Structuralists seek to view the market economy in its entirety. Because they believe that the economic structure is the strongest influence on society, the free market system envisioned by liberals will create class conflicts between the proletariat and the bourgeoisie. While liberals believe that the state is a dangerous force, structuralists see that "the state and the bourgeoisie are intertwined to such an extent that the two cannot be separated". This basically means that liberals see the state as an opposing force while from the structuralist view point, only the proletariat sees the state as a dangerous force because of the cooperation between the bourgeoisie and the state. Viewing the economy in its whole, it is easy to understand that the government supports and defends the elite class of bourgeois essentially because they are the capital owners. This is extremely evident in the current state of affairs in the United States. For example, rich oligopolies, such as the banking companies, have an extremely tight connection to the government. Many companies contribute heavily to the campaigns of politicians who, if elected, pass regulation that helps the oligopolies. The government recently passed a bill that makes it harder to file for bankruptcy. The bill was lobbied heavily by the banking industry, which holds much of the capital of the nation. It only benefits the banking industry. It will make it extremely hard for people to file for bankruptcy, and also makes them have to pay back the money. This legislation hurts the working class tremendously while benefiting the banking industry. Thus, it is evident that the government does indeed support and defend the interests of the elite class.

This tight bond between the government and bourgeois leads to the exploitation of the laborers and one of the pitfalls of liberalism. What leads to class conflict? There are many remarkable findings when looking at this problem from a global point of view. According to Leninists', the profit-seeking capitalists would not use surplus capital to raise the standard of living of the proletariat. "Therefore, capitalists societies would remain unevenly developed ones, with some classes prospering as others were mired in poverty". In reality, the standard of living has risen for the majority of people worldwide because of the effects of modernization. V.I. Lenin was wrong when it came to the standard of living for the proletariat, but he was correct in his analysis that capitalists societies would be unevenly developed and that the proletariat would still get the short end of the stick. Lenin's imperialist theory of capitalism seeks to "explain how it was that capitalism shifted from internal to international exploitation, and how the inequality among the classes had as its parallel the law of uneven development among nations". Lenin believed that the imperial phase of capitalism exported exploitation to poor peripheral countries as wealth and poverty were put onto the world stage. Looking at the world's economy, this made a new class of proletariats that was not bound within nations. For Lenin, imperialism was a tool that rich capitalist nations sought to use to increase revenue by making poor nations dependent on them for manufactured goods, jobs, and financial resources. It also made these poor nations heavily in debt, thus making them more dependent on the rich capitalism nations. This leads to a cycle of dependency. The bourgeois (by owning the means of production) and the government benefit from this 'tool' while the proletariats suffer tremendously. Why do the proletariats suffer? Imperialism heavily exploited the working class, especially of the colonized countries, by denying them basic workers rights and keeping them impoverished through a cycle of debt. Basically, structuralists see the bond between the rich and the government as detrimental to the working class.

When it comes to competition, liberals believe that it "constrains self-interest and prevents it from becoming destructive to the interests of others". Producers must push prices down because of competition, thus benefiting the working class by creating low prices. This is countered with Marx's "law of concentration (or accumulation of capital)". The theory is that the capitalist system produces "inequality in the distribution of income and wealth. As the bourgeoisie continue to exploit the proletariat and weaker capitalists are swallowed by stronger, bigger ones, wealth and the ownership of capital become increasingly concentrated in fewer and fewer hands". The law of disproportionality also counters the liberal view that competition benefits the working class. According to the law of disproportionality, "capitalism, because of its anarchic, unplanned nature, is prone to instability". Capitalism can be subject to overproduction or underconsumption. "Capitalists are not able to sell everything they produce at a profit and workers cannot afford to buy what they make". This disproportionality between supply and demands leads to economic fluctuations and increases the chance of social unrest and revolution. The Keynesian Theory of economics can further prove this disproportionality.

John Marynard Keynes developed his theory just as the Great Depression spread poverty all over the United States. In his view, "individuals and markets tended to make decisions that were particularly unwise when faced with situations where the future is unknown". Basically, Keynes believed that people were concerned about being unemployed in the future. So, everybody spent less money, saved more, and the result was that fewer goods were purchased and produced. Thus, "the recession and unemployment that everyone feared...[was] caused by the very actions that individuals took to protect themselves from this eventuality". This is called the paradox of thrift. The wealth gap in the country continued to grow and all the capital was concentrated within the hands of the few elite. Competition vanished at this point because the means of production was halted. "Keynes argued that the state should spend and invest when individuals would not...". Keynes was a liberal at heart, yet even he envisioned the Great Depression and the consequences of it. Structuralists seek to end this instable cycle of booms and busts by creating a socialist society where everybody is as equal in class as possible. No competition will exist because the state will set the prices. There will be virtually no wealth gap because everybody will contribute equality and earn equal capital. There will see be an elite group of people who basically run the country. These people will have a great deal of power because they run the government. Using Keynes views, a checks and balances system would be setup to make sure the people in power will not exploit the population.

THE MARXISM THAT INDIA INHERITED

Marxism has played a central role in Indian political thinking since the time of the foundation of an independent, if truncated, Indian "nation-state" in 1947. And indeed Marxist ideas became highly influential within the nationalist movement from the 1920s. This was not especially related to the role of the communist party or parties, whose electoral strength has been largely confined to one of two regions of the country (although their political and intellectual influence has often been far greater than their numerical size), but to the much wider sway held by Marxist thought amongst other political parties and institutions in post-independence India. Marxist-derived ideas were at the heart of the economic thinking of leading figures in Congress, most notably Jawaharlal Nehru. And the main opposition to these Congress leaders in the period before and after independence, first the Congress Socialists and later the Socialists, were profoundly influenced by a Marxist worldview. This intellectual predominance found expression in institutions such as the Planning Commission and in many universities. In prestigious institutions such as Jawaharlal Nehru University in Delhi, Marxism has been almost the dominant paradigm.

But Marxism is many different things. Far from being a monolithic body of thought as is often implied by its supporters and detractors alike, it is an evolving tradition of many often competing streams articulated by people in the singular historical circumstances in which they find themselves. To paraphrase Marx himself, people make their own history, but they do so under circumstances inherited from the past. But Marx also observed that inheritances and traditions from "the dead generations [weigh] like a nightmare on the brain of the living". Such a image seems, unfortunately, to be only too apt because India and Indians, in inheriting Marxism as one of the traditions of post-Enlightenment thought, mainly inherited a particular version of Marxism, albeit the dominant version. And that version of Marxism was dominant not because of its intellectual or philosophical force but because of the force of political circumstances. It was dominant because it was articulated and propagated by a powerful state, the Soviet Union, which appeared, at once, to provide an alternative model for economic development and to be the only force capable of resisting first Fascism and then US hegemony.

The central theme of this paper is that this dominant or mainstream Marxism, Soviet Marxism, was a Marxism that had been transformed over the preceding decades of political conflict and debate. In the process, a philosophy motivated by a vision of human liberation through proletarian revolution had been transformed, metamorphosed, into an ideology to justify and legitimise an authoritarian regime. The ideology retained its capacity for inspiration mainly for the leaderships of various nationalist movements in the colonial world as a means of forcing imperial powers to grant independence and as an alternative path to economic advancement and industrialisation free from the influence of the capitalist world. From a view of social change whose historical actors were classes, Soviet Marxism was one where the agents of conflict and change were nations and nation-states. India inherited a translated and reformulated version of Marxism because events which occurred far from India and with little apparent significance to India. These events were political rather than philosophical, yet they critically determined how one of the key philosophical traditions of the twentieth century came to be represented in India and how they came to represent India.

From Berlin to Bombay via Moscow

The mainstream of the Marxist tradition before 1917, what might be called "classical Marxism" or perhaps even "Marxian Marxism", was focused on the possibilities for social change in the industrially advanced capitalist West. Given Marx's own German origins and the fact that the largest party which claimed allegiance to Marxism was the German Social-Democratic Party clearly placed Berlin as the symbolic home for this pre-Bolshevik Marxism.

This was the Marxist tradition that argued that capitalism could only be transcended where the productive forces of society had reached such a level as to place the working class into the position of comprising the vast majority of society. This would thereby create the material circumstances for resolving the great contradiction of capitalist society - that it provided the productive capacity for abundance, but its exploitative social arrangements condemned humanity to immense inequality and alienation. The political project of Marxism, then, was to win the class struggle in the advanced capitalist world.

Where did this leave the working class in the less developed regions of the world where the proletariat was not only not in the majority but where it was a tiny minority confined to those parts of the economy where capitalist production relations prevailed. There was little discussion in Marx's writings about the role that workers could play in the colonial world and in countries just beginning their integration into the capitalist economy. A crucial example of such a country was, of course, Russia, where capitalist relations of production existed only in certain enclaves of the economy and the political structures of Tsarism hindered the free and further development of capitalism. The Menshevik position was that in such circumstances the working class could only support the political struggle of the liberal bourgeoisie and that working class demands could not be placed on the agenda until such time as the Russian economy had developed to a level comparable with the industrial West. Lenin and the Bolsheviks, on the other hand, developed the argument that the Russian bourgeoisie was too weak to perform what could be its historic tasks and that it was not only possible, but necessary, for the working class to take the initiative and take independent political action to overthrow Tsarism. This would mean transcending or bypassing the stage of capitalist economic development under the rule of bourgeois democracy and moving directly on to the establishment of a state run by and for the working class - a state would protect an economic system controlled by labour in the cities and by the peasantry in the countryside.

The key caveat, however, which is often written out of accounts of these debates, was that such a pivotal role for the working class in a backward country was seen as only a temporary one. A workers' state, the Bolsheviks argued, could not survive for long if it was isolated in a sea of hostile imperialist powers. The point of a working class seizing power in a backward country like Russia was that the country was the weak link in the chain of European capitalism and to break that link would open up the possibility of sparking revolution in the countries of the advanced capitalist West. Only revolution in these states, first of all in Germany, could ensure the survival of a beleaguered workers' state in backward Russia and help advance the process of economic development and strengthen the social and demographic position of the working class in Russia. In other words, while the locus of Marxism might shift temporarily to Petrograd and Moscow, the leading centres of a transcended capitalist world - an international workers' state - would be in Berlin, Paris, London, New York and so on.

As events developed, of course, the centre of a revolutionary workers' movement did shift to Petrograd and then to Moscow and these cities became the centres which dominated the course of debate on Marxist theory and strategy. Ultimately, however, the Bolshevik project failed. There were indeed, as hoped in Moscow, revolutionary upheavals in Germany, Hungary and Italy, three empires collapsed and there was a wave of working class unrest from England, to India, to America and Australia. But, nevertheless, the upsurge waned, capitalism survived and the Bolshevik regime was left isolated in backward Russia.

The result of the developments was to distort the development of Marxist thinking for decades afterwards. Because although the regime in Moscow was isolated and was almost toppled in civil war and foreign intervention, it did survive without the revolution spreading. But in the process of surviving, the Soviet regime destroyed the very features which a classical Marxist would have seen as crucial to identifying a workers' state along lines similar to Marx's analysis of the Paris Commune - most notably control of production by the producers and control of the state by organs controlled directly by working people. Instead the Soviet regime was characterised by the harshest discipline and exploitation of labour, the expropriation of the peasants, the destruction of the soviets and trade unions as effective instruments and their replacement by dictatorial state forms.

But all of this was carried out without a bourgeoisie as it was understood in Marx's writings – a class of private property owners with legal title as well as control over the means of production. Instead, in Stalinist Russia, the economy and the state were controlled by a bureaucratic party structure, without legal title but with effective control, claiming to act on the behalf of the working class and legitimising its actions in the language of Marxism. At the most basic level, the regime was legitimised by a claim that it represented "socialism in one country", a claim which to the internationalism of pre-1917 Marxism was a contradiction in terms. In the understanding of classical Marxism, capitalism was a world system and its overthrow could only be accomplished on an international scale.

Despite the reconstituting of fundamental Marxian conceptions implicit in the doctrine of "socialism in one country", Moscow became established as a permanent rather than a transitory centre dominating debate on Marxist theory and strategy. Soviet Russia appeared to be the only bulwark against fascism and imperialism and the startling economic transformation of the country during a time when the West was mired in Depression was an inspiration to political movements across the world seeking social change.

When Marxist ideas began to filter through the screens of British political control into the Indian subcontinent from the 1920s, the process of the transformation of mainstream Marxism was almost complete. For the young activists attracted to the fledgling Communist Party of India (CPI) in Bombay, Moscow was the unquestioned centre of Marxist thought and the Comintern, increasingly an instrument of Stalin's foreign policy, ensured that any questioning of the view from the Kremlin was expunged from communist parties internationally. The Marxist stream at which the CPI drank was, from the very beginning, the metamorphosed mainstream of Soviet Marxism. The only exception to the intellectual domination of Indian communists by Moscow was M.N Roy who, significantly, came under Marxist influence well before the rise of Stalin. As discussed below, Roy in fact conducted a major debate with Lenin over the political nature of national independence movements in the colonial world.

The Inheritance of Soviet Marxism

As a philosophy of practical politics whose adherents were keen to make an impact on the world around them, the dominance of Soviet Marxism in India had a critical affect on the political direction of the Left in India. The two key elements of the inheritance of Soviet Marxism were the ascendancy of nationalism and what might be called "developmentalism" or more precisely "state-centred developmentalism".

Sanjay Seth, in his important study of the engagement between Marxism and nationalism in India observed that "the definition of what it meant to be a communist" in India became those who argued for "a necessary relation between the class struggle and the national struggle". As he also points out, however, there was no theoretical imperative or logical necessity governing this conclusion. The reality was that most of the activists drawn to Marxism in India were fundamentally nationalists seeking a more militant inspiration to their nationalism than was provided by the Indian National Congress and who wanted to find a link between the economic demands of the workers and peasants and the fight for independence. The Comintern said that the link could be made by declaring, as distinct from theoretically or practically demonstrating, that independence could only be achieved through the workers' fight for socialism. Seth tends to argue as if the acceptance of this particular relationship between Marxism and nationalism can be understood in largely philosophical terms, when the ascendancy of nationalism in Soviet Marxism was the outcome of political expediency rather than the working out of contending philosophical notions.

On the first question - nationalism - there were a number of major debates within the Comintern during its earliest years of existence, from 1919 to 1922, about the nature and political role of nationalism in what were termed the colonies and semi-colonies. The example uppermost in the minds of the participants in the debate was India, particularly during the time of the first non-cooperation movement. Lenin argued that capitalism had passed into a new and final stage - that of imperialism - where a worldwide capitalist system had developed which depended on the "superprofits" to be gained in the colonies. He therefore concluded that the independence movements rising throughout Asia, led by the colonial middle class and bourgeoisie, were movements of oppressed nations attempting to throw off the yoke of oppressor nations in the West. In arguing in this way Lenin made the first important introduction of non-class categories as key actors in Marxist political analysis.

M.N. Roy, on the other hand, argued that to draw a parallel or analogy between the class struggle between labour and capital with that of oppressed versus oppressor nation was false and misleading. He made a case which pointed to the development of indigenous capitalism and hence of an indigenous capitalist class in India which British policies either allowed or, especially in the years after WWI, deliberately facilitated. He concluded that the nationalist movement of the Indian bourgeoisie was essentially a fraternal or internecine struggle between rival national bourgeoisie and not a struggle that could lead to the overthrow of capitalism. He therefore also concluded that the working class in India (and by implication, the working class in other colonies) should not be limited by political program of the nationalist movement but had to place its own class demands on the agenda. The working class should even, if circumstances allowed, actively work towards the overthrow of its "own" bourgeoisie and the establishment of a workers' state on the Russian model.

The outcome of the debate was that Lenin's position was largely adopted, but was modified to note that any assessment of the nationalist movement in a particular country should take account of the relationship between the indigenous bourgeoisie and imperialism. This was a potentially crucial modification in that it suggested that nationalist movements were not necessarily progressive and depended for their anti-imperialist content on the nature and origin of the indigenous capitalist class - whether it was entirely dependent on imperial capital for its existence or whether it had a degree of autonomy giving a material interest in resisting imperialist power. Bourgeois nationalist movements were not necessarily forces that would weaken capitalism as a whole, but were to be assessed on a case by case basis.

It should be noted here that Roy's ideas were adopted as a "Supplementary Thesis on the Colonial Question" at the second Congress of the Comintern, affirming that were given a comparable status to the line in the official Thesis, even though they had been voted down by the Congress. This was in stark contrast to the way in which the views of colonial delegates were regarded (or disregarded) in subsequent Comintern Congresses in the 1920s when the Comintern had been taken over by the Stalinist dictatorship. Roy himself was expelled from the Comintern in 1926, the same year that Trotsky was exiled.

Back in India, from the mid-1920s onwards the CPI followed every twist and turn of Stalin's Comintern as the needs of the survival of the his regime were translated into directives to change and rechange strategy, each change being justified in a *post hoc* theoretical re-formulation. The first line foisted on the CPI (and all other parties throughout the world affiliated to the Comintern) was that of the short but strategically disastrous ultra-Left period from 1928 to 1935 when all bourgeois nationalist movements in the colonies and social-democratic parties in the West were branded as agents of imperialism who were as equally dangerous to the working class as were the forces of fascism. The CPI thus isolated itself from the nationalist movement and from most elements in the labour movement. Then, from 1935, Stalin instituted the line of the Popular Front in which communist parties were directed to ally themselves closely with the liberal bourgeoisie in their own country and to play down independent working class organisation. The change was driven was Stalin's concern about the threat presented to the Soviet Union by the rise of Nazi Germany and Stalin's decision to seek rapprochement with the West, a possibility which could be enhanced if the threat of communist-inspired labour unrest was eliminated. In the colonies such as India this meant that the communists should all but dissolve themselves into the nationalist movement, regardless of its class character or anti-imperialist potential.

The political consequences of the embrace of Soviet Marxism became particularly clear during WWII when the CPI first followed the Comintern line during the period of the Nazi-Soviet pact that the war was an inter-imperialist struggle in which all progressive organisations should refuse to participate, and then faithfully took up the contrary position after the invasion of the Soviet Union and called for support of the "people's war". The change of line provided the opportunity for the CPI to operate legally and to cooperate with the British war effort, but caused bitter alienation between itself and the mainstream of nationalist thought and was to taint the CPI with air of betrayal for years after the war. The Comintern itself was, of course, dissolved during the war as a gesture of conciliation to the Western allies, the ultimate gesture which indicated the extent of its degeneration from a coalition of anti-capitalist parties to a bureaucratic arm of the Soviet state.

But beyond these more extreme examples of obeisance to Moscow, the phenomenon of close political direction from the Kremlin declined in the post-War period following Stalin's death, Krushchev's "secret speech" and the damage to Soviet standing following the invasion of Hungary in 1956. Yet with the gradual disappearance of overt political influence from Moscow, the stamp of nationalist thinking which emerged during the early days of the Comintern remains indelibly attached to the Left in India. Apparently dissident versions of Soviet Marxism, such as that emanating from Beijing in the 1960s, in fact had more in common with the Moscow version than seemed to be the case to many at the time. And on the critical issue of the role of the nation as an agent for political change, Maoism took the effective jettisoning of class categories to even further extremes. Thus the Left in India has most of its life striven to appear more nationalist than the nationalists. At times the CPI claimed leadership of the nationalist movement, as during the ultra-Left periods from 1928 to 1935 and immediately after WWII, or saw the protection of the Soviet Union as the immediate priority, as after the Nazi invasion of 1941. But whatever the peculiarities of the time, the Left in general has held to the position that India is an oppressed nation and that the natural allies of the working class is the liberal or "progressive sections" of the "national bourgeoisie" and that the indigenous capitalist state defended the interests of the entire Indian nation against the depredation of imperialism.

"State Developmentalism" and the Problem of Differentiation

The practical political effect of the nationalist orientation which pervades the Left and the labour movement has been that it has constantly been confronted with the problem of how to differentiate itself effectively from the party identified as the representative of the national bourgeoisie, the Congress Party. Congress was always able to identify itself as the leading party of Indian nationalism and the CPI left in a "me-too" role over what it saw as the key issue facing the country. While other Marxist-influenced currents such as the Socialists mounted a major challenge to the predominance of Congress in the pre and post-independence periods, their influenced had waned by the 1960s. The split in the CPI in the early 1960s has often been portrayed as a reflecting the split between Moscow and Peking, but was fundamentally over the question of how to analyse the place of Congress in social change in India and how to relate to the party politically.

The problem of differentiation has been particularly acute concerning the other key inheritance of Soviet Marxism - state-centred developmentalism. One of the main points of inspiration provided by Soviet Marxism was that the Soviet Union itself seemed to demonstrate that there was an alternative way to bring about the development of the forces of production which did not involve the creation of a bourgeois ruling class or a surrender to international capital. Soviet Marxism was centred not on the project of transcending capitalism through class struggle, but on the project of using the state to mobilise the resources of an independent nation-state, behind autarchic economic barriers, in order to defend the new state's autonomy and to allow it to join the ranks of the economically developed and politically powerful states of the advanced world. The phrase "building socialism" in the Soviet Union or China was synonymous with building heavy industry and farming with tractors. It was this Marxism that Nehru found attractive. The model of the Soviet Union led to the state-directed planning and strict regulation on the movement of capital and technology in and out of India that has dominated the policies of the Indian state since independence.

Marxism, presented in this way, with developmentalism virtually its central idea, was readily able to be co-opted and was indeed ideologically integrated into the edifice of the Indian state. Being thus co-opted Marxism was largely stripped of its oppositional possibilities and the Left was reduced to being a number of alternative parliamentary parties offering a political program which appeared not fundamentally different from that of Congress. At the height of Left influence in the 1960s and 1970s the CPI became the handmaiden of Indira Gandhi's campaign of empty populism. The CPM took office in West Bengal on a wave of working class unrest, but soon found itself locked into an enclave which limited rather than expanded its options for political activity. After a brief flirtation with using the office to facilitate class struggle by withdrawing police intervention in labour disputes, the CPM came to realise that to occupy even a relatively minor seat in the house of the bourgeois Indian state necessitated crushing more radical challenges to the status quo such as the Naxalites and discouraging independent initiative from labour organisations.

Thus the construction of India (and the rest of the developing world) which was implicit in the version of Marxism that India inherited was such that Marxism was absorbed into the mainstream of Indian political discourse. In the process, most of the potential for Marxism to provide inspiration and direction for organisations of the millions of working people in India being drawn into the capitalist economy, both in industry and agriculture, was also absorbed. Rather Marxism became one of the tools of the Indian state in its developmental project.

After the Fall: What's Left of Marxism?

The collapse of the Soviet Union and the collapse of Soviet Marxism have thrown much of the Left in India into a confused and disoriented condition. The political practice of the communist parties in India has, at least since the 1950s, been little different from any social-democratic party in the world, but the example of the Soviet Union provided an inspiration for what communists were, in theory, fighting for. This ideological veneer was also very important for the cadre of the party in maintaining their sense of difference from the Congress and the Socialists and for sustaining the idea that the communists were the most principled fighters for state direction over the economy, even though planning was part of mainstream thinking in post-independence India.

Economic liberalisation has presented the Left with a challenge in two senses: firstly because the economic restructuring with which it is associated has had major effects, both positive and negative, on the social groups which have been the Left's traditional constituency, and secondly in the sense that liberalisation has resulted from and facilitated the collapse of the post-independence economic nationalist consensus that India's path to development lay through a relative disengagement with the global capitalist economy. Economic nationalism, together with state planning and control of resource allocation, was seen as a progressive idea and the special ideological property of the Left. The institutionalisation of these ideas created a constituency of supporters amongst the state bureaucracy, the managers, administrators and workers of state-owned corporations, the owners of industries shielded against foreign competition and agriculturalists supported by subsidies and tax-free income. Some people amongst these groups were drawn to support Left parties. But unfortunately there does not seem to be any evidence of fundamental rethinking of the issues facing socialist and labour organisations in India today. Instead, on key issues such as ways to respond to the effects of economic liberalisation, there is little more than a repetition of the economic nationalist mantras of the past.

One recent contributor to the *Economic and Political Weekly*, for example, argued that the nationalist movement: should be revived and led by the working class by boycotting foreign goods... and preventing if required physically the entry of MNCs, the offspring of the old East India Co, now out to deindustrialise the country.

And although ideas of Third World solidarity have probably the least substance that they have ever had, there is still a school of thought which argues that: At no time was there a greater need for the concept of the nation state; and the need for the banding together of developing nations greater.

Even considerably more sophisticated analyses, when applied in practical political terms, frequently do little more than return by more complicated routes to old nationalist presumptions. Partha Chatterjee, for example, has attacked ideas of going "beyond nationalism" when rethinking the position of the Indian state in the world economy, arguing that it would "strengthen inequalities and defeat the struggle for democracy the world over".

At the same time, sections of the Left with a niche in the state machinery are increasingly adapting themselves to the most conventional of solutions to issues of economic development. The CPM in West Bengal, while rhetorically subscribing to anti-MNC positions in some forums, has been actively developing policies designed to welcome and facilitate the entry of international capital into the state. It is, of course, understandable that a government in its position would take such action, faced with the realities of the domestic and international economy. But it is also these realities which expose the ideological pretentions that the CPM has fundamentally different political priorities from other parliamentary parties. The nationalist starting-point for many Left organisations on questions such as nuclear disarmament has also left them open to accusations of being unable to develop a position which is significantly different from the chauvinism the Hindutva brigade.

A starting point for the reinvigoration of Indian Marxism would be a rediscovery of analyses based on the international class nature of capitalism as distinct from analyses which begin with a conception of oppressed and oppressor nations. This needs to be accompanied by a rediscovery of the politics of the movement rather than the politics of the state. The dominant tradition of the Indian Left has been fixated on attempts to influence the direction of the policies of the state, based on a view that the developmentalist state was in a position to free the mass of Indians from poverty, in contrast to the classical Marxist conception of revolutionary change as possible only by the action of workers themselves.

Rather than persisting with increasingly quixotic and irrelevant efforts to lobby the state to somehow, by administrative fiat, prevent the continued integration of India into the world economy, a far more productive route (from the point of view of the empowerment of workers, both urban and rural) would be to attempt to organise those workers and peasants who are actually being drawn into the increasingly internationalised Indian capitalist economy. For example in Bombay, one the principal linkages between the Indian economy and global economy, the key reality confronting workers in their daily lives is not whether their employers are Indians or foreigners, but whether or not they are employed in the formal organised sector or, like increasing numbers of workers, are employed in the appalling conditions of the informal, unorganised sector. But so many Left trade unions have been focused on defending the interests of ever-diminishing numbers of workers in the declining sectors of the textile mills and on the small numbers employed by state-owned services and corporations, and have neglected the difficult work of organising in the ever-expanding informal and service industries which now dominate the Bombay labour market.

A MARXIST PERSPECTIVE

The political resolution adopted by the 17th congress gives an insight into the CPI(M)'s views on the national and international situations.

Unlike many other mainstream political parties, the communist parties hold meetings periodically, not only to review their policies and decide action programmes, but also to elect their leaderships at all levels. In fact, in this specific sense they are the most consistently democratic parties, quite unlike many a mainstream party where the national leader may appoint the entire State executive. The first level of organisation in a communist party is the so-called branch or unit in which a person who joins the party is placed. This unit holds a "conference", usually once in three years, to review its political work and to elect its secretary and also its delegates to the conference at the next level, usually an area or a block. The process is repeated at higher territorial levels, such as the block, taluk, district and State. The delegates for the conferences at each of these levels are persons who have been elected at the conference at the immediately lower level. Finally, the conferences in various States elect the delegates to the highest decision-making body of the party, namely, the all-India conference, which by convention is also called the party congress. The CPI(M), which was born in 1964 following the split in the Indian communist movement, held its 17th congress in Hyderabad at the end of precisely such a process. Given its position as the largest contingent of the political Left in the country, the leader of ruling coalitions in two States, and the leader of the main Opposition in another State, the deliberations at the CPI(M)'s congress and the decisions arrived at it merit attention.

The congress was held at a time of great turmoil in the country - against the background of the communal carnage in Gujarat and attempts to whip up communal hysteria over Ayodhya which saw a sovereign, elected government being held hostage by a fanatical organisation like the Vishwa Hindu Parishad. Also important, although relegated to the back burner because of Gujarat and Ayodhya, was the economic crisis, which even the carefully sanitised Economic Survey of the Government of India could not entirely conceal. The congress discussed and adopted two important documents - the political resolution and the Political-Organisational Report - which between them provide a detailed statement of the party's understanding of the political situation and its own organisational experience, strengths, weaknesses and tasks ahead.

Again, unlike in the case of other mainstream non-communist parties, a draft of the political resolution ultimately adopted by the congress after discussion had been prepared by the Central Committee of the party more than three months prior to the Hyderabad meet, translated into all major Indian languages, and sent to reach all party members two months before the congress. Over 5,000 amendments to the draft were received from members, apart from hundreds of suggestions. The delegates at the congress debated the draft further before final adoption. The Political-Organisational Report, on the other hand, was discussed only by the delegates to the congress and then adopted. It has not yet been made public. Since the political resolution adopted by the congress is said to be substantially the same as the draft already made public, one can get an insight into the CPI(M)'s views based on it.

In the CPI(M)'s view, the most important features of the international situation are the growing offensive of the G-7 countries led by the United States seeking to "strengthen its economic and political hegemony over the world", and the growing resistance to this offensive, as witnessed in various struggles and protest actions in both advanced and Third World countries. Post-September 11, 2001, the U.S. "links all aspects of globalisation with the fight against terrorism". The CPI(M) is of the view that "both the U.S.' 'war against terrorism' and the threats posed by terrorism based on all varieties of fundamentalism will have to be challenged".

Turning to the national situation, the CPI(M) takes a dim view of the four years of Bharatiya Janata Party-led National Democratic Alliance rule at the Centre. Noting that NDA rule has involved both a "continuous assault on the secular principles of the state...", and an "accelerated pursuit of the economic policies of liberalisation, which has increased the exploitation of people and social inequalities", the political resolution documents at length the ruinous implications for national unity and people's well-being as well as the country's economic and political sovereignty of these policies. It does not spare minority fundamentalism either, which it points out is harmful to democracy and progress, and demands that it be countered.

The party also takes an unequivocal view on terrorism, noting that "state terrorism and individual acts of terrorism... only feed each other" and also that "terrorist violence, whatever be the motivation, has to be firmly combated as it disrupts the unity of working people and helps reactionary forces to divert attention from the real problems facing the people".

An aspect of the BJP's policies of particular concern is its stand on federalism. The BJP dispensation at the Centre has been eroding the already limited powers of the States by reducing Central assistance and tying such assistance to States falling in line with the Centre on economic reforms. More ominously, it has discarded the principle of State formation on the basis of linguistic nationality, and has been breaking up States to suit its own political interests. The CPI(M) notes: "The BJP wishes to create small States so that the Centre can dominate them. Small states with limited resources would mean weaker States incapable of resisting Central encroachment." Expressing its opposition to the break-up of linguistic States "which were formed after a powerful mass movement for democratising the state structure", the CPI(M) states: "The problems of national unity in a multi-lingual and multi-national country like India can be addressed and resolved only within the framework of a federal and secular polity which recognises and respects the diversities of our society and harnesses these forces for strengthening unity."

The CPI(M) notes that the Congress(I) and the BJP are wedded to the same liberalisation/privatisation/globalisation policies and rules out the possibility of any alliance or united front with the Congress(I). Although the Congress(I) is not a communal party like the BJP, it "displays vacillations" on the question of secularism. On the regional parties, the CPI(M)'s view is that while they vary in character "with some representing the regional bourgeoisie and landlords and articulating the linguistic/nationality aspirations of their State while others are caste-based", there has been a change in the outlook of regional parties. The political resolution notes: "They have changed their attitude to foreign capital and are favourable to the liberalisation policies..." Based on this assessment, the CPI(M) will take a "differentiated attitude" towards regional parties, cooperating with those which oppose communal forces and opposing those who join with the BJP. Where does this leave the CPI(M) in terms of political tactics and allies? The party says that it is "committed to strengthening and deepening Left unity" and that its key present task is to build a third alternative, a combination of non-Congress(I), non-BJP secular forces. The People's Front, consisting of the Left parties, the Samajwadi Party and the Rashtriya Janata Dal at the moment, is seen as "a partial expression of the immediate need for a third force".

In terms of its future direction, the CPI(M)'s main concern is how to strengthen its independent role and influence, in which respect it self-critically admits that it has not made much advance over a considerable period. While the third alternative represents an immediate need, the CPI(M) argues, basic policy and structural changes are needed to solve the problems facing the people and the country. It puts forward what it calls a Left and Democratic Alternative and calls for a radical land reforms programme; an economic policy framework based on self-reliance; more direct taxation of the well-to-do; promotion of small and medium non-monopoly industry; support for agricultural labour and the peasantry, especially the poor and middle peasants; regulation of capital flows and an end to the indiscriminate import liberalisation; selective use of foreign capital in line with chosen national priorities; commitment to secularism and federalism; democratisation of state structure and repeal of repressive laws; electoral reforms and proportional representation; protection of the rights of the working people; and sustainable development with caste and gender equality.

Given the current state of the Indian polity, it is refreshing to see a political party engage its own activists in a serious and self-critical discussion of its policies and programmes. However, the fact remains that the CPI(M) and the Left remain confined in terms of mass political strength to a few States, though in terms of population these States will surpass that of several sovereign nations put together. While the Left's and the CPI(M)'s political influence in the debates on the nation's agenda and priorities far exceed its numbers and geographical spread, it must surely be a matter of concern for the CPI(M) that its membership and that of the mass organisations led by it have grown rather slowly over the last decade. Admittedly, this was the decade that saw major setbacks to socialism in the collapse of the Soviet Union and the restoration of capitalism in Eastern Europe, and the rise of capitalist triumphalism. It is also true, as the CPI(M) says, that capitalism's record over the long haul shows that it is incapable of solving humanity's basic problems. However, the CPI(M) and other Left formations will need to engage in much deeper reflection to cope with the series of new challenges that have emerged, globally and in India, if the vision of a more progressive and humane social order is to be realised. In the interest of the Indian people and of working people all over the world, one can only wish that they succeed.

7

Gender Inequality in India

For several reasons India is an interesting country to study in the context of gender equality. Although China has a larger population, it is fair to say that India is the country in which the highest number of women suffer discrimination. India is also an example of failed attempts to implement pro-women policies. Since independence, the Indian government has imposed several laws to protect women, which for the most part have not been applied. Consequently, India has been named "a good example of a country with an abyssal gap between policy and practise" (Rhoodie, 1989). India is therefore a prime example to illustrate the limitations of a sound legal framework. Finally, India is characterised by the impact of religion on the status of women. In many cases, Hinduism (accounting for some 80% of the population) is more important than the officials laws and regulations. Similarly for the Muslim population the Islamic code is frequently the reference.

FAMILY CODE

The State has fought against child marriage since the 19th century and the legal age of marriage for girls has been raised continuously: from 12 in 1891, 14 in 1929, 15 in 1955, and finally to 18 in 1976. However, a high percentage of women married before the age of 20 shows that the law is not respected. An estimated 30 percent of girls between 15 and 19 years of age are currently married, divorced or widowed. What is more, in rural areas in the North, more than 50% of women are believed to be married even before the age of 15 (C. Morrisson 2004).

Polygamy is legal for Muslims and it also exists to some extent among Hindus, particularly in cases where the first wife has not given birth to any sons. Repudiation is also legal for Moslems. For persons of other religious believs, the divorce proceedings have been equal for men and women since 1976. Divorce by mutual consent is legal but in reality, any woman who initiates a divorce is condemned by the public opinion. For that reason, divorces are very rare. The father alone detains parental authority in Hindu and Muslim families. His authority is partially limited only in educated and urban families. In the event of divorce, the law assures some equality with regards to child custody, but any advantages granted to the mother in this aspect are rarely exercised as divorces are not common practice. The old Hindu traditions privileged men in matters of inheritance: only sons – not daughters - could inherit their parents. After independence, however, these traditions were abolished by law. But in the North, nothing has really changed and women are still deprived of inheritance. Contrary to laws passed by the Indian Union, several local states allow the exclusion of widows and daughters for land inheritance. The conditions for women are most favourable in the South, where the national laws tend to be respected more often. For the Muslim population, inheritance practices are discriminatory. A daughter, for example, inherits half as much as a son. This is commonly justified by the fact that a woman has no financial responsibility towards her husband and children.

PHYSICAL INTEGRITY

Violence against women is very frequent in India. Statistics show that wives are often the victim of domestic violence: in half the states, the percentages of women that are beaten by their husbands vary between 10% and 20%. The practise of dowry has been maintained and thousands of women are murdered every year by their husbands because the dowry is too low. An estimated 6000 women are killed every year. However, this figure most likely underestimates the reality as the majority of murders do not get registered. Selective abortions are more and more frequent in India, which explains a high percentage of missing women. Census data show that almost 40 million Indian women were missing in 2001. This practice is linked to an old tradition: during the past centuries, young girl killings were frequent. In 1870, the authorities prohibited this practice and demanded the registration of all births. But especially in rural areas, girl killings have continued and now, owing to technological progress, it is even getting easier to be sex-selective before birth. Moreover, when children are ill, the fathers prefer to pay treatment for sons than for daughters, so that more girls die.

CIVIL LIBERTIES

Women are not free to move in the villages of the North and suffer severe restriction of their movement in the South. In the North the tradition of the purdah prevails except in large towns: 80% to 85% of women do not have any freedom. Purdah imposes at the same time the veil and reclusion at home: the wife must ask permission to go to the village market or to visit friends.

Before the 10th century purdah did not exist. The Muslim invasion at that time lead the Hindu husbands to enforce this practise because they feared Muslims who imposed the purdah on their wives. But the purdah is less respected in large towns: in Delhi nearly half the women can move freely. In the South, Muslims ruled only for a short time during the 18th century. As a consequence, purdah affects less than half the women in this region. Restrictions on freedom of dress only affect 50-60% of women if the following facts are taken into account: in the villages of the North the obligation to wear of a veil and reclusion are always linked, but in the South the obligation of the veil is less frequent. On the other hand, freedom of dress prevails often in towns.

OWNERSHIP RIGHTS

In principle, several laws guarantee that women have access to property, including land. In the North, however, these laws are not respected. On average half the women may not even have access to money (e.g. they must ask their husbands for a small amount of money before going shopping). In these cases, women naturally do not have access to other forms of property as well, including credit. The situation is worse for land ownership which is always restricted to men. In the South, women can sometimes inherit land and frequently have access to money: between 70 and 80% according to surveys.

Seven Types of Inequality

IT was more than a century ago, in 1870, that Queen Victoria wrote to Sir Theodore Martin complaining about "this mad, wicked folly of 'Woman's Rights'." The formidable empress certainly did not herself need any protection that the acknowledgment of women's rights might offer. Even at the age of eighty, in 1899, she could write to A.J. Balfour, "We are not interested in the possibilities of defeat; they do not exist." That, however, is not the way most people's lives go - reduced and defeated as they frequently are by adversities. And within each community, nationality and class, the burden of hardship often falls disproportionately on women.

The afflicted world in which we live is characterised by deeply unequal sharing of the burden of adversities between women and men. Gender inequality exists in most parts of the world, from Japan to Morocco, from Uzbekistan to the United States of America. However, inequality between women and men can take very many different forms. Indeed, gender inequality is not one homogeneous phenomenon, but a collection of disparate and interlinked problems. Let me illustrate with examples of different kinds of disparity.

(1) Mortality inequality: In some regions in the world, inequality between women and men directly involves matters of life and death, and takes the brutal form of unusually high mortality rates of women and a consequent preponderance of men in the total population, as opposed to the preponderance of women found in societies with little or no gender bias in health care and nutrition. Mortality inequality has been observed extensively in North Africa and in Asia, including China and South Asia.

(2) Natality inequality: Given a preference for boys over girls that many male-dominated societies have, gender inequality can manifest itself in the form of the parents wanting the newborn to be a boy rather than a girl. There was a time when this could be no more than a wish (a daydream or a nightmare, depending on one's perspective), but with the availability of modern techniques to determine the gender of the foetus, sex-

selective abortion has become common in many countries. It is particularly prevalent in East Asia, in China and South Korea in particular, but also in Singapore and Taiwan, and it is beginning to emerge as a statistically significant phenomenon in India and South Asia as well. This is high-tech sexism.

(3) Basic facility inequality: Even when demographic characteristics do not show much or any anti-female bias, there are other ways in which women can have less than a square deal. Afghanistan may be the only country in the world the government of which is keen on actively excluding girls from schooling (it combines this with other features of massive gender inequality), but there are many countries in Asia and Africa, and also in Latin America, where girls have far less opportunity of schooling than boys do. There are other deficiencies in basic facilities available to women, varying from encouragement to cultivate one's natural talents to fair participation in rewarding social functions of the community.

(4) Special opportunity inequality: Even when there is relatively little difference in basic facilities including schooling, the opportunities of higher education may be far fewer for young women than for young men. Indeed, gender bias in higher education and professional training can be observed even in some of the richest countries in the world, in Europe and North America. Sometimes this type of division has been based on the superficially innocuous idea that the respective "provinces" of men and women are just different. This thesis has been championed in different forms over the centuries, and has had much implicit as well as explicit following. It was presented with particular directness more than a hundred years before Queen Victoria's complaint about "woman's rights" by the Revd James Fordyce in his Sermons to Young Women (1766), a book which, as Mary Wollstonecraft noted in her A Vindication of the Rights of Women (1792), had been "long made a part of woman's library." Fordyce warned the young women, to whom his sermons were addressed, against "those

masculine women that would plead for your sharing any part of their province with us," identifying the province of men as including not only "war," but also "commerce, politics, exercises of strength and dexterity, abstract philosophy and all the abstruser sciences." Even though such clear-cut beliefs about the provinces of men and women are now rather rare, nevertheless the presence of extensive gender asymmetry can be seen in many areas of education, training and professional work even in Europe and North America.

(5) Professional inequality: In terms of employment as well as promotion in work and occupation, women often face greater handicap than men. A country like Japan may be quite egalitarian in matters of demography or basic facilities, and even, to a great extent, in higher education, and yet progress to elevated levels of employment and occupation seems to be much more problematic for women than for men. In the English television series called "Yes, Minister," there is an episode where the Minister, full of reforming zeal, is trying to find out from the immovable permanent secretary, Sir Humphrey, how many women are in really senior positions in the British civil service. Sir Humphrey says that it is very difficult to give an exact number; it would require a lot of investigation. The Minister is still insistent, and wants to know approximately how many women are there in these senior positions. To which Sir Humphrey finally replies, "Approximately, none."

(6) Ownership inequality: In many societies the ownership of property can also be very unequal. Even basic assets such as homes and land may be very asymmetrically shared. The absence of claims to property can not only reduce the voice of women, but also make it harder for women to enter and flourish in commercial, economic and even some social activities. This type of inequality has existed in most parts of the world, though there are also local variations. For example, even though traditional property rights have favoured men in the bulk of India, in what is now the State of Kerala, there

has been, for a long time, matrilineal inheritance for an influential part of the community, namely the Nairs.

(7) Household inequality: There are, often enough, basic inequalities in gender relations within the family or the household, which can take many different forms. Even in cases in which there are no overt signs of anti-female bias in, say, survival or son-preference or education, or even in promotion to higher executive positions, the family arrangements can be quite unequal in terms of sharing the burden of housework and child care. It is, for example, quite common in many societies to take it for granted that while men will naturally work outside the home, women could do it if and only if they could combine it with various inescapable and unequally shared household duties. This is sometimes called "division of labour," though women could be forgiven for seeing it as "accumulation of labour." The reach of this inequality includes not only unequal relations within the family, but also derivative inequalities in employment and recognition in the outside world. Also, the established fixity of this type of "division" or "accumulation" of labour can also have far-reaching effects on the knowledge and understanding of different types of work in professional circles. When I first started working on gender inequality, in the 1970s, I remember being struck by the fact that the Handbook of Human Nutrition Requirement of the World Health Organisation (WHO), in presenting "calorie requirements" for different categories of people, chose to classify household work as "sedentary activity," requiring very little deployment of energy. I was, however, not able to determine precisely how this remarkable bit of information had been collected by the patrician leaders of society.

FOCUSSING ON SOUTH ASIA

It is important to take note of the variety of forms that gender inequality can take. First, inequality between women and men cannot be confronted and overcome by any one set of all-purpose remedy. Second, over time the same country can move from one type of gender inequality to harbouring other forms of that inequity. I shall presently argue that there is new evidence that India is undergoing just such a transformation right at this time. Third, the different forms of gender inequality can impose diverse adversities on the lives of men and boys, in addition to those of women and girls. In understanding the different aspects of the evil of gender inequality, we have to look beyond the predicament of women and examine the problems created for men as well by the asymmetric treatment of women. These causal connections, which (as I shall presently illustrate) can be very significant, can vary with the form of gender inequality. Finally, inequalities of different kinds can also, frequently enough, feed each other, and we have to be aware of their interlinkages.

Even though part of the object of this paper is to discuss the variety of different types of gender inequality, a substantial part of my empirical focus will, in fact, be on two of the most elementary kinds of gender inequality, namely, mortality inequality and natality inequality. I shall be concerned, in particular, with gender inequality in South Asia, or the Indian subcontinent. While I shall separate out the subcontinent for special attention, I must also warn against the smugness of thinking that the United States or Western Europe is free from gender bias simply because some of the empirical generalisations that can be made about the subcontinent would not hold in the West. Given the many faces of gender inequality, much would depend on which face we look at.

For example, India, along with Bangladesh, Pakistan and Sri Lanka, has had female heads of governments, which the United States or Japan has not yet had (and does not seem very likely to have in the immediate future, if I am any judge). Indeed, in the case of Bangladesh, where both the Prime Minister and the Leader of the Opposition are women, one might begin to wonder whether any man could possibly rise to a leadership position there in the near future. To take another example, I had a vastly larger proportion of tenured women colleagues. To take another type of example (of a rather personal kind), in preparing my last book, Development as Freedom, when I was looking for a suitably early formulation of the contrast between the instrumental importance of income and wealth, on the one hand, and the intrinsic value of human life, on the other (a point of departure for my book), I found it in the words of Maitreyee, a woman intellectual depicted in the Upanishads (from the eighth century B.C.).

The classic formulation of this distinction would, of course, come about four centuries later, from Aristotle, in Nicomachean Ethics, but it is interesting that the first sharp formulation of the value of living for men and women should have come from a woman thinker in a society that has not yet - three thousand years later - been able to overcome the mortality differential between women and men. Indeed, in the scale of mortality inequality, India - as well as Pakistan and Bangladesh - is close to the bottom of the league in gender disparity. And, as I shall presently argue, natality inequality is also beginning to rear its ugly head very firmly and very fast right at this time in the subcontinent.

EXCEPTIONS AND TRENDS

In the bulk of the subcontinent, with only a few exceptions (such as Sri Lanka and the State of Kerala in India), female mortality rates are very significantly higher than what could be expected given the mortality patterns of men (in the respective age groups).

This type of gender inequality need not entail any conscious homicide, and it would be a mistake to try to explain this large phenomenon by invoking the occasional cases of female infanticide that are reported from China or India; these are truly dreadful events when they occur, but they are relatively rare. Rather, the mortality disadvantage of women works mainly through a widespread neglect of health, nutrition and other interests of women that influence survival.

It is sometimes presumed that there are more women than men in the world, since that is well-known to be the case in Europe and North America, which have a female to male ratio of 1.05 or so, on the average (that is, about 105 women per 100 men). But women do not outnumber men in the world as a whole; indeed there are only about 98 women per 100 men on the globe. This "shortfall" of women is most acute in Asia and North Africa. For example, the number of females per 100 males in the total population is 97 in Egypt and Iran, 95 in

Bangladesh and Turkey, 94 in China, 93 in India and Pakistan, and 84 in Saudi Arabia (though the last ratio is considerably reduced by the presence of male migrant workers from elsewhere who come to Saudi Arabia).

It has been widely observed that given similar health care and nutrition, women tend typically to have lower age-specific mortality rates than men do. Indeed, even female foetuses tend to have a lower probability of miscarriage than male foetuses have. Everywhere in the world, more male babies are born than female babies (and an even higher proportion of male foetuses are conceived compared with female foetuses), but throughout their respective lives the proportion of males goes on falling as we move to higher and higher age groups, due to typically greater male mortality rates. The excess of females over males in the population of Europe and North America comes about as a result of this greater survival chance of females in different age groups.

However, in many parts of the world, women receive less attention and health care than men do, and particularly girls often receive very much less support than boys. As a result of this gender bias, the mortality rates of females often exceed those of males in these countries. The concept of "missing women" was devised to give some idea of the enormity of the phenomenon of women's adversity in mortality by focusing on the women who are simply not there, due to unusually high mortality compared with male mortality rates. The basic idea is to find some rough and ready way to understand the quantitative difference between (1) the actual number of women in these countries, and (2) the number we could expect to see if the gender pattern of mortality were similar in these countries as in other regions of the world that do not have a significant bias against women in terms of health care and other attentions relevant for survival.

For example, if we take the ratio of women to men in sub-Saharan Africa as the standard (there is relatively little bias against women in terms of health care, social status and mortality rates in sub-Saharan Africa, even though the absolute numbers are quite dreadful for both men and women), then its female-male ratio of 1.022 can be used to calculate the number of missing women in women-short countries.

For example, with India's female-male ratio of 0.93, there is a total difference of 9 per cent (of the male population) between that ratio and the standard used for comparison, namely, the sub-Saharan African ratio of 1.022. This yielded a figure of 37 million missing women already in 1986 (when I first did the estimation). Using the same sub-Saharan standard, China had 44 million missing women, and it was evident that for the world as a whole the magnitude of shortfall easily exceeded 100 million. Other standards and different procedures can also be used, as has been done by Ansley Coale and Stephan Klasen, getting somewhat different numbers, but invariably very large ones (Klasen's total number is about 80 million missing women). Gender bias in mortality does take an astonishingly heavy toll.

How can this be reversed? Some economic models have tended to relate the neglect of women to the lack of economic empowerment of women. While Ester Boserup, an early feminist economist, discussed how the status and standing of women are enhanced by economic independence (such as gainful employment), others have tried to link the neglect of girls to the higher economic returns for the family from boys compared with girls. I believe the former line of reasoning, which takes fuller note of social considerations that take us beyond any hard-headed calculation of relative returns from rearing girls vis-a-vis boys, is both appropriately broader and more promising, but no matter which interpretation is taken, women's gainful employment, especially in more rewarding occupations, clearly does play a role in improving the deal that women and girls get. And so does women's literacy, and other factors that can be seen as adding to the status, standing and voice of women in family decisions. An example that has been discussed in this context is the experience of the State of Kerala in India, which provides a sharp contrast with many other parts of the country in having little or no gender bias in mortality.

Indeed, not only is the life expectancy of Kerala women at birth above 76 (compared with 70 for men), the female-male ratio of Kerala's population is 1.06 according to the 2001 Census (possibly somewhat raised by greater migration for work by men, but certainly no lower than the West European or North American ratios, which are around 1.05 or so). With its 30 million population, Kerala's example also involves a fair number of people. The causal variables related to women's empowerment can be seen as playing a role here, since Kerala has a very high level of women's literacy (nearly universal for the younger age groups), and also much more access for women to well paid and well respected jobs.

One of the other influences of women's empowerment, namely a fertility decline, is also observed in Kerala, where the fertility rate has fallen very fast (much faster, incidentally, than China, despite the rigours of Chinese coercive measures in birth control), and Kerala's present fertility rate around 1.7 or 1.8 (roughly interpretable as an average of 1.7 or 1.8 children per couple) is one of the lowest in the developing world (about the same as in Britain and France, and much lower than in the United States). All these observations link with each other very well in a harmonious causal story.

However, there is further need for causal discrimination in interpreting Kerala's experience.

There are other special features of Kerala which may also be relevant, such as female ownership of property for an influential part of the Hindu population (the Nairs), openness to and interaction with the outside world (with the presence of Christians - about a fifth of the population - who have been much longer in Kerala - since around the fourth century - than they have been in, say, Britain, not to mention Jews who came to Kerala shortly after the fall of Jerusalem), and activist left-wing politics with a particularly egalitarian commitment, which has tended to focus strongly on issues of equity (not only between classes and castes, but also between women and men).

ISSUES THAT NEED INVESTIGATION

We begin by noting four substantial phenomena that happen to be quite widely observed in South Asia.

(1) Undernourishment of girls over boys: At the time of birth, girls are obviously no more nutritionally deprived than boys are, but this situation changes as society's unequal treatment takes over from nature's non-discrimination. There has, in fact, been plenty of aggregative evidence on this for quite some time now.

But this has been accompanied by some anthropological scepticism of the appropriateness of using aggregate statistics with pooled data from different regions to interpret the behaviour of individual families. However, there have also been some detailed and concretely local studies on this subject, which confirm the picture that emerges on the basis of aggregate statistics. One case study from India, involved the weighing of every child in two large villages. The time pattern that emerged from this micro study, which concentrated particularly on weight-for-age as the chosen indicator of nutritional level for children under five, brings out clearly how an initial condition of broad nutritional symmetry turns gradually into a situation of significant female disadvantage. The detailed local studies tend to confirm rather than contradict the picture that emerges from aggregate statistics.

In interpreting the causal process, it is important to emphasise that the lower level of nourishment of girls may not relate directly to their being underfed vis-a-vis boys. Often enough, the differences may particularly arise from the neglect of health care of girls compared with what boys get. There is, in fact, some direct information of comparative medical neglect of girls vis-a-vis boys in South Asia. Indeed, when one studied, admissions data from two large public hospitals in Bombay (Mumbai), it was very striking to find clear evidence that the admitted girls were typically more ill than boys, suggesting the inference that a girl has to be more stricken before she is taken to the hospital. Undernourishment may well result from greater morbidity, which can adversely affect both the absorption of nutrients and the performance of bodily functions.

(2) High incidence of maternal undernourishment: In South Asia maternal undernutrition is more common than in most other regions of the world. Comparisons of Body Mass Index (BMI), which is essentially a measure of weight for height, bring this out clearly enough, as do statistics of such consequential characteristics as the incidence of anaemia.

(3) Prevalence of low birthweight: In South Asia, as many as 21 per cent of children are born clinically underweight (in accepted medical standards) - more than in any other substantial region in the world.. The predicament of being low in weight in childhood seems often enough to begin at birth in the case of South Asian children. In terms of weight for age, South Asia has around 40 to 60 per cent children undernourished compared with 20 to 40 per cent undernourishment even in sub-Saharan Africa. The children start deprived and stay deprived.

(4) High incidence of cardiovascular diseases: South Asia stands out as having more cardiovascular diseases than any other part of the third world. Even when other countries, such as China, have greater prevalence of the standard predisposing conditions, the Indian population seems to have more heart problems than these other countries have.

It is not difficult to see that the first three observations are very likely causally connected. The neglect of the care of girls and of women in general and the underlying gender bias that they reflect would tend to yield more maternal undernourishment, and through that more foetal deprivation and distress, underweight babies, and child undernourishment. But what about the last observation - the higher incidence of cardiovascular diseases among South Asian adults? On some pioneering work of a British medical team, led by Professor D.J.P. Barker. Based on English data, Barker has shown that low birth weight is closely associated with higher incidence, many decades later, of several adult diseases, including hypertension, glucose intolerance, and other cardiovascular hazards. The robustness of the statistical connections as well as the causal mechanisms involved in intrauterine growth retardation can, of course, be further investigated, but as matters stand these medical findings offer a possibility of causally interconnecting the different empirical observations related to South Asia, tried to discuss in a joint paper with Siddiq Osmani. The application of this medical understanding to the phenomenon of high incidence of cardiovascular diseases in South Asia strongly suggests a causal pattern that goes from the nutritional neglect of women to maternal undernourishment, from there to foetal growth retardation and underweight babies, and thence to greater incidence of cardiovascular afflictions much later in adult life (along with the phenomenon of undernourished children in the shorter run). What begins as a neglect of the interests of women ends up causing adversities in the health and survival of all - even at an advanced age. Given the uniquely critical role of women in the reproductive process, it would be hard to imagine that the deprivation to which women are subjected would not have some adverse impact on the lives of all - men as well as women and adults as well as children - who are "born of a woman" (as the Book of Job describes every person, not particularly daringly). Indeed, since men suffer disproportionately more from cardiovascular diseases, the suffering of women hit men even harder, in this respect. The extensive penalties of neglecting women's interests rebounds, it appears, on men with a vengeance.

WHAT WOMEN'S AGENCY CAN ACHIEVE

These biological connections illustrate a more general point, to wit, gender inequality can hurt the interests of men as well as women. There are other - non-biological - connections that operate through women's conscious agency. The expansion of women's capabilities not only enhances women's own freedom and well-being, but also has many other effects on the lives of all. An enhancement of women's active agency can, in many circumstances, contribute substantially to the lives of all people- men as well as women, children as well as adults. As many studies have brought out, the greater empowerment of women tends to reduce child neglect and mortality, cut down fertility and overcrowding, and more generally, broaden social concern and care. These illustrations can be supplemented by considering the functioning of women in other areas, including in economic and political fields. Substantial linkages between women's agency and social achievements have been noted in many different countries.

There is, for example, plenty of evidence that whenever social and economic arrangements depart from the standard practice of male ownership, women can seize business and economic initiative with much success. It is also clear that the result of women's participation is not merely to generate income for women, but also to provide many other social benefits that come from women's enhanced status and independence. The remarkable success of organisations like the Grameen Bank and the Bangladesh Rural Advancement Committee (BRAC) in Bangladesh is a good example of this, and there is some evidence that the high profile presence of women in social and political life in that country has drawn substantial support from women's economic involvement and from a changed image of the role of women. While the Revd James Fordyce might disapprove of "those masculine women," as he called them, straying into men's "province," the nature of modern Bangladesh reflects in many different ways the increasing agency of women. The precipitate fall of the total fertility rate in Bangladesh from 6.1 to 3.0 in the course of two decades (perhaps the fastest such fall in the world) is clearly related to the changed economic and social roles of women, along with increases in family planning facilities. There have also been cultural influences and developments in that direction. Similar changes can be observed also in parts of India where women's empowerment has expanded, with more literacy and greater economic and social involvements outside the home.

BEHIND A SPLIT INDIA

While there is something to cheer in the developments I have just been discussing, and there is considerable evidence of a weakened hold of gender disparity in several fields in the subcontinent, there is also, alas, some evidence of a movement in the contrary direction, at least in one aspect of gender inequality, namely, natality inequality. This has been brought out particularly sharply by the early results of the 2001 decennial national Census of India, which are now available. Early results indicate that even though the overall female to male ratio has improved slightly for the country as a whole (with a corresponding reduction of the proportion of "missing women"), the female-male ratio for children has had a substantial decline. For India as a whole, the female-male ratio of the population under age 6 has fallen from 94.5 girls for hundred boys in 1991 to 92.7 girls per hundred boys in 2001. While there has been no such decline in some parts of the country (most notably Kerala), it has fallen very sharply in others, such as Punjab,

Haryana, Gujarat and Maharashtra, which are among the richer Indian States.

Taking together all the evidence that exists, it is clear that this change reflects not a rise in female child mortality, but a fall in female births vis-a-vis male births, and is almost certainly connected with increased availability and use of gender determination of foetuses. Fearing that sex-selective abortion might occur in India, the Indian Parliament banned some years ago the use of sex determination techniques for foetuses, except when it is a by-product of other necessary medical investigation. But it appears that the enforcement of this law has been comprehensively neglected, and when questioned by Celia Dugger, the energetic correspondent of The New York Times, the police often cited difficulties in achieving successful prosecution thanks to the reluctance of mothers to give evidence of use of such techniques.

We do not believe that this need be an insurmountable difficulty (other types of evidence can in fact be used for prosecution), but the reluctance of the mothers to give evidence brings out perhaps the most disturbing aspect of this natality inequality, to wit, the "son preference" that many Indian mothers themselves seem to have. This face of gender inequality cannot, therefore, be removed, at least in the short run, by the enhancement of women's empowerment and agency, since that agency is itself an integral part of the cause of natality inequality. Policy initiatives have to take adequate note of the fact that the pattern of gender inequality seems to be shifting in India, right at this time, from mortality inequality (the female life expectancy at birth is by now two years higher than male life expectancy in India) to natality inequality.

Indeed, there is clear evidence that traditional routes of changing gender inequality, through using public policy to influence female education and female economic participation, may not serve as a path to the removal of natality inequality. A sharp pointer in that direction comes from countries in East Asia, which all have high levels of female education and economic participation. Despite these achievements, compared with the biologically common ratio across the world of 95 girls being born per hundred boys, Singapore and Taiwan have 92 girls, South Korea only 88, and China a mere 86. In fact, South

Korea's overall female-male ratio for children is also a meagre 88 girls for 100 boys and China's 85 girls for 100 boys. In comparison, the Indian ratio of 92.7 girls for 100 boys (though lower than its previous figure of 94.5) still looks far less unfavourable.

However, there are more grounds for concern than may be suggested by the current all-India average. First, there are substantial variations within India, and the all-India average hides the fact that there are States in India where the female-male ratio for children is very much lower than the Indian average. Second, it has to be asked whether with the spread of sex-selective abortion, India may catch up with - and perhaps even go beyond - Korea and China. There is, in fact, strong evidence that this is happening in a big way in parts of the country.

There is, however, something of a social and cultural divide across India, splitting the country into two nearly contiguous halves, in the extent of anti-female bias in natality and post-natality mortality. Since more boys are born than girls everywhere in the world, even without sex-specific abortion, we can use as a classificatory benchmark the female-male ratio among children in advanced industrial countries. The female-male ratio for the 0-5 age group is 94.8 in Germany, 95.0 in the U.K., and 95.7 in the U.S., and perhaps we can sensibly pick the German ratio of 94.8 as the cut-off point below which we should suspect anti-female intervention.

The use of this dividing line produces a remarkable geographical split of India. There are the States in the north and the west where the female-male ratio of children is consistently below the benchmark figure, led by Punjab, Haryana, Delhi and Gujarat (with ratios between 79.3 and 87.8), and also including, among others, Himachal Pradesh, Madhya Pradesh, Rajasthan, Uttar Pradesh, Maharashtra, Jammu and Kashmir, and Bihar (a tiny exception is Dadra and Nagar Haveli, with less than a quarter million people altogether). On the other side of the divide, the States in the east and the south tend to have female-male ratios that are above the benchmark line of 94.8 girls per 100 boys: with Kerala, Andhra Pradesh, West Bengal and Assam (each between 96.3 and 96.6), and also, among others, Orissa, Karnataka and the northeastern States to the east of Bangladesh (Meghalaya, Mizoram, Manipur, Nagaland, Arunachal Pradesh).

One significant exception to this neat pattern of adjoining division is, however, provided by Tamil Nadu, where the female-male ratio is just below 94, which is higher than the ratio of any State in the deficit list, but still just below the cut-off line used for the partitioning (94.8). The astonishing finding is not that one particular State seems to provide a marginal misfit, but how the vast majority of the Indian States fall firmly into two contiguous halves, classified broadly into the north and the west, on one side, and the south and the east, on the other. Indeed, every State in the north and the west (with the slight exception of the tiny Union Territory of Dadra and Nagar Haveli) has strictly lower female-male ratio of children than every State in the east and the south (even Tamil Nadu fits into this classification), and this indeed is quite remarkable.

The pattern of female-male ratio of children produces a much sharper regional classification than does the female-male ratio of mortality of children, even though the two are also fairly strongly correlated. The female-male ratio in child mortality varies between 0.91 in West Bengal and 0.93 in Kerala, on one side, in the southern and eastern group, to 1.30 in Punjab, Haryana and Uttar Pradesh, with high ratios also in Gujarat, Bihar and Rajasthan, in the northern and western group.

The north and the west have clear characteristics of anti-female bias in a way that is not present - or at least not yet visible - in most of the east and the south. This contrast does not have any immediate economic explanation. The States with anti-female bias include rich ones (Punjab and Haryana) as well as poor States (Madhya Pradesh and Uttar Pradesh), and fast-growing States (Gujarat and Maharashtra) as well as growth failures (Bihar and Uttar Pradesh). Also, the incidence of sex-specific abortions cannot be explained by the availability of medical resources for determining the sex of the foetus: Kerala and West Bengal in the non-deficit list, both with the ratio of 96.3 girls to 100 boys (comfortably higher than the benchmark cut-off of 94.8), have at least as much medical facilities as in such deficit States as Madhya Pradesh or Rajasthan. If commercial facilities for sex-selected abortion are infrequent in Kerala or West Bengal, it is because of a low demand for those specific services, rather than any great supply side barrier.

This suggests that we have to look beyond economic resources or material prosperity or GNP growth into broadly cultural and social influences. There are a variety of potential connections to be considered here, and the linking of these demographic features with the rich subject matter of social anthropology and cultural studies would certainly be important to pursue. There is perhaps a common link with politics as well. Indeed, it has been noted, in other contexts, that the States in the north and the west have, by and large, given much more room to religion-based sectarian politics than have the east or the south, where religion-centred parties have had very little success. For example, of the 197 members of Parliament from the Bharatiya Janata Party (BJP) and the Shiv Sena elected in 1999, as many 169 won from States in the north and the west. Even if we take out the BJP members who, though elected from Bihar or Madhya Pradesh, come from the recently formed relatively "eastern" States of Jharkhand and Chhatisgarh (which, incidentally, do have "eastern" female-male ratios above the benchmark line), the predominance of the north and the west in the representation of the Sangh Parivar remains strong. It is not easy to settle, without further scrutiny, how significant these regional, cultural or political associations are, and how (and even in which direction) the causal influences operate. But the remarkable geographical division of India into two largely contiguous parts in terms of female-male ratio among children (reflecting the combined influence of inequality in natality and post-natal mortality) does call for acknowledgement and further analysis. It would also be important to keep a close watch on whether the incidence of sex-specific abortions will significantly increase in States in which they are at this time quite uncommon.

GENDER EQUALITY AND ECONOMIC GROWTH: COMPETING HYPOTHESES

A final set of studies, which take a macro-level approach to gender analysis, are based on cross-country and, in some cases, time series comparisons. Their findings have been somewhat varied and often conflicting. Some suggest a positive relationship between gender inequality and economic growth. Seguino, for example, found that gender inequality in wages led to higher levels of economic growth while another study found that high levels of gender inequality in secondary education had a similar effect. On the other hand, Dollar and Gatti found that: (a) gender equality in education and legal rights led to an increase in per capita economic growth; and (b) increases in per capita GNP led to increases in equality for women. Similarly, a study found that gender inequalities had a significant negative impact on economic growth.

The 'positive synergy' hypothesis: The study by Dollar and Gatti is one of the few of its kind that explores both the effects of gender inequality on economic growth and, conversely, the effects of economic growth on gender inequality. It also includes a measure of gender equality of rights and looks at social as well as economic variables. It found that:

- Economic growth only affected gender inequality when countries moved from lower middle income to higher income levels;
- Muslim and Hindu majority populations had higher levels of gender inequality for most of the measures used; and
- Japan had higher levels of gender inequality than other countries at similar levels of per capita GNP, except in relation to secondary education.

A second set of findings found that female educational attainment – mainly measured by secondary education – had a positive effect on economic growth. The effects of both male and female education on per capita income were low for less developed countries where female secondary attainment covered less than 10 per cent of the population. Once countries had achieved a certain level of female education, however, an increase of 1 per cent in the share of women with secondary school education implied a 0.3 per cent increase in per capita income. The authors suggest that the absence of a relationship between gender equality in education and economic growth in poor, primarily agrarian economies is due to the limited returns that female secondary education brings. There is little reason to invest in it if men have preferred access to types of employment for which secondary education is a qualification. Certain aspects of the study will be returned to in the course of the discussion in the rest of this book:

1. Gender equality has a positive effect on per capita economic growth once a certain stage of development has been reached. Thus the growth-based rationale for reducing the gender gap in education in poorer countries is in terms of long-run rather than immediate returns.
2. Regional as well as religious differences are important sources of variation in the relationships between gender equality and economic growth.
3. While the focus on education as a measure of inequality reflects the increasing importance given to 'human capital' in the international development agenda, 'capital' can also include material and financial resources and social relationships and networks. Gender inequalities in access to credit, land, wages, capital equipment and trade networks may be more relevant for economic growth in poorer countries than inequalities in education or even formal rights.
4. It is crucial to distinguish between intrinsic and instrumental arguments for policies relating to gender inequality.

The trade-off hypothesis: Seguino's study focused on the relationship between gender inequality and economic growth in the context of export- oriented industrialisation. It looked at the relationship between economic growth and gender inequality in wages. Her sample was drawn from lower and middle-income countries (as defined by the 1995 *World Development Report*).

The findings from the cross-country analysis suggested that, along with levels of human capital and investment, inequality in male and female wages was positively associated with economic growth. A 10-point increase in the gap between male and female returns per year of secondary education was seen to raise GDP growth by .10 per cent. Or to put it another way, 4 percentage points of the gap between the rate of GDP growth in the Republic of Korea (9.2%) and Costa Rica (3.9%)

between 1985 and 1989 could be explained by the gender wage gap. The results from the time-varying country specific analysis confirm the significance of investment as well as human capital, but suggest that female educational attainment has a more significant effect than male. The wage gap variables remain significant.

Gender disparities in wages were found to increase levels of investment. The study concludes that gender inequality in returns to labour have led to higher rates of growth in countries that have relied on export-oriented industrialisation.

Seguino notes that the gender disparities in earnings are only partly related to a country's GNP. Other factors that play a role include policy regimes as well as the 'gender regimes' prevailing in different countries. It is striking that of the Asian countries for which she provides data, three of the four fast-growing 'miracle' economies, all East Asian, report the largest gender disparities in earnings (Republic of Korea, Singapore and Taiwan). However, it also suggests that economic growth is likely to be higher in this set of countries if investments in female education co-exist with greater gender disparities in wages.

Overall, Dollar and Gatti's findings provide support for gender equality on 'efficiency' grounds and for greater economic growth on equity grounds. Seguino's findings suggest that there may be a trade-off between gender equality and economic growth due to the intensified competition unleashed by globalisation. However, the findings clearly need to be explored further through more detailed analysis at the country level.

DEFINING SEX AND GENDER

Sociologists have traditionally differentiated the terms sex and gender to emphasise the social dimensions of gender relations. *Sex,* used to refer to one's biological identity as male or female, is not necessarily the same *as gender*—the socially learned behaviours and expectations associated with members of each sex. Normally, humans are born as either male or female, but learn to become masculine or feminine. For example, studies of newborn infants have found that, even controlling for objective measures such as size, parents describe their girl babies as softer, smaller, and less attentive, while parents of boys describe them as strong and alert. The distinction between sex and gender, like the distinction between biology and culture, is not a perfect one, but it emphasises that gender is a cultural, not a biological, category. Social expectations pattern male and female behavior and, often, what men and women expect of themselves. In addition, because social institution are organised around gender inequality, the system of gender relations also patterns one's life chances and directs men's and women's social, economic, and political experiences.

The societal system of gender relations affects us on different levels, including individual subjectivity, social interaction, and institutional structures. At the level of individual subjectivity, gender expectations can influence our sell definition, including our sense of competency, our self-esteem, and our emotional state of mind. For example, women who internalise traditional expectations of femininity may become dependent on men for their sense of self-worth. It is important to note, however, that not all persons, men or women, internalise sex-typed expectations to the same extent. In fact, rejection of gender expectations can be a source of resistance to the oppressive limitations imposed by traditional gender expectations.

At the second level of societal experience, that of social interaction, gender relations are easy to observe. Gender structures the social interaction of groups. Consider the example of touching. Research on patterns of touch indicates that men touch women more often and on more different parts of the body than women touch men. Differences in oral communication, too, can be observed by sex. Researchers have pointed out women "work" more in conversations with men, meaning that they make more effort to keep the conversation going even though they have less control over what the conversation is about. And studies of male-female conversations show that men interrupt women more often than vice versa, and that, in mixed sex groups, men spend more time talking than do women, despite sexist images to the contrary. Since it is higher status people who are given more license to touch, interrupt, and dominate those of lower status, these patterns are indicatiye of the power relations between men and women in society.

Finally, at the social structural level gender patterns the distribution of privileges and the organisation of institutions.

In education, for example, the majority of elementary school teachers are women, but the higher one moves in the educational system, the more likely it is that the teachers will be men. Not only do women receive fewer rewards, in terms of earnings and prestige, for the work they do as teachers, but the inequality conveys the misleading message that men make better educational leaders. Patterns of gender relations in public institutions also interest with gender relations in families. So, for example, the assumption that men are responsible for family earning while women ate responsible for child care creates many strains for families since institutional supports for men to be more involved in child care are lacking, as is adequate day care for employed patents.

How does gender come to be so significant in social organisation? From birth we begin to learn the significance of gender in how we will think of ourselves, what others will think of us, and what our opportunities in life may be. Gender influences most aspects of our lives, including our health,- attitudes, friendship patterns, and earning potential, to name just a few. Gender is so significant in structuring social relations that many people think that gender differences stem from biological differences between the sexes. But the idea that gender differences are social, not natural, in their origins is central to the sociological perspective.

BIOLOGY AND CULTURE

The belief that "biology is destiny" is a long-standing claim that, though it has little basis in fact, has influenced cultural beliefs about men's and women's abilities and character, and it continues to influence public concepts of gender inequality. For example, claims that women do less well than men in quantitative reasoning, though largely unsubstantiated by research studies, discourage many women from pursuing studies in mathematics and statistics. The idea that male hormones make men more aggressive, though also scientifically questionable, is popular and indicates that men, as well as women, are stereotyped by biologically determinist arguments.

Biological determinism and *biological reductionism* are theories that attribute gender differences to biological causes. A reductionist argument is one that reduces a complex event to a single cause. One example is the claim that women's capacity to bear children is the basis for their social status. A determinist argument is one that assumes that a given condition (for example, the presence of male hormones) inevitably produces a given result. Explaining sex differences as natural and inevitable consequences of biological differences between the sexes is both a biologically reductionist and determinist argument. Such arguments assume that one's biological nature is more significant than one's social experience in determining social identities and social privileges.

What is the reliable scientific evidence for biological differences between the sexes? While many biologically based claims have been made, one of the most common is the assumption that differences in aggression between men and women are caused by differences in the sex hormones. To begin with, research does not find consistent differences in levels of aggression between boys and girls or men and women. Furthermore, aggression is not consistently defined, either in the research literature or in people's minds. But suppose that we assume that boys are more aggressive than girls at an early age. Can this be attributed to differences in their sex hormones? After puberty, males do produce greater amounts of testosterone while in females the ovaries secrete additional estrogens and progestins. However, before puberty there are few or no differences in the sex hormones produced in either sex since all of the sex hormones are at very low levels. It is only logical to conclude that sex hormones explain little about observed differences between the sexes in the prepubescent period. Moreover, following menopause, women actually have lower levels of the so-called female hormones (estrogen and progestin) than do men; few have argued that older women are therefore less feminine than older men. And neither chemical castration of human beings nor actual castration of male rhesus monkeys results in a consistent reduction of male aggression. Taken together, we can conclude that hormonal influences are a poor explanation of observed social differences between the sexes.

Sexually dimorphic traits are those that appear in different frequencies between males and females. They include physical as well as social and cultural differences; for example, height is a sexually dimorphic trait since, among human beings, men tend to be taller than women. But, sexually dimorphic traits are not precise differences between the sexes. For most sexually dimorphic traits, variation within a sex group is greater than the variation across groups. Body weight provides an example. While, on the average, men weigh more than women, weight differences among men and among women exceed the weight difference between men and women as separate groups. Thus, while weight may be a sexually dimorphic trait, the difference may not be found among any given male-female pair.

Biological explanations of gender inequality assume that human biology is a fixed entity that does not change in response to social circumstances. Biological researchers know that this is not true. Even the simplest physical traits such as body size, weight, and height are known to be strongly influenced by the environment. More complex traits, such as intelligence and strength, are also strongly conditioned by environmental factors. Even those traits thought to have a genetic basis cannot be said to be solely genetically caused, since most genetic traits are known to interact with the environment in which they are found.

Studies of hermaphrodites clearly demonstrate that genetic sex identity does not by itself determine one's masculine or feminine identity. *Hermaphroditism* is a "condition of prenatal origin in which embryonic and/or fetal differentiation of the reproductive system fails to reach completion as either entirely female or entirely male." In cases of hermaphroditism, infants may be born with the complete genetic makeup of a male or a female, but with improperly differentiated sexual anatomy. For example, an infant may be born with the complete genetic makeup of a female, but with a penis (though often incomplete) and no clitoris or vagina. Such cases often result in a sex reassignment, involving the complex reconstruction of sex identity, including anatomical surgery, hormonal treatment, and cultural socialisation. Studies of such cases consistently show that surgical reassignment alone does not result in new gender identities; rather, the sex reassignment also involves an intricate process of new social expectations. Therefore, one of the first steps in reclassification is giving the child a new name, hairdo, and clothing appropriate to his or her new gender identity. Though there are statistically few such cases, they demonstrate the importance of cultural expectations in the evolution of gender identity.

While human biology is relevant in determining the basis of possibilities for social behavior, biology sets extremely broad limits for behavior among human beings. Even the development of human biological life involves a complex process of adaptation to the environment. Given the interplay of human biological organisms with their environment, it is difficult, if not impossible, to separate biological influences from social influences. As biologists and sociologists alike understand, simply knowing a person's sex is not a good predictor of his or her behavior.

What is so remarkable about biological explanations of gender inequality is that we seem so concerned about finding biological differences between the sexes. As with race, alleged biological differences between sex groups have historically been used as the basis for justifying group exploitation. Biological explanations of inequality have frequently appeared during historical periods of rapid social change in traditional societal arrangements.

For example, following the Civil War, racist ideas attributed the inequality of blacks to their innate inferiority and defined white privilege as a sign of biological and cultural superiority. Likewise, in the post-Civil War period, women's exclusion from educational institutions was explained as necessary to protect their reproductive organs. Educational leaders warned that women's wombs dominated their mental life and that studying hard would damage their reproductive systems. Young girls were even warned not to study at all during menstruation for fear of draining their reproductive power! These historical examples indicate that biological explanations of sex and race differences have been used to justify existing social arrangements.

Although biological differences between the sexes do exist, they cannot be seen as separate from the cultural context in which men and women develop. Human biology and cultural systems exist as dynamically interrelated systems. All in all, biological sex differences alone tell us very little about the experience of men and women in society.

SOCIAL CONSTRUCTION OF GENDER IDENTITIES

From the moment we are born, expectations for each sex begin to shape our gender identities. Parents talk with and touch their girl infants more than their boys; fathers are more likely to mock-wrestle with their sons than with their daughters. These patterns of social interaction teach us how others see us, how we are supposed to see ourselves, and what our options in society might be. Sociologists use the concept *social roles* to refer to the culturally prescribed expectations that define relations between persons in society. *Socialisation* is the process by which roles are learned. Gender socialisation is an ongoing process that continues throughout life. As we encounter new roles, we are socialised to new sets of expectations for our behavior and beliefs. Seen from this perspective, our gender identities as men and as women evolve over our lifetime and change as we encounter new situations.

Gender Roles Can be Hazardous to Your Health

It has been said that traditional gender roles are hazardous to our health. For men, adherence to traditional sex roles seems related to shorter life expectancy and a greater likelihood of death by violent means. Men are more likely than women to be homicide victims, for example, though these patterns are further complicated by race since black women are more likely to be homicide victims than are white men and black men are six times more likely than white men to die by homicide. As we have seen in our earlier discussion of violence, women are also much more likely than men to be victims of sexual abuse and assault in this culture. Attitudinal data suggest that sexual violence is learned behavior—it is tied to men's conceptions of male power. For instance, surveys of college students find that 30 per cent of males report that they would be aroused by forcing a woman to do something she would not want to do. Such findings paint a disturbing picture of the association between learned male roles and the high degree of sexual violence directed against women in this society.

But we do not have to look to acts of violence to see the damage done to both men and women by sex role stereotypes and behavior. Men's roles, which discourage intimacy and self-disclosure, shape not only men's relations with women, but their relations with other men. Research on male friendships, for example, finds that men report that they have more friends than do women, but women have more diverse, intense, and intimate friendships than do men. The higher degree of homophobia—fear of homosexuality—found among men also discourages them from expressing so-called feminine traits: caring, nurturing, and gentleness. For women, strict adherence to feminine roles also has negative consequences, including high rates of mental illness and lowered self-esteem.

Research on the culture of college classrooms shows that gender roles influence the nature of teacher-student and student-student interactions in these settings. In mixed-sex classes, faculty may call on male students more often than females and may coach male students toward fuller answers. Students, too, may ignore the comments of women students or challenge the authority of women professors.

Sexist comments by professors or other students in the classroom also make women angry and can leave them feeling vulnerable, thereby lessening their ability to learn. As the result of these behaviours, women may avoid some classes and departments. The costs in terms of educational development are then borne not only by the individuals, but by the society as a whole, since it results in a loss of the available talent.

The degree to which individuals adhere to traditional sex roles can influence their mental health. Studies show that men and women who are the most integrated into traditional roles have higher rates of mental illness. Men and women with androgynous orientations—that is, showing a balance of so-called masculine and feminine traits—tend to have more positive images of themselves and report themselves to be more healthy than do persons typed as very masculine or very feminine.

In addition to the consequences for mental health, traditional gender roles divide men and women from each other by polarising human traits along lines of sex. Andrew Tolson in his discussions of masculinity argues that traditional gender expectations condemn men and women to one-sided existences, denying women access to the public world of power, achievement, and independence while also denying men the nurturant, other-oriented, and emotive world associated with the women's roles.

Traditional gender roles limit the psychological and social possibilities for all human beings.

Socialisation Across the Life Span

Interest in patterns of gender socialisation has generated many studies of how sex roles are learned. Much of this research has focused on childhood as a particularly significant time for the establishment of gender identity among boys and girls. Research on sex role socialisation suggests that childhood play and games are significant in defining expectations for boys and girls. Drawing form the work of sociologist George Herbert Mead, Janet Lever argues that through play and games children learn skills of social interaction, cognitive and analytical abilities, and the values and attitudes of their culture. Using observations of children's play school playgrounds, she measured the complexity of children's play according to six criteria: the degree of role differentiation, the interdependence of roles, group size, the presence or absence of explicit goals, the number and specificity of the rules, and whether the play involves team formation or individual activity. Based on these measurements, she concludes that boys" games are more complex than girls, but, more important, that they involve the mastery of skills deemed essential to adult work in complex organisations. She finds that girls" games have fewer and less explicit rules than boys'; that girls are more likely to play in activities requiring only single roles, while boys' play more likely involves the formation of teams with interdependent role; girls play more cooperatively, while boys are competitive; and girls' games more likely involves ritualistic play, while games boys play have elaborate rules. She also discovers that, when girls do play games involving preestablished rules, they are more likely to ignore or bend the rules, while boys adhere to the rules more rigidly.

Lever concludes that childhood forms of play better prepare boys for the hierarchical forms of organisation characteristic of industrial, bureaucratised societies that they encounter in their adult lives. However, it is important to point out that neither girls' nor boys' play always follows such sex-stereotypic lines. Even when it does, must we assume that complexity and competence should only be measured in terms of "masculine" traits? While girls may not learn to be competitive and rule-oriented, sex-typed play also prevents boys from learning to be cooperative and flexible. However we interpret Lever's findings, they do impress upon us the importance of childhood learning in the elaboration of gender roles later in life.

Other studies demonstrate this as well. Observations of children's toys show that boys' toys tend to encourage play outside the home, while girls' toys are more domestic. Many experts have also argued that the recent popularity of military toys and dress for boys encourages the development of militaristic values of aggression, violence, and stereotyping of "enemies." And, despite modest improvements in recent years, children's literature, both fiction and textbooks, continues to show female characters as more conforming, more verbal than physical, and more engaged in fantasy than are male- characters. One limitation of the research on sex role socialisation is that so much of it has been based primarily on white subjects. We know that black women, like white women, are socialised to place primary emphasis on nurturing, though black women are more likely than white women to also be socialised to be self-sufficient, to hold high educational and occupational aspirations, and to expect paid employment to be an important part of their roles as women. In fact, studies of black women find that almost all of them (90 per cent) believed as they were growing up that they would have jobs as adults. These expectations are greatly influenced by the fact that black girls are more likely than white girls to have working mothers, although, with the increased labour force participation of white women in recent years, we might expect these differences to narrow. For Asian women, socialisation occurs in the context of a culture with devalued and subordinate roles for women; for Hispanic women, like other women of colour, conditions of exclusion, marginality, and hostility based on race are part of the context in which sex role socialisation occurs.

Research literature on the socialisation patterns of black, Hispanic, and Asian men is scarce. What limited research exists tends to be bound by a framework that defines black culture as deficient and dysfunctional. Despite these problems in the literature, there is some evidence that black men are more egalitarian in their sex role orientation than are white men; poll data also indicate that black men are more supportive of feminist issues than are white men. Other evidence suggests that because of pervasive racial discrimination, many black men are unable to meet the expectations of the traditional male role as provider and protector; as a result, some may develop roles of exaggerated masculinity—the "tough guy" or the "player of women." Since this may be particularly prevalent among lower class black men, it suggests the extent to which sex role socialisation is influenced by race as well as by class location.

For all persons in the society, sex role socialisation is a lifelong process. As we grow older, we continue to encounter different expectations based on our sex. White men, for example, tend to gain prestige as they age, while aging is seen as a liability for women. In fact, for women, aging is popularly depicted as something to be feared. Myths about aging and gender do not necessarily conform to reality, however, since research finds that women's self-esteem increases with age. Older women describe themselves as more assertive, competent, independent, and effective than do younger women. And, in black and Hispanic communities, the aged (both women and men) tend to be accorded high esteem.

Influence of the Media

One source of the cultural expectations associated with gender in this culture is the popular media. The media bombard us with cultural messages about who we should be, how we should feel, and how we should associate with others. Whether in popular music, in television programming, advertisements, or magazines, gendered definitions of men and women convey images of ourselves, our relationships to others, and how we define the world around us. Even the simple act of buying a greeting card can become problematic if one wants to avoid sex role stereotyping. Birthday cards for women typically depict fear of aging or show women as helpless sex objects. Likewise Father's Day cards portray fathers as the persons who do the outside chores and who are strong and serious, but not frilly or feminine, as is suggested by the designs Mother's Day cards.

Television is a particularly influential source of gender socialisation since it a estimated that the average person watches seven and a half hours of television per day. Television programming is especially influential in shaping children's perceptions of the world, since by the time a child is 15, he or she will have spent more hour watching television than attending school. With a few exceptions, what children and adults see is a world in which sex, race, and class are stereotyped, and that world is one of the few bases for a common culture among American people. On televisions programmes women are typically depicted as sidekicks to men, but it is men who engage in the main action. Soap operas, while including predominantly female character, typically cast powerful, successful women as villains, while the good women art vulnerable, sweet, and easily manipulated. While new programmes do exist that show women in strong and intelligent roles, they remain the exception. Men are also narrowly cast in television roles and are less often seen in family roles than are women. Black men and women are not only under represented on television, but systematic observations show that they are most often cast as cooks, entertainers, athletics to servants. Black women are most frequently depicted as comical; Asians and Hispanics when they appear at all, are usually in the background, silently working as domestics or appearing as criminals and villains. Two-thirds of Hispanic characters on television are criminals, though in the 1984 season, of the 264 speaking roles, Hispanics held only three.

Together, the popular media form an important system of authority in contemporary culture. By presenting stereotypes of appropriate behaviour for men and women, the media limit the range of acceptable behaviour for each sex, direct our feelings, shape our self-concepts, and frame our ideas. Those who have studied the media describe women's depiction as one of 'symbolic annihilation,' meaning that, overall, women are condemned, trivialised, and ignored. By creating the framework through which we view and interpret reality, the media have a powerful influence on how we see or world and ourselves.

8

Social Movements in India

THE REFORM MOVEMENT 1860-1886

In India during the 1860's, marriage meant girls getting married below 8 or 9 years old. Socio-reform religious movements such as the Brahmo Samaj and the Arya Samaj pioneered work against child marriage. Late in the 1860's some success was met when the Indian Penal Code prohibited intercourse with a wife who had not reached ten years of age. Nevertheless, it wasn't until 1880 that child marriage as a problem became a public issue in India during the debate on the Age of Consent Bill. Towards the end of the debate a child wife of eleven years old, Named Phulmani, died when her husband raped her. More than 500 women doctors sent a memorandum to the Viceroy requesting him to stop marriage of girls below 14 years of age. The resulting bill compromised at 12 years old.

On August 15, 1884 a Parsee reformist, Behramji Malabari, circulated two notes which highlighted the evils of child marriage and enforced widowhood. The Honourable J. Gibbs added his comments to Malabari's notes saying that, "Young mothers become stunted in growth, and often become invalids for life, while children were too often pony and weak." Kadhavdas added to the list of evils, "Early marriage is a great obstacle in the progress of female education." Shortly thereafter, in 1886 the first petition against 'Hindu Infant Marriage' was proposed to the Government by the natives of Meerut. It was finally passed in 1927. It declared that no marriage would be valid unless the girl had completed her twelfth year. In spite of laws prohibiting the practice, child marriage continues to be a widespread custom in India. After looking at the debate which raged in the 1880's, I look at Hindu scriptures and their mandates for the practice.

The Malabari Letters-1887

Between 1884 and 1887 Behramji Malabari collected opinions for and against infant marriage and enforced widowhood from "representative Hindu gentlemen and official and other authorities." The "Hindu gentlemen" were mostly selected from Brahmins educated in English universities. The resultant letters, dedicated to the Duke and Duchess of Connaught were published in the Voice of India. Malabari argued that infant marriage was "a practice more evil than infanticide." His arguments against infant marriage can be summarized as a too early consummation of the nuptial troth, breaking down the constitutions and the ushering in of disease, the birth of sick children, the necessity of feeding too many mouths, poverty and dependence, and a disorganized household leading perhaps to sin.

A response by Ramanujchari's typifies the reformer's view of child marriage, an evil which he thought that even the reformers were unaware, ".the practice of the selling of girls by their parents has become so rife in these parts of the country that girls are disposed of in marriage to the highest bidders like goods at an auction sale. Girls are married, as a rule, before they attain their 8th or 9th birthday-an age when they are utterly incompetent to comprehend the contract they enter into." The authors included in Malabari's publication nearly universally condemned infant marriage as a "great physical and moral evil." Infant marriage was considered "one of two evils that, if not remedied in time, are sure to destroy the vitality of the whole native community of India." Infant marriage was not confined to the Hindus, but was also "practiced by Parsis and Mohamedans." Two related issues were being discussed, child marriage and infant widowhood. Shirgaonkar, not so interested in child marriage, objected to child widowhood. He said, "I condemn infant marriages not because I think that they afterwards prove unhappy-which statement I will not accept unsupported by statistics-but because such marriages increase infant widows"

How child marriage works to increase infant widows and their misery is hinted at by Colonel E.W. West, "I have known many cases of old men marrying girls not yet emerged from childhood and it needs but little knowledge of human nature to realize the misery during the husband's lifetime, and of Hindu ways to realize the misery after his death, of the girl." Many authors felt that government action was a necessity: "The reason for this is that for the last 2000 years the Hindus have lost the power of refection, and even that of following or imitating what is good.. The masses still grope in darkness. They are bound by their customs and the foolish teachings of their priests."

Of the eighty-seven respondents, only a few suggested that the evil wasn't as great as Malabari considered it to be. For example, Dr. Rajendralala Mitra from Calcutta said, "I have also yet to learn that disparity in age of marriage does more harm in India than it does in Europe."

Mozoomdar objected and offered some statistics, arguing that the problem of infant widowhood wasn't nearly so serious as propounded. According to the census there were only 28,369 widows between the ages of 14 and 19 out of twenty million total widows in India. More than a few of the respondents objected to Malabari's proposal for prohibition of child marriage. Taleyar Khan from Baroda argued that, "Our English ideas actually jar with their (the Hindus) sympathies, the antipathies, and all important affections of their heart and mind."

He goes on to explain that 'marriage seasons' can be at intervals as many as twelve years apart. In the case cited a girl of four couldn't be married until she was sixteen, "A horrible purgatory, according to the Shastras, for the parents to keep her unmarried at that age." He continues by saying, "It is a wonder how this nation has succeeded for ages in preserving such a marked harmony of their homes. If we have weakly children the homes are happy, contented, well regulated and economical."

Reformers Ignored Hindu Scriptures and Epics

Malabari claims that, "No Shastra enforces marriage proper on a girl under 12 years of age, when presumably the boy must be between 15 and 20." That being Malabari's only comment on the religious basis of the nearly universal custom of child marriage he concluded, "So much as to the social or so-called religious aspect of the practice." The writers who supported Malabari, with one or two exceptions, also denied the religious-spiritual background of infant marriage. Lakshmiram, for example, said, "There is one foolish text, I know, which enjoins the marriage of every girl before she is eleven years old."

One exception to this denial is found in the letter of Keshaveal Madhavadas who says, "The Hindu law gives clear injunction not to keep a girl unmarried beyond 12 years old." While it does appear to be arguable that the Vedic literature, written before 400 B.C. advised that children not be married before puberty, in the following compilation I show that the British and their Brahmin supporters ignored the long Hindu scriptural tradition of child marriage during Vedic times and after the fourth century BC. The citations also help us understand the point of view of a civilization that allowed for child marriage.

SELF-RESPECT MOVEMENT

The Self-Respect Movement was founded in 1925 by Periyar E. V. Ramasamy (also known as Periyar) in Tamil Nadu, India. The movement has the aim of achieving a society where backward castes have equal human rights, and encouraging backward castes to have self-respect in the context of a caste based society that considered them to be a lower end of the hierarchy. The movement was extremely influential not just in Tamil Nadu, but also overseas in countries with large Tamil populations, such as Malaysia and Singapore. Among Singapore Indians, groups like the Tamil Reform Association, and leaders like Thamizhavel G. Sarangapani were prominent in promoting the principals of the Self-Respect Movement among the local Tamil population through schools and publications.

A number of political parties in Tamil Nadu, such as Dravida Munnetra Kazhagam (DMK) and All India Anna Dravida Munnetra Kazhagam (AIADMK) owe their origins to the Self-respect movement, the latter a 1972 breakaway from the DMK. Both parties are populist with a generally social democratic orientation. The movement has been in political power in Tamil Nadu since 1967, when the DMK under C. N. Annadurai defeated the ruling Congress Party. The incumbent (as of 2009) Chief Minister is M. Karunanidhi of the DMK.

The Tenets of Self-Respect

Periyar was convinced that if man developed *self respect*, he would automatically develop individuality and would refuse to be led by the nose by schemers. One of his most known quotes on Self-Respect was, "we are fit to think of 'self-respect' only when the notion of 'superior' and 'inferior' caste is banished from our land". Periyar did not expect personal or material gain out of this movement. He used to recall in a very casual manner that as a human being, he also was obligated to this duty, as it was the right and freedom to choose this work. Thus, Periyar opted to engage himself in starting and promoting the movement.

Periyar declared that the *Self-Respect Movement* alone could be the genuine freedom movement, and political freedom would not be fruitful without individual self-respect. He remarked that the so called 'Indian freedom fighters' were showing disrespect of self-respect, and this was really an irrational philosophy.

Periyar observed that political freedom as conceived by nationalists not excluding even Gandhi and Jawaharlal Nehru did not cover individual self-respect. To him neither revival of the original spirit of Hindu religion and ancient traditions which formed part of Gandhi's conception of freedom, nor complete liberation from the British rule which was considered by Nehru to be the meaning of freedom or both of them together could ensure individual self-respect or remove the ills from Indian societies. In his opinion the task of fulfilling the need for self-respect would have to be faced whatever be the extent of political freedom gained. Pointing out that even the British monarch in a sovereign independent nation had no freedom to marry a person of his choice and had to abdicate his kingdom, Periyar raised a question whether Gandhi's vision of freedom or Nehru's concept of independence contained even an iota of individual self-respect.

Periyar believed that self-respect was as valuable as life itself and its protection is a birth right and not *swaraj* ('political freedom'). He described the movement as *Arivu Vidutalai*

Iyakkam, that is, a movement to liberate the intellect. The terms *tan-maanam* or *suya mariyadai* meaning 'self-respect' are traceable in ancient Tamil literature considered a virtue of high valor in Tamil society. Periyar once claimed that to describe the ideology of his movement, no dictionary in the entire world, implying that no other language, could provide a word better than or equal to *suya mariyadai*.

Started as a movement (*Iyakkam* in Tamil) to promote rational behaviour, the *Self-Respect Movement* acquired much wider connotation within a short period of time. Periyar speaking with M.K. Reddy at the *First Self-Respect Conference* held in 1929, explained the significance of self-respect and its principles. The main tenets of the *Self-Respect Movement* in society were to be: no kind of inequality among people; no difference as rich and poor in the economic life; men and women to be treated as equals in every respect without differences; attachments to caste, religion, *varna*, and country to be eradicated from society with a prevalent friendship and unity around the world; and every human being seeing to act according to reason, understanding, desire, and perspective, and shall not be subject to slavery of any kind or manner. Equality with stress on economic and social equality formed the central theme of the *Self-Respect Movement* was due to Periyar's determination to fight the inequalities ingrained in the caste system and religious practices. Working on the theme of liberating the society from the baneful social practices perpetrated in the name of *dharma* and *karma*, Periyar developed the idea of establishing this movement as the instrument for achieving his objective.

Anti-Brahmanism

Tamil Brahmins (Iyers and Iyengars) were frequently held responsible by followers of Periyar for direct or indirect oppression of lower-caste people on the canard of "Brahmin oppression" and resulted in attacks on Brahmins and which among other reasons started a wave of mass-migration of the Brahmin population. Periyar in regards to a DK member's attempt to assassinate Rajagopalachari, "expressed his abhorrence of violence as a means of settling political differences". Eventually, the anti-Brahmanism subsided with the replacement of the DMK party by the AIADMK.

Self-Respect Marriages

One of the major sociological changes introduced through the self respect movement was the self-respect marriage system, where by marriages were conducted without being officiated by a Brahmin priest. Periyar had regarded the then conventional marriages were mere financial arrangements and often caused great debt through dowry. Self-Respect marriages encouraged inter-caste marriages and arranged marriages to be replaced by love marriages. It was argued by the proponents of self-respect marriage that the then conventional marriages were officiated by Brahmins, who has to be paid for and also the marriage ceremony was in Sanskrit which most people did not understand, and hence were ritual and practices based on blind adherence.

THE NATIONAL MOVEMENT FOR INDEPENDENCE

An aspect of Asia that must always be seen as a historical backdrop while discussing its social movements are a variety of national liberation movements against colonial occupation in many countries of the region. Contemporary social movements can not really be well understood without identifying the elements of continuity and change from such liberation movements. And nowhere else is that as important as in India. The Indian national independence movement, as is well known, was greatly influenced by the leadership provided by Mahatma Gandhi. The sheer number of people who participated in this movement, particularly from about 1910 to the time of independence in 1947 is staggering. Apart from gaining political independence for India, the movement influenced a nation of 300 million people in 1947 and over a billion today in nearly all aspects of politics and life. Apart from its main characteristics of nonviolence and struggle based on truth satyagraha Gandhian thought penetrated areas like governance, decentralization, ethics and morality of politics, education, rural and national development, self-reliance, volunteerism, caste and untouchability and much more.

After gaining independence, and even after Gandhi's assassination by a Hindu religious fanatic in 1948, his thought spurred a wide varicty of Gandhian movements and civil society formations that continue till today. The persistence and resilience of his thoughts can also be discerned today in movements that may not be direct descendents of Gandhian movements, like the environmental, adivasi and local governance movements. The more direct Gandhian movements would include the Sarvodaya movement that concentrated on the redistribution of land in the fifties and sixties but is fairly dormant now, the movement for bringing in Panchayati Raj (local governance), and a plethora of Gandhian institutions all over the country, of which the Gandhi Peace Foundation in Delhi, Sewagram Ashram in Wardha, Gandhigram in Tamil Nadu, Gandhi University and Sabarmati Ashram in Gujarat would be prominent. His notion of self reliance, symbolized by the hand-spun local cloth, khadi, and a variety of other locally produced products is promoted by the state through a vast organization called the Khadi and Village Industries Commission, with an extensive network of still popular retail outlets.

Gandhian thought finds popularity amongst groups and movements that seek to establish a more ethical, moral and harmonious relationship between human activities and nature, and who are seeking another world that draws away from centralization of political power and economic production. It would therefore seem to confront and resist both forms of capital, private or state-owned, putting much more emphasis on community ownership.

ENVIRONMENTAL MOVEMENT

Chipko Movement, India

The forests of India are a critical resource for the subsistence of rural peoples throughout the country, but especially in hill and mountain areas, both because of their direct provision of food, fuel and fodder and because of their role in stabilising soil and water resources. As these forests have been increasingly felled for commerce and industry, Indian villagers have sought to protect their livelihoods through the Gandhian method of satyagraha nonviolent resistence. In the 1970s and 1980s this resistance to the destruction of forests spread throughout India and became organised and known as the Chipko Movement.

The first Chipko action took place spontaneously in April 1973 and over the next five years spread to many districts of the Himalaya in Uttar Pradesh. The name of the movement comes from a word meaning 'embrace': the villagers hug the trees, saving them by interposing their bodies between them and the contractors' axes. The Chipko protests in Uttar Pradesh achieved a major victory in 1980 with a 15-year ban on green felling in the Himalayan forests of that state by order of India's then Prime Minister, Indira Gandhi. Since then the movement has spread to Himachal Pradesh in the North, Karnataka in the South, Rajasthan in the West, Bihar in the East and to the Vindhyas in Central India. In addition to the 15-year ban in Uttar Pradesh, the movement has stopped clear felling in the Western Ghats and the Vindhyas and generated pressure for a natural resource policy which is more sensitive to people's needs and ecological requirements.

The Chipko Movement is the result of hundreds of decentralised and locally autonomous initiatives. Its leaders and activists are primarily village women, acting to save their means of subsistence and their communities. Men are involved too, however, and some of these have given wider leadership to the movement. Prominent Chipko figures include: Sunderlal Bahuguna, a Gandhian activist and philosopher, whose appeal to Mrs. Gandhi results in the green-felling ban and whose 5,000 kilometre trans-Himalaya footmarch in 1981-83 was crucial in spreading the Chipko message. Bahuguna coined the Chipko slogan: 'ecology is permanent economy'.

Chandi Prasad Bhatt, one of the earliest Chipko activists, who fostered locally-based industries based on the conservation and sustainable use of forest wealth for local benefit. Dhoom Singh Negi, who, with Bachni Devi and many village women, first saved trees by hugging them in the 'Chipko embrace'. They coined the slogan: 'What do the forests bear? soil, water and pure air'.

Ghanasyam Raturi, the Chipko poet, whose songs echo throughout the Himalaya of Uttar Pradesh. Indu Tikekar, a doctor of philosophy, whose spiritual discourses throughout India on the ancient Sanskrit scriptures and on comparative religion have stressed the unity and oneness of life and put the Chipko Movement in this context.

A feature published by the United Nations Environment Programme reported the Chipko Movement thus: 'In effect the

Chipko people are working a socioeconomic revolution by winning control of their forest resources from the hands of a distant bureaucracy which is concerned with selling the forest for making urban-oriented products.'

"The solution of present-day problems lie in the re-establishment of a harmonious relationship between man and nature. To keep this relationship permanent we will have to digest the definition of real development: development is synonymous with culture. When we sublimate nature in a way that we achieve peace, happiness, prosperity and, ultimately, fulfilment along with satisfying our basic needs, we march towards culture." Sunderlal Bahuguna

WOMEN'S MOVEMENT IN INDIA

The women's movement in India is a rich and vibrant movement which has taken different forms in different parts of the country. Urvashi Butalia contends that the absence of a single cohesive movement, rather than being a source of weakness, may be one of the strengths of the movement. Although scattered and fragmented, it is a strong and plural movement.

ONE of the most enduring cliches about India is that is a country of contradictions. Like all cliches, this one too has a grain of truth in it. At the heart of the contradiction stand Indian women: for it is true to say that they are among the most oppressed in the world, and it is equally true to say that they are among the most liberated, the most articulate and perhaps even the most free. Can these two realities be simultaneously true?

During the 18 years that India had a woman as Prime Minister the country also saw increasing incidents of violence and discrimination against women. This is no different from any other time: a casual visitor to any Indian city-for example Mumbai-will see hundreds of women, young and old, working in all kinds of professions: doctors, nurses, teachers, engineers, scientists... and yet newspapers in India are full of stories of violent incidents against women, of rape, sexual harassment, sometimes even murder. But to have a woman in the highest office of the State and to simultaneously have extreme violence against women are merely the two ends of the scale. As always, a more complex reality lies in between. Fifty years ago when India became independent, it was widely acknowledged that the battle for freedom had been fought as much by women as by men. One of the methods M K Gandhi chose to undermine the authority of the British was for Indians to defy the law which made it illegal for them to make salt. At the time, salt-making was a monopoly and earned considerable revenues for the British. Gandhi began his campaign by going on a march-the salt march-through many villages, leading finally to the sea, where he and others broke the law by making salt. No woman had been included by Gandhi in his chosen number of marchers. But nationalist women protested, and they forced him to allow them to participate.

Sarojini Naidu

The first to join was Sarojini Naidu, who went on to become the first woman President of the Indian National Congress in 1925. Her presence was a signal for hundreds of other women to join, and eventually the salt protest was made successful by the many women who not only made salt, but also sat openly in marketplaces selling, and indeed, buying it.

Sarojini Naidu's spirit lives on in thousands of Indian women today. Some years ago, Rojamma, a poor woman from the southern state of Andhra Pradesh, attended a literacy class. Here, she read a story which described a life very like her own. It talked about a poor woman, struggling to make ends meet, who was regularly beaten by her husband. Whatever he earned, he spent on liquor, and then, drunk and violent, he attacked her because she had no food to give him. Unable to stand the continuing violence, the woman went from house to house, to find every other woman who had the same story to tell. They got together, and decided they would pitch their attack where it hurt most: they would picket liquor shops and stop liquor being sold.

Their husbands then would have no liquor to drink, and the money they earned would be saved. Inspired by the story, Rojamma collected her friends together, and they began to picket liquor shops. The campaign spread like wildfire. In village after village, women got together, they talked, they went on strike, they beat up liquor shop owners, they refused to allow their husbands to squander money on liquor. And, they succeeded. The sale of liquor was banned in Andhra Pradesh, reluctantly, by the government for liquor brings in huge amounts of money. As a result, savings went up, violence levels dropped, and the lives of poor women began to improve.

The hundreds of thousands of Rojammas and Sarojini Naidus who are to be found all over India form part of one of the most dynamic and vibrant of political movements in India today, the women's movement. The trajectory of this movement is usually traced from the social reform movements of the 19th century when campaigns for the betterment of the conditions of women's lives were taken up, initially by men. By the end of the century women had begun to organise themselves and gradually they took up a number of causes such as education, the conditions of women's work and so on. It was in the early part of the 20th century that women's organisations were set up, and many of the women who were active in these later became involved in the freedom movement.

Independence brought many promises and dreams for women in India-the dream of an egalitarian, just, democratic society in which both men and women would have a voice. The reality, when it began to sink in was, however, somewhat different. For all that had happened was that, despite some improvements in the status of women, patriarchy had simply taken on new and different forms.

Unfulfilled Promises

By the 1960s it was clear that many of the promises of Independence were still unfulfilled. It was thus that the 1960s and 1970s saw a spate of movements in which women took part: campaigns against rising prices, movements for land rights, peasant movements. Women from different parts of the country came together to form groups both inside and outside political parties. Everywhere, in the different movements that were sweeping the country, women participated in large numbers. Everywhere, their participation resulted in transforming the movements from within.

Worried at this increase in political activity, Indira Gandhi's government declared a State of Emergency in 1975, putting a stop to all democratic political activity. Activists, both young and old, women and men, were forced to go underground or to stop all political work. It was only when the Emergency was lifted, some 18 months later, that overground political activity resumed. It was around this time that many of the contemporary women's groups began to get formed, with their members often being women with a history of involvement in other political movements.

One of the first issues to receive countrywide attention from women's groups was violence against women, specifically in the form of rape, and what came to be known in India as 'dowry deaths'-the killing of young married women for the 'dowry' or money/goods they brought with them at marriage. This was also the beginning of a process of learning for women: most protests were directed at the State. Because women were able to mobilise support, the State responded, seemingly positively, by changing the law on rape and dowry, making both more stringent. This seemed, at the time, like a great victory. It was only later that the knowledge began to sink in that mere changes in the law meant little, unless there was a will and a machinery to implement these. And that the root of the problem of discrimination against women lay not only in the law, or with the State, but was much more widespread.

In the early campaigns, groups learnt from day to day that targeting the State was not enough and that victims also needed support. So a further level of work was needed: awareness raising or conscientisation so that violence against women could be prevented, rather than only dealt with after it had happened. Legal aid and counselling centres were set up, and attempts were made to establish women's shelters. It was only when groups began to feel sucked into the overwhelming volume of the day-to-day work of such centres that they began to feel that it was not enough to do what they now saw as 'reformist' and 'non-campaign' work. Knowledge was recognised as an important need. India is such a vast country; what did activists in Karnataka, a state in southern India, know of what was going on in Garhwal in north India? And yet, everywhere you looked, there was women's activity, activity that could not necessarily be defined as 'feminist', but that was, nonetheless, geared towards improving the conditions of women's lives. In recent years, the euphoria of the 1970s and early 1980s, symbolised by street-level protests, campaigns in which groups mobilised at a national level, the sense of a commonality of experience cutting across class, caste, region and religion-all this seems to have gone, replaced by a more considered and complex response to issues. In many parts of India, women are no longer to be seen out on the streets protesting about this or that form of injustice. This apparent lack of a visible movement has led to the accusation that the women's movement is dead or dying.

Other whipping sticks have been brought out: little has happened to improve women's lives, so how can the movement be called successful? Activists within the movement are urban, Western, and middle class, so the movement was considered an alien thing, a Western product. It has little to do with the lives of thousands of poor, rural, underprivileged women all over India. These allegations make the classic mistake: they judge a complex reality by that part of it that is most visible. Because urban, middle-class women are visible and articulate, therefore they must be the only participants in the women's movement.

Backbone

The reality is somewhat different. While the participation of urban, middle class women is undeniable, it is not they who make up the backbone of the movement, or of the many, different campaigns that are generally seen as comprising the movement. The anti-alcohol agitation in Andhra Pradesh, and similar campaigns in other parts of India were started and sustained by poor, low-caste, often working-class women. The movement to protect the environment was begun by poor women in a village called Reni in the northern hill regions of India, and only after that did it spread to other parts of the country. There are any number of such examples.

One of the biggest challenges women have had to face in recent years is the growing influence of the religious right in India. Right-wing groups have built much of their support on the involvement of women: offering to help them with domestic problems, enabling them to enter the public space in a limited way, and all the while ensuring that the overall ideology within which they operate remains firmly patriarchal. For activists too, this has posed major problems. It has forced them to confront the fact that they cannot assume a solidarity as women that cuts across class, religion, caste, ethnic difference. And yet, they must hold fast to such an assumption if they are to work with women: for how, as an activist, do you deal with a woman who takes part in a violent right wing demonstration one day, and comes to you for help as a victim of domestic violence the next?

Perhaps the most significant development for women in the last few decades has been the introduction of 33% reservation for women in local, village-level elections. In the early days, when this move was introduced, there was considerable scepticism. How will women cope?

Are they equipped to be leaders? Will this mean any real change, or will it merely mean that the men will take a backseat and use the women as a front to implement what they want? While all these problems still remain, in a greater or lesser degree, what is also true is that more and more women have shown that once they have power, they are able to use it, to the benefit of society in general and women in particular.

The women's movement in India today is a rich and vibrant movement, which has spread to various parts of the country. It is often said that there is no one single cohesive movement in the country, but a number of fragmented campaigns. Activists see this as one of the strengths of the movement which takes different forms in different parts. While the movement may be scattered all over India, they feel it is nonetheless a strong and plural force.

It is important to recognise that for a country of India's magnitude, change in male-female relations and the kinds of issues the women's movement is focusing on, will not come easy. For every step the movement takes forward, there will be a possible backlash, a possible regression. And it is this that makes for the contradictions, this that makes it possible for there to be women who can aspire to, and attain, the highest political office in the country, and for women to continue to have to confront patriarchy within the home, in the workplace, throughout their lives. As activists never tire of repeating: out of the deepest repression is born the greatest resistance.-

Week 3 Lecture 2

The women's question is still widely debated among Indian historians. On the one hand, it is argued that it was "resolved" by the Indian nationalists by constructing the modern Indian woman as the guardians of the (constructed) "authentic" realm of the inner or spiritual realm, i.e. the home.

This argument is based on the reasoning that:

1. Indian women were now understood as different from men but venerated, not demeaned.
2. The difference was the grounds of women's' special relation to the nation. They became guardians of what was authentically Indian.
3. Consequently, the battle for the new idea of womanhood-who the new woman was--was moved to the home.

The implications of this resolution of the women's question for social movements are:

1. As the fight over the women's question moved to the home the focus of social movements became those concerned with the private sphere: for education and for control of reproduction, labour, sexuality.
2. The fight over women's issues became subordinated to the main cause of nationalism. In particular, Indian nationalism.

On the other hand, it is argued that the women's question as "resolved" by Indian nationalists in the late 19th century, did not preclude the self-emancipation of women.

This argument is based on the reasoning that:

1. Women continued to organize and fight for various rights in the public sphere.
2. Women demanded from Gandhi and the INC a recognition of women not simply as the bearers of Indian "tradition" but as bearers of Indian "modernity."
3. Women took part in other movements, peasant, regional, and radical anti-caste struggles, like the Self Respect Movement, and revolutionary peasant movements, like the Telengana People's Struggle.

Women and Gandhi

1. Gandhi's entrance into the freedom movement changed the perception of women from "objects" of reform to participants.
2. It led to the mass participation of women.
3. Gandhi's ideas on women changed over time often in response to women's critiques and depending on the strategies of the freedom movement Gandhi's strategies.
    1. Convinced women and men that national movement could not succeed without women.
    2. Made possible women's involvement without shifting them out domestic sphere through spinning.
    3. Moved "home" into nationalist space as where Swadeshi could be upheld.
    4. Characterized nonviolence as women's particular strength to withstand violence and brutality.

As a political strategy, this was used to shame British and call the bluff on their civilizing mission.

How did women go from "tradition" bearer to national citizen? In the fight for vote women argued that unlike Britain where only women above 30 and those who owned property could vote India must give women the vote on equal terms to men Indian feminists challenged the INC to be more democratic than the British by recognizing a citizen above considerations of gender, caste, class, and community.

In so doing it also provided ideological cover to a singular and dominant form of nationalism that compromised actually existing differences of gender, caste, religion, class.

What is Liberalism?

Individual liberty and human dignity through a political process that involves: representative and democratic institutions guaranty of individual property rights freedom of expression, association, conscience Both British and INC expressed commitment to liberalism.

For British, the backwardness of India justified imperial governance towards a better future. Civilization is a precondition for self-governance.

For the Indian freedom movement, the precondition of civilization was achieved long ago; it is empire that is uncivil.

In liberal politics violence does not have a place.

What is Communism?

A social theory and political movement for the direct and communal control of society towards the common benefits of all members.

Its main features are:

A classless society in which all property is owned by the community as a whole and where all people enjoy equal social and economic status.

Like liberalism, communism was a major intellectual resource for social movements in India.

Communist Party of India (CPI) was established by MN Roy in 1920, inspired by 1917 Bolshevik Revolution.

The CPI set up unions and organized strikes in textile, jute, railways through 1920s.

Telengana People's Struggle

Conditions for movement as conjuncture

Women in the movement

Writing women's' history.

Conjunctures

1. Land regime under Nizam of Hyderabad
    a. Under feudal nobles as jagirs, samsthans, imams: 40%
    b. Under direct administration as khalsa or divani lands under deshmukhs: 60%
2. Labour regime
    a. Vetti or free services by castes according to various occupations.
    b. Baghela or bonded labour especially in Tribal areas.
    c. Adi bapas: concubines and other sexual services provided by women to landlords.
3. Religious and Caste distribution:

   Muslim ruler and feudal nobles. Muslims also 9% of

general population in state, but majority Hindu population. Mala and Madiga labouring "untouchable" castes Reddy and Kamma rich and middle peasants-later politicized Komati and Marwadi money lenders, traders Chenchus, Lambadas, Konda reddys tribal poplulations.

4. Rise of Muslim fundamentalist organizations like, Ittehad ul Mussalmeen, in response to Hindu fundamentalist organizations like Hindu Maha Sabha and eventually of militant wing, the Razakars.
5. Andhra Maha Sabha formed in 1921 as cultural organization for Telugu and telugu speakers on whom Urdu had been imposed.
6. Regional Communist Party of India in Andhra was strong and later, differed from national CPI as more Maoist than Leninist. Eventually, the movement was called off after Indian Army marched in to force the recalcitrant Nizam to join the Indian. Union in September 1948. The Indian Army first subdued the Razakars who quickly disbanded and then turned attention to the communist, peasant squads. As rich peasant support evaporated, in 1951 the CPI called off the armed insurrection.

Though movement ended, it led to:

1. Land redistribution and Land reform.
2. Abolishment of bonded labour.
3. Tenancy reform.
4. Ideological shift in CPI from United Front to Maoist ideology.
5. Involvement of large numbers of men and women across classes and from 2000 villages.
6. For a time, established People's courts, village "soviets". That Magic Time" Women participated in the Telengana Struggle as supports to men. Women participated in the Telengana Struggle as heroines. In fact, oral histories are testimonies to the contradictoryness of experience and memories of it. Telegana Movement was not just a seried of events but a process of struggle. The becoming conscious as women, as peasants, as revolutionaries is what was and is important.

FARMERS' MOVEMENTS

The farmers in India had to do a great struggle in all the states to get rid of exploitation by the Jagirdars and zamindars. Some of the movements were successful but some failed. The farmer movements in 1907 under the leadership of Sardar Ajit Singh and in 1921 under Sardar Vallabhbhai Patel were a grand success but the farmers were subjected to great sufferings in Chauri Chaura, Avadh and Mopla farmer movements.

At the global level the French Revolution had changed the course of history. Since then it was the working class which became the vanguard of revolution in Europe. But when during the first half of the 20th century, national liberation struggles started against colonisation, there was very little industry in the colonies and their working class, if it existed at all, was still in infancy. So the impetus for these struggles had to come from somewhere else. It was Mao's peasant revolution in China which became a role model for national liberation movements in many a colony, including India.

Farmer Movements in Punjab

In India it was in Punjab that India's first farmers' movement emerged. The role played by Ghadar party, led by Raja Mahendra Pratap, in the political awakening of India was an important step. The Sikhs of Punjab were the first to migrate to the United States and Canada in the 19th century. They financed and helped the formation of Ghadar party which when gave the call to Indians abroad to return home and fight British imperialism, had its call immediately heeded to. The majority of those who did return--8000 of them--comprised Punjab's (Sikhs). Despite its apparent failure, the Ghadar Movement was to have a powerful impact on Punjab politics and especially on the peasants. It established a tradition of militant and secular anti-imperialism, enriched in subsequent years by social radicalism, which was to continue to inspire subsequent generations.

The peasant conferences were held in Lahore, Lyallpur and other places of West Punjab--the most famous of them being 1938-39 Long Morcha in Lahore when peasants from all over Punjab courted arrests for nine months in front of the assembly building.

The slogan of Pagri Sambhal O' Jatta (Hold your head high, O peasant) was first raised at a mass gathering in Lyallpur in 1907. Ten Thousand people--the Hindus, the Muslims and the Sikhs alike--attended this gathering.

Farmers' Movements in Gujarat

Mahatma Gandhi had led two great revolts of communities of poor Indian farmers against the tyranny of the British government and allied landlords in Champaran, Bihar, and Kheda, Gujarat. Success in both struggles had helped win the farmers economic and civil rights, and electrified India's people.

In 1920, the Indian National Congress under Gandhi's leadership launched the Non-Cooperation Movement. Millions of Indians revolted against the British, boycotting the courts, government services, schools and disavowing titles, pensions and British clothes and goods. The freedom fighters, known as Satyagrahis, peacefully protested authoritarian British laws, and called for India's independence. Many thousands were beaten, tortured and arrested.

Bardoli Satyagraha

Bardoli Satyagraha of 1925 in the state of Gujarat, India during the British Raj was a major episode of civil disobedience and revolt in the Indian Independence Movement.

In 1925, the taluka of Bardoli in Gujarat suffered from floods and famine, which hurt the crop produce, leaving farmers facing great financial troubles. However, the Government of the Bombay Presidency had raised the tax rate by 30% that year, and despite petitions from civic groups, refused to cancel the rise in face of the calamities. The situation for the farmers was grave enough, that they barely had enough property and crops to pay-off the tax, let alone for feeding themselves afterwards.

The Gujarati activists Narhari Parikh, Ravi Shankar Vyas and Mohanlal Pandya talked to village chieftains and farmers, and solicited the help of Gujarat's most prominent freedom fighter, Vallabhbhai Patel. Patel had previously guided Gujarat's farmers during the Kheda struggle, and had served recently as Ahmedabad's municipal president. He was widely respected by common Gujaratis across the state. Patel and Gandhi decided that the struggle be left entirely to the people of Bardoli taluka. Governor of Bombay ignored the request made by Patel to reduce taxes but reciprocated by announcing the date of collection. Patel then instructed all the farmers of Bardoli taluka to refuse payment of their taxes. Aided by Parikh, Vyas and Pandya, he divided Bardoli into several zones-each with a leader and volunteers specifically assigned. Patel also placed some Gujarati activists close to the government, to act as informers on the movements of government officials. Patel instructed the farmers to remain completely nonviolent, and not respond physically to any incitements or aggressive actions from officials. He reassured them that the struggle would not end until not only the cancellation of all taxes for the year, but also when all the seized property and lands were returned to rightful owners.

The Government declared that it would crush the revolt. Along with tax inspectors, bands of Pathans were gathered from northwest India to forcibly seize the property of the villagers and terrorize them. The Pathans and the men of the collectors forced themselves into the houses, took all property, including cattle.

The government began to auction the houses and the lands. But not a single man from Gujarat or anywhere else in India came forward to buy them. Patel had appointed volunteers in every village to keep watch. As soon as he sighted the officials who were coming to auction the property, the volunteer would sound his bugle. The farmers would leave the village and hide in the jungles. The officials would find the entire village empty. They could never find out who owned a particular house. Members of the legislative councils of Bombay and across India were angered by the terrible treatment of the protesting farmers. Indian members resigned their offices, and expressed open support of the farmers. Even many in the Raj's offices heavily criticized the Government.

In 1928, an agreement was finally brokered by a Parsi member of the Bombay government. The Government agreed to restore the confiscated lands and properties, as well as cancel revenue payment not only for the year, but cancel the 30% raise until after the succeeding year. While Patel credited Gandhi's teachings and the farmers' undying resolve, people across the nation recognized his vital leadership. Gandhi and his fellow satyagrahis called him Sardar for the first time, which in Gujarati and most Indian languages means Chief or Leader. It was after Bardoli, that Sardar Patel became one of India's most important leaders.

Farmer Movements in Rajasthan

Rajasthan is known as the land of kings and palaces and whose history is replete with encomium of their kings, the land known for "Sati", the land known for its vast tracts of deserts was witness to a history in making, the successful agitation of farmers and peasants for their right to livelihood.

The twenty-two princely states of erstwhile Rajputana state did not form a common political collectivity which can be termed as a unified political action model. Each state had its own territorial area, which was exclusive politically in that it had its separate administration nag and army. Each state retained its cultural and linguistic distinctiveness. Political authority varied from ruler to ruler depending upon the terms of contract or covenant with the paramount power dating back to the period of subsidiary alliance of Lord Wellesley. Obviously in a state like this, freedom movement was bound to be divided and segmented, depending upon the degree of unity and cohesiveness among political players in each state. The two states of Jaipur and Jodhpur provided differential patterns of political movements.

Justice Kan Singh Parihar, the retired Judge of High Court of Rajasthan, has written about exploitation of farmers by Jagirdars prior to Independence as under:

"Every thing that the Kisan had, never treated as his own. In Jagir areas all cultivators were really landless. There was no tenancy law and one could be thrown away from the land one cultivated at the pleasure of Jagirdar, his "malik". In most of the Jagirs a Jagirdar would in the first instance be taking fifty percent of the produce. This would be taken by actual division of the produce on the thrashing floor or by appraisal of the standing crop (kunta). Then over and above the share of the produce the Kisan had to pay numerous "lags" or cesses.

Together with the share of the produce known as "Hasil" these cesses meant that the Kisans had to part with more than eighty percent of their produce. The findings of the Sukhdeonarain Committee in the years 1940-42 bear this out. If a Kisan had to marry his daughter he had to pay "Chavri Lag" if he held a dinner then a "Kansa Lag"; if members of the family separated then "Dhunwa Lag" and so on. If the Jagirdar had a guest then fodder for his mount had to be supplied. Then there was "begar" that is forced labour, for tilling the personal lands of the Jagirdar. The homestead in which the Kisan lived in the Abadi had to be vacated in case he ceased cultivating the land. He could not alienate the plot to anyone."

Shekhawati Farmers' Movement

The farmers of the Sekhawati region are considered to be the most advanced in the state of Rajasthan. The Shekhawati region has the highest literacy in the state. The most dominating farmer community in the rural areas of Shekhawati is Jat. The Jats are politically and economically very sound. The major land holdings in the present times are with Jats. Then comes the Rajput community who were the jagirdars before independence. The farmers of the region have done great struggle to come to the present status.

Before independence the conditions of the farmers were worst. The farmers of the Shekhawati region were exploited and oppressed by the Jagirdars during British Raj. They were deprived of fundamental rights. They were given inhuman treatment when the Jagirdars did not get cesses known as leg (tax) or beger (unpaid work) in time, they were given hard punishments and their crop used to be destroyed. There were 37 kinds of begers (work without pay) prevalent in Shekhawati. A newly married bride was forced to go first to Jagirdar.

The Shekhawati Jat farmers' movement had its genesis in the Jat Praja Pati Maha-Yagna a socio-religious festival held in January, 1934. It lasted ten days and was the biggest of its kind in Rajputana. It facilitated a widespread involvement of Jats in a community festival. Each Jat household attending it was to contribute some cash and an unspecified quantity of ghee. A total of two hundred maunds of ghee were used in the sacrificial flame. The function concluded with a triumphal elephant ride hitherto prohibited by the rules of Sikar Thikana. The success of this movement encouraged the Jats to hold more meetings on local levels and print literature to glorify Jat history. The Yagna became a dominant symbol of folklore which glorified it as the beginning of an anti-feudal struggle. The peasants demanded remissions in taxes and finally a Jat-Sikar Thikana Agreement was signed on August 23, 1934, by which the Thikana authorities conceded to abolish various lags (taxes) and agreed to provide for a mobile dispensary.

The following year, the Kisan Sabha formally came into existence and under its aegis the famous Sikar Andolan of 1935 was launched. With outside mediation efforts of Jamnalal Bajaj, Sir Chhotu Ram-a renowned Jat leader of Punjab and Ratan Singh of All India Jat Mahasabha, a settlement was arrived at and the Jats were promised remissions of rent, abolition of internal cesses and an introduction of fixed rent tenure. The Jats were also promised equal opportunities in Thikana administration and were permitted to ride elephants and horses and to construct schools for their children.

The formation of a Jat Kisan Panchayat was officially sanctioned and the right to agitate for redressal of grievances in non-Khalsa areas was conceded. Much however, could not be made out of these agreements for two reasons. First, the subordinate Thikanedars of Sikar did not fully cooperate with Sikar authorities to ensure compliance with the terms of these agreements. Secondly, the beginning of settlement operations and reform of revenue administration was a time-consuming process which entailed enormous delay. This was interpreted by the Jats as a breach of agreement and hence, they indulged in acts of disorder and violence, which were perceived by Thikana authorities as signs of bad faith. In the meanwhile two unsavoury incidents led to a termination of agreements. The first, occurred at Khudi village, where the sight of Jat bridegroom riding a horse incensed the local Rajputs and the two sides readied themselves for an armed combat. The state authorities asked the two parties to disperse but the Jats refused. The state police charged and in the melee that followed, several people were injured. The second incident took place at Kudan village, where about one hundred armed Jats attacked Sikar revenue officials. The police fired upon the armed mob, which resulted in several casualties and injuries. A total of 104 Jats were arrested.

Farmers of the Shekhawati, mainly the Jats, united against oppression of Jagirdars by forming 'Sikar Jat-Kisan-Panchayat' and stopped giving "lags" or cesses to the Jagirdards. The 'Jaipur Praja-Mandal' also supported the Shekhawati farmers' movement against abolition of Jagirdari system. The leaders of 'Bijoria-Kisan-Movement' of 1922, 1931, and 1932 supported the movement of Shekhawati farmers. The Jagirdars tried to suppress the movement in many ways. Many farmers were killed and a large number were sent to jail. A Jat farmer was beaten to death in the market of Sikar town; his dead body was thrown and insulted. This movement got support from famous Kisan leaders like, Baldev Ram Mirdha, Nathuram Mirdha and Kumbharam Arya. After a long struggle the farmers got rid of oppression and got the ownership right over the land they were cultivating.

The leading Jat farmers of Shekhawati region, who played important role in the movement for abolition of the Jagirdari system, were:

- Iswar Singh Bhamu Bhairupura,
- Hari Singh Burdak and Hardeva Palthana,
- Prithvi Singh Gothra,
- Ganeshram Kudan,
- Panne Singh Bataranau,
- Goru Singh Katrathal,
- Deva Singh Bochalya,
- Chandrabhan Singh,
- Hardev Singh Harsawa.

Shekhawati farmers' movement against abolition of Jagirs got great support from outside Kisan leaders like Sir Chhotu Ram from Haryana, Kunwar Ratan Singh and Thakur Deshraj from Bharatpur, Kunwar Hukum Singh from Aangai.

Marwar Farmers' Movement

The farmers of the Marwar region are considered to be the most simple in the state of Rajasthan. The most dominating farmer community in the rural areas of Marwar is Jat. The Jats are politically and economically very sound. The major land holdings in the present times are with Jats.

Though the position of Kisan (farmer) in what was Khels? (under the direct control of the state) was better in comparison to a Kisan of the Jagir areas, he was only a little above a beast of burden. In Jagir areas of Marwar state before independence all cultivators were really landless. There was no tenancy Law and one could be thrown away from the land one cultivated at the pleasure of Jagirdar, his "malik". In most of the Jagirs a Jagirdar would in the first instance be taking fifty percent of the produce. This would be taken by actual division of the produce on the thrashing floor or by appraisal of the standing crop (kunt?). The latter method proved at times more onerous as the appraisal depended on the whims of the Kamdar. Then over and above the share of the produce the farmer had to pay numerous "lags" or cesses. There were 64 kinds of begars (work without pay) prevalent in Marwar. Then the bigger Jagirdars had judicial powers including magisterial powers. Further they had their own police force besides the revenue staff. This enabled them to keep their stronghold on the farmers. Over and above this policy of divide and rule was fully practiced. By offering the temptation of giving better land for cultivation one farmer would be set against another. There were no schools worth the name in rural areas and the masses were steeped in ignorance.

The oppression of the public by traditional Samantas (chiefs) and Jagirdars (feudatories) of Marwar state made their life difficult, which led to a class war. In urban areas, Jaynarayan Vyas started agitation against oppression, under the banner of "Marwar Lok Parishad" founded on 16th May 1938. This movement was supported by National Congress. The persons who played important role in "Marwar Lok Parishad" were: Shiv Dayal Dave and Jorawar Singh Oswal of Nagaur, Kishanlal Sahu, Manak Chand Konari and Sari Mal of Kuchaman City, Tulsiram of Didwana, Srikishan Pandit of Kolia and Sukhdev Dipankar of Ladnu.

Rural masses of Marwar were united by Kisan Kesari-Baldev Ram Mirdha under the banner of "Marwar Kisan Sabha" founded in 1940. After the formation of Rajasthan, Baldev Ram Mirdha who had by then retired from Government service formed the "Rajasthan Kisan Sabha" and unified the Kisans of Rajasthan under its banner. He was its first president. Since the broad objectives of the Kisan Sabha and the congress were identical the congress leaders approached Baldev Ram Mirdha to unite the Rajasthan Kisan Sabha with the Congress. Baldev Ram Mirdha was a visionary and he realized that the two could not and should not remain separate. Therefore, he just made one demand from the national leaders that the Jagirs be abolished forthwith in Rajasthan. This was agreed to by the Congress high command with the result that the Jagirs were soon abolished. A tenancy law was passed and the cultivating farmers were made the owners of the land.

Bibliography

Ahir, D.C.: *Dr. Ambedkar, Buddhism and Social Change*, BR Publishing, Delhi, 1993.

Appadurai, A. : *The Social Life of Things; Commodities in Cultural Perspective*, Cambridge: CUP., 1986.

Bailey, F.G. : *Stratagems and Spoils: A Social Anthropology of Politics*, Oxford: Basil Blackwell & Moll, Ltd., 1969.

Bandopadhyay Arun : *Tribes, Forest and Social Formation in Indian History*, Manohar, Delhi, 2004.

Banton, M. : *Political Systems and the Distribution of Power*, London: Tavistock, 1965.

Barbara R.: *Untouchable! Voices of the Dalit Liberation Movement,* London, Zed Books, 1986.

Beacon. Mair, Lucy : *Primitive Government*, Baltimore: Penguin, 1962.

Beckmann, F. : *Property in Social Continuity; Continuity and Change in the Maintenance of Property Relationships Through Time in Minangkabau*, West Sumatra, The Hague: Martin Nijhoff, 1979.

Benjamin, Joseph: *Scheduled Castes in Indian Politics and Society*, Ess Ess Publications, New Delhi, 1989.

Berreman, Gerald D., : *Social Inequality: Comparative and Developmental Approaches*, New York: Academic Press, 1981.

Bond, G. and A Gilliam : *The Social Construction of the Past: Representation as Power*, New York: Routledge, 1997.

Bose, N. K.: *The Scheduled Castes and Tribes and Their Present Conditions*, Calcutta, University of Calcutta, 1969.

Chatterjee, Partha: *Caste and Subaltern Consciousness*, Oxford University Press, Delhi, 1994.

Chaudhury Sukant K. : *Indian Tribes and the Mainstream*, Rawat, Delhi, 2008.

Clastres, Pierre : *Society Against the State*, New York: Urizen Books, 1977.

Cohan, B. N.: *The Changing Status of a Depressed Class*, Chicago, The University of Chicago Press, 1955.

Deshpande, Vasant: *Towards Social Intergration: Problems of Adjustment of SC Elites*, Shubhada- Saraswat, Pune, 1978.

Donham, Donald : *History, Power, Ideology: Central Issues in Marxism and Anthropology*, Berkeley, CA: University of California Press, 1999.

Ekta Singh: *Caste System in India : A Historical Perspective*, Kalpaz, Delhi, 2005.

Ghosh Abhik : *History and Culture of the Oraon Tribe : Some Aspects of Their Social Life*, Mohit Pub, Delhi, 2003.

Glen, M. and Johnson, S. B.: *Social Mobility Among Untouchables*, Vikas, New Delhi, 1979.

Goody, J. : *Death, Property and the Ancestors,* Stanford: Stanford University Press, 1962.

Gorhe, Neelam: *Social Development and Dalit Women*, Gyan Pub. House, New Delhi, 1995.

Gornick, V. : *Women and Science: Portraits from a World in Transition,* New York, Simon & Schuster, 1983.

Gudeman, S. : *Economics as Culture,* London: Routledge, 1986.

Humphrey, C. : *Karl Marx Collective; economy, society and religion on a Siberian collective farm,* Cambridge: CUP, 1983.

Jadhav, N.: *Dr. Ambedkar's Economic Thought and Philosophy*, Popular Prakashan, Bombay, 1993.

Johnson, Glen and Bose, Sipra: *Social Mobility Among Untouchables,* Cohesion and Conflict in Modern India, New Delhi, 1978.

Judith D. Toland : *State Formations and Political Legitimacy*, New Brunswick, NJ: Transaction Books, 1988.

Karve, Irawati: *Hindu Society: An Interpretation*, Poona, Sangam Press, 1961.

King, Margaret L." *Women of the Renaissance*. Chicago: University of Chicago Press, 1991.

Kourany, Janet A. : *The Gender of Science*, Upper Saddle River, New Jersey, Prentice Hall, 2002.

Krishnaiah Chetty, V.B.: *Scheduled Castes and Development Programmes in India,* Vohra, Allahabad, 1991.

Kurtz, Donald V. : *Political Anthropology: Paradigms and Power*, Boulder, CO: Westview, 2001.

Lakshmanna, C.: *Caste Dynamics in Village India*, Nachiketa Publications, Bombay, 1973.

Leons, M.B., & F. Rothstein : *New Directions in Political Economy: An Approach from Anthropology*, London: Greenwood, 1979.

Majumdar, D. N.: *Caste and Communication in an Indian Village*, Asia Publishing House, Bombay, 1958.

Mallik, Suneila: *Social Integration of the Scheduled Castes*, New Delhi, Abhinav, 1979.

Mann, K.: *Tribal Women in a Changing Society*, Mittal Publications, Delhi, 1987.

Mayer, A.: *Caste in an Indian Village: Change and Continuity 1954-1992*, Delhi, OUP, 1996.

Meyer, Mark J.: *Religion as Social Vision: The Movement Against Untouchability in 20th Century in Punjab*, University of California Press, Berkeley, 1982.

Misra Pramod : *Ecology, Culture and Health : A Primitive Tribe*, Serials Pub, Delhi, 2004.

Mumtaz Ali: *Identity Formation and Self Identity Among Harijan Elite*, New Delhi, Uppal Publishing House, 1994.

Nagaraj, D. R.: *The Flaming Feet: A Study of the Dalit Movement*, South Forum Press, Bangalore, 1993.

Naidu, Ch. M.: *Salt Satyagraha in the Coastal Andhra*, Mittal Publications, Delhi, 1986.

Neelima Yadav: *Gender, Caste and Class in India*, Pragun Pub, Delhi, 2006.

O'Malley, L. S. S.: *Indian Caste Customs*, Vikas Publishing House, Delhi, 1974.

Ong, Aihwa : *Flexible Citizenship: The Cultural Logics of Transnationality*, Durham, NC: Duke University Press, 1999.

Partha, C.: *Caste and Subaltern Consciousness*, Oxford University Press, Delhi, 1994.

Patel, Arjun: *Dalits in Modern India,* New Delhi, Vistaar, 1999.

Penner, J. : *The Idea of Property in Law,* Oxford: Clarendon Press, 1997.

Ram, Jagivan: *Caste Challenge in India*, New Delhi, Vision Books, 1980.

Robertson, A. F. : *The Dynamics of Productive Relationships,* Cambridge: CUP, 1987.

Sarkar, J.: *Caste, Occupation and Change*, B. R. Publishing Co., Delhi, 1984.

Schlicht, E. : *Custom in the Economy,* Oxford: Clarendon Press, 1998.

Shah, Ghanshyam: *Caste Association and Political Processes in Gujarat*, Popular Prakashan, Bombay, 1975.

Silverberg, James: *Social Mobility in the Caste System in India*, Mouton Publishers, The Hague, 1968.

Singh, S. N.: *Reservation: Problems and Prospects*, New Delhi, Uppal Publishing House, 1987.

Suvira Jaiswal: *Caste : Origin, Function and Dimensions of Change*, Manohar, Delhi, 1998.

Venkateshwarlu, D.: *Harijan-Upper Class Conflicts*, Discovery, New Delhi, 1990.

Verdery, K. : *Uncertain Transition; Ethnographies of change in the Postsocialist World,* Lanham MD: Rowman and Littlefield, 1999.

Walder, A. G. : *Property Rights and Economic Reform in China,* Stanford: Stanford University Press, 1999.

Wolf, Eric R. : *Envisioning Power: Ideologies of Dominance and Crisis,* Berkeley: University of California, 1999.

Yogesh, A.: *The Changing Frontiers of Caste*, National Publishing House, Delhi, 1968.

Index

M

N

O

P

R

S

T

V

W

❑❑❑